ROUTLEDGE LIBRARY EDITIONS:
RESPONDING TO FASCISM

I SPEAK OF GERMANY

I SPEAK OF GERMANY

A Plea for Anglo-German Friendship

NORMAN HILLSON

Volume 5

Routledge
Taylor & Francis Group
LONDON AND NEW YORK

First published in English 1937

This edition first published in 2010
by Routledge
2 Park Square, Milton Park, Abingdon, Oxon, OX14 4RN

Simultaneously published in the USA and Canada
by Routledge
711 Third Avenue, New York, NY 10017

Routledge is an imprint of the Taylor & Francis Group, an informa business

First issued in paperwork 2013

British Library Cataloguing in Publication Data
A catalogue record for this book is available from the British Library

ISBN 13: 978-0-415-57699-4 (Set)
eISBN 13: 978-0-203-85012-1 (Set)
ISBN 13: 978-0-415-57947-6 (Volume 5)
ISBN 13: 978-0-415-84888-6 (Volume 5)
eISBN 13: 978-0-203-85020-6 (Volume 5)

Publisher's Note
The publisher has gone to great lengths to ensure the quality of this reprint but points out that some imperfections in the original copies may be apparent.

Disclaimer
The publisher has made every effort to trace copyright holders and would welcome correspondence from those they have been unable to trace.

ADOLF HITLER

NORMAN HILLSON

★

I SPEAK OF GERMANY

A PLEA FOR ANGLO-GERMAN FRIENDSHIP

★

LONDON
GEORGE ROUTLEDGE & SONS, LTD.
BROADWAY HOUSE 68–74 CARTER LANE, E.C.
1937

Printed in Great Britain by Butler & Tanner Ltd., Frome and London

TO

ALAN BLAND

" *More matter for a May morning* "

CONTENTS

LIST OF ILLUSTRATIONS

I SPEAK OF GERMANY

CHAPTER I

FACE OF BERLIN

LESS than twenty years after the greatest war in history Europe is getting ready for a bigger and better war. This is no cynicism: it is statement of fact. The problem of world unemployment is being solved largely in war munition factories. There is scarcely a steelworks or naval dockyard or aeroplane factory on the Continent which is not working at full pressure. And this is true largely of Great Britain. The race for rearmament is already making fun of accepted principles of political economics. On all sides politicians are searching for new shibboleths which they hope will be heaven-sent formulæ. In the blind fatuity of their own past shortcomings and incompetence, they are declaring that the only way to avoid another war is to be prepared to fight in that same war. For them history has no lessons to teach and the next generation, or even that which is now growing to manhood, may have to pay a bitter bloody price for the follies of their rulers. In the varying names of democracy, autocracy and oligarchy the world is gradually drifting to a similar bankruptcy of statesmanship that precipitated the catastrophe of 1914. It is as if the world has learned nothing and forgotten everything.

In the changing face of Europe one vitally important

feature emerges—the new Germany. A short time ago a former British Foreign Minister, Sir Austen Chamberlain, who once gratuitously declared that he loved France like a mistress, recorded on paper that certain important members of the National Socialist Government in Berlin looked on Great Britain as Public Enemy Number One. It was a mischievous statement in the light of the public declarations of Herr von Ribbentrop, the newly appointed German ambassador to London. Von Ribbentrop announced that his mission was one of understanding between the German and British peoples—an understanding devoutly to be wished for and one which, I sincerely believe, is desired by the ordinary citizen (may be not the politician in all cases) in both Germany and Great Britain. If, in Germany, certain ministers in reviewing the general situation referred to the fact that the Reich had 70,000,000 people and no overseas dominions to which to export the surplus population it could not possibly maintain at home, this was hardly the occasion for Sir Austen Chamberlain to talk of hostility and forget how much the world has changed in outlook, ideals and possibilities in the last two decades. Such a statement was indicative of the Versailles mentality—that mentality which is once more transforming Europe into an armed camp.

In certain quarters of England there are those who view every move or accomplishment in the Third Reich with something like suspicion. To-day the old diehard "fight-to-a-finish" section who persist in calling an honourable enemy "Huns" are reinforced by the former Pacifist and milk-and-water element who saw nothing but good in Germany when she was threatened by Communist revolution and now find a well-governed Germany the invention of the devil. Unhappily both extremes of opinion are so voluble that one is apt to lose sight of the fact that a great revolution has been accomplished in Germany and that the German people are anxious to set their house in order, and obtain from life something which stress of circumstances denied them for fifteen years after the armistice—a sense of self-respect, some measure of security, a feeling of national pride. When Hitler threw over the military clauses of the Treaty of Versailles, invaded the demilitarised zone and re-introduced conscription his acts were regarded as just reversions to the pre-war German military mentality. It was conveniently forgotten that internal anarchy had rapidly reduced Germany to something like chaos and that she was surrounded by powerful states which, armed to the teeth, persistently refused to disarm. Such a situation was, in any case, intolerable to a nation which had for four years fought three-quarters of the world to a standstill and well-nigh prevailed on more than one occasion. The fact remained—and in some quarters still remains—that Germany had once more shown signs of aggressiveness. Her new policy was plainly military. Conscription was the forerunner of war. France, which had never abandoned conscription, had built the Maginot line, and wrecked the disarmament conference, was loud in her complaints. Stalin, fresh from a review of tens of thousands of troops in Red Square, sent Maxime Litvinoff to Geneva to register protest against this latest Nazi crime against mankind. It appeared plainly a crime for Germany to assert that she was after all a great power entitled to means of self-defence. What was a delinquency in the case of the Reich was an honourable virtue in everyone else.

But what in the meantime did the ordinary German

think of all this? And what does he think to-day? It is a question which ought to have been asked and which can still be asked. It was to find an answer to that question that I recently made an extensive tour of Germany.

My travels took me far afield—from the Rhine to the Oder; from the Baltic to the Bavarian Alps. And I discovered a new Germany inhabited by Germans who seem suddenly to have re-found their self-respect and pride of spirit. In three years of revolution something remarkable, new and strange had emerged from the grim period of post-war distress and uncertainty. I found a Germany that had raised her eyes from the ground to look at the hills. In many ways it was a revelation: in some, an inspiration. It was all so different from the Germany just after the war, when men and women were dying of starvation and murder was committed for a tin of bully beef or a bar of soap. It was different from the Germany of that wild, vicious time after the inflation, when money was dissipated with almost criminal folly and the vicious dancing halls of Berlin's Kurfürstendam became synonymous with the lowest depths of human depravity. It was different from the weary, anxious, feverish Germany of the revolution days early in 1933, when the chief political weapon on both sides was the revolver or rubber pipe. It was a land of work and sacrifice, where people had little but were content with what they got, and where such modest pleasures as were to be had were enjoyed with zest and not with that bored resignation accorded to places of amusement in this England of ours, which I have come to feel may be very rich and prosperous but is not so fundamentally happy as we would have ourselves believe.

It is my aim in the succeeding pages to record my impressions of the new Germany. I will endeavour to be as impartial as possible, recognising that, although my sympathies favour the régime, which has resurrected Germany from something like despair, nothing is perfect in this distracted world. There are many things in the Third Reich which must cause resentment in the minds of observers brought up in the freer atmosphere of the British Empire. At the same time not everything which has been done in the interests of discipline should be condemned as a denial of the liberty of the individual. In England we talk a great deal of cant in the name of liberty and profess to abhor any interference with so-called rights of expression and equality while paradoxically accepting without question the domination of the new despotism of our bureaucratic system and insolent delays in the most vital issues in the sacred name of the democratic Parliamentary system. In approaching the new Germany we must bear in mind that what we should regard as outrageous interference with personal rights is accepted as a matter of course by the average German citizen. There is a more ruthless spirit in Germany and in Europe generally than prevails in our own islands. There is no doubt that the Nazi régime is severe and that the methods of its leaders in acquiring power were sometimes harsh. But it is equally true that, if the advanced Socialist and Communist elements had prevailed, then the régime would have been equally uncompromising towards its enemies and the so-called inspired democratic leaders would have had equally short shrift with their Nazi opponents. It is a point which ought not to be forgotten in an examination of the issues which led to the establishment of the Third Reich. And it is just plain humbug to imagine that a victory of the Left in Germany on a big scale would have ushered in a millennium of personal liberty. It would have been the exact reverse. In any case the ordinary German would not know what to do with his life if he was without the knowledge of all-powerful authority somewhere in the background. He is content to serve the State provided that the Government is working steadfastly for the welfare of the beloved, sacred Fatherland. It is his idea of personal liberty, certainly it is his ideal of conduct.

I desire to take my readers to various parts of the Reich—to Cologne, to Frankfurt am Main, to Nuremburg, Dresden, Breslau and Hamburg, to name but a few German centres where there is so much outward evidence of the achievements of the Nazis. But it is necessary to start with Berlin, for Berlin is the most important city in Germany. Berlin is the political capital of the Reich. Here Hitler directs the country from his room in the Chancellery in the Wilhelmplatz. The Nazis look on Munich as a special headquarters of their movement—a place of particular sentiment that contains the historic Brown House. They may further glow with pride at the mention of Nuremburg, the city where the party has so often demonstrated its strength to the world. But Berlin is the city from which both party and country is really directed.

It is true of practically every country in Europe that the capital is by no means a reliable criterion of the rest of the State. The French go to Paris when they want to spend their savings but their true loyalty is given to their local town and province. The citizen of Milan often looks upon Rome as an interesting historical survival having none of the amenities of

Lombardy. From the point of view of the North Countryman London has an altogether exaggerated sense of its own importance. It is the same with regard to Berlin which many Germans, and especially Bavarians, regard as a quite artificial capital, in fact an historical parvenu. Not even the Nazi Revolution, so thorough in nearly everything, has induced a feeling of affection among the provincial Germans for the northern city and capital of Prussia and the Third Reich. Berlin is a vast metropolis of over 4,000,000 people, the scene of intense active city life, the seat of government, the centre of vast industry. To the Berliners—a people with a pawky humour and enormous appetite—it is the only city in the world. For the Munchener it is a good place to get away from. And it will always be so in a world where men and women conceive love for the place where they were born. In modern Berlin people are too busy making or spending money to take an active concern in anything outside their immediate interests, and thus it is that one often finds in the smaller and perhaps more leisurely cities outside the capital a more intense political feeling and appreciation of the Revolution.

As I stepped out of the Friedrichstrasse station I remembered with a shudder my last visit to the German capital. It was before the final accession to supreme power of Hitler and the Nazi party. I was on my way to Poland but a missed connection caused some hours delay. Outside on the rise of ground near the famous music-hall called the Admirals Palast were drawn up in the drizzling rain about five hundred men, of all shapes and sizes, wearing jack-boots and weather-worn brown shirts. Hurrying to the Unter den Linden I came across about a score of police lorries with rows of police, fully armed, and looking very smart but very impatient, drawn up on the broad pavements. A battalion of infantry stood to attention opposite the war memorial near the old Imperial Palace. It was like visiting a war-time base —which in a measure it was. There had been fierce rioting during the previous night, and a further outbreak was expected at dusk on the notorious Alexanderplatz. Both Communists and Nazis had been killed by revolver and rifle bullets.

It was all a little unnerving for the stranger unaccustomed to such spectacles. Later on at luncheon in the quiet luxurious atmosphere of the Adlon Hotel I was told not to pay too much attention to such things for the riots would be confined to the east end, that is, if they were resumed. But somehow I could not efface from my memory that spectacle of armed men and the tramp of hob-nailed boots that went on all day, and was apparently a commonplace of everyday life in the capital. One was aware that at the least sign of disturbance those police reinforcements would be hurried to Berlin's east end and there would be more useless bloodshed.

This recent arrival at the Friedrichstrasse was much pleasanter. The autumn sun was shining and there were no armed men with the exception of a solitary policeman who was struggling with a sudden stream of traffic brought about by the arrival of the afternoon express from the Hook of Holland. There was a sense of vivid movement in the air. In the Linden there was the normal crowd of shoppers and loiterers looking at the windows of jewellers or displays in the numerous shipping offices. There was only an occasional uniform—an officer of the Reichswehr on leave or a black-coated S.S. man attached to one of the government departments. The Linden itself looked immensely broad: I did not realise the reason for a minute or two—the construction of a new subway railway had necessitated the destruction of the famous lime trees from Brandenburger Tor right to the far end. When I reached the Kaiserhof dozens of people were seated in the lounge listening to jazz music, and a very attractive American girl was seated on the couch which Hitler used to occupy in other days when he came to the hotel in the afternoon to drink chocolate and eat cream buns. It was all very different.

Circumstances have made entry and exit from Germany, so far as possession of actual money is concerned, a little difficult for everybody. Much has been said concerning the attitude of Dr. Schacht to the conservation of currency within the Reich. The restrictions on the movement of money have been used by many critics of the Nazi régime as an appropriate flail with which to thresh the new Germany of everything useful except the more worthless chaff. It is always forgotten that such restrictions were rendered imperative by the conditions in which an impoverished Germany found herself. It is surely not necessary, nevertheless, to hark back to the grim months of inflation and remember the fortunes subsequently made by German subjects who, having established their competencies abroad, now, in exile, are such virulent enemies of the Third Reich.

It so happened that, along with many others in the Berlin express, I possessed a book of registered marks cheques, purchased in London before my departure. They were exchangeable at something like twenty marks to the pound—a rate which makes living in Germany cheaper than in any other great country in Europe. On arrival at the Hook of Holland I was informed by a Dutch official that I could exchange some of my registered marks at Benkheim on the German frontier. In the meantime I was invited to dispense four shillings and sixpence for a roll, a cup of coffee, a minute pot of jam and an abhorrent slice of tasteless Edam cheese, in Dutch gilders because I was privileged to land in Holland. It was the normal introduction to Europe experienced by so many who have made that bleak crossing of the North Sea in the early hours of the morning in the autumn season. It was a comfort to take one's place in the commodious Mitropa wagon of the direct express and to watch, as the train made its way across the flats, a country rouse itself to the business of the day with the knowledge that it was not necessary for you to emerge from those trim, smug, red-bricked houses and make your way on top of a bicycle over the narrow roads between the canals to an office or factory somewhere on the far side of the grey horizon. I have never quite understood how Rembrandt Van Ryn and Vermeer of Delft obtained their inspiration from a landscape which has not changed in essential details and a people who are so dreary in their outlook. After the shivering cold of the endless platforms and buffets of the Hook, the Mitropa Speisewagen seemed like Paradise Regained. The geniality of the conductors and waiters was contagious. But at Benkheim there was to be disillusionment.

For here it was found that there were no facilities for the exchange of registered marks. The well-mannered official of the customs who had courteously examined the luggage of all, and the young man who politely asked the amount of foreign currency carried by each individual, in order that he might possess himself of a certificate of self-protection, had explained that it would not be possible to exchange money before arrival at Berlin. There was some expostulation but the officials pointed out that it would be only a matter of a few hours in any case and that the issue of registered marks was a privilege given to foreigners and not vouchsafed to Germans.

It was noteworthy that from the moment the frontier was passed the restaurant-car was almost denuded of passengers. There was one particularly noisy party of American young men who had flourished their money about while crossing Holland, who were conspicuously absent when they discovered they could not take advantage of the traveller's exchange. Later I saw them on the platform of Hanover station eating sausages with characteristic piles of mustard smeared over the edges of cardboard platters. Although they were well equipped with dollar money they were not prepared to spend a few shillings extra on a comfortable meal in the restaurant-car although they must have been well aware that in the weeks ahead they were to enjoy the advantages of a specially regulated exchange. I found it difficult to understand the attitude of the handsome English commercial traveller on his way to Stockholm who denied himself luncheon because he could obtain no registered marks. The following day I saw him paying the bill for a most expensive young lady after dinner at the Hotel Bristol on the Linden. I suppose that time he had visited the appropriate bank or travel agency.

Actually on arrival in Berlin my only small change consisted of a mark and a few pfennig, apart from the flotsam and jetsam of silver and copper which are always left over in the pocket of the traveller from England. A courier of the America Express Company sensed my predicament and told me I could change money on the station. He conducted me through the subway of the station to where dozens of travellers stood in a queue brandishing their books of registered marks. It would have involved a wait of a quarter of an hour and I was tired after my journey. The courier said :

" If you tell me your hotel I will pay the porter and arrange for your big luggage. I can come along later."

One might have thought that he was looking for an elaborate tip, but in the circumstances I did not much care. Later on the head porter of the Kaiserhof told me that the courier had only asked for the actual charges plus the universal ten per cent *pourboire.* I wondered afterwards if a traveller arriving in any other great capital in Europe would have had his entry made so pleasant. I have a nodding acquaintance with Victoria ; I am familiar with the Gare du Nord ; I have even reached the Pennsylvania Terminus in a state of temporary penury. My mind still goes back to the spectacle of those young men on the platform at Hanover grimacing over sausages they did not like instead of eating the restaurant-car roast veal which they could well have afforded.

Sauntering into the Wilhelmplatz and down the famous Leipzigerstrasse to the broad space in front of the Potsdam station, I was quickly aware that nearly everybody in Berlin was well dressed and walked with an air. The people of Berlin have never been very emotional nor outwardly very gay. In the Berlin streets there is—and ever has been—the resilience of the Grands boulevards. But on this occasion I sensed a feeling of definite well-being. The flower-girls reminded one of their more celebrated counterparts in Piccadilly Circus with their good-humoured attempts at *badinage.* The big Aeschinger café was packed to the doors and the approach to the Vaterland restaurant was crowded. As dusk came so the lights went up in a blaze and life moved with the anticipatory swiftness of the pleasures of evening. I wandered from one end of Berlin to the other. On all sides there was movement and a restrained gaiety of people who had not a great deal to spend but were determined to spend it to the utmost advantage. It was pleasant to see husbands and wives, young men and their sweethearts, rejoicing round glasses of beer and goblets of wine and plates of sausage and *delicatessen.* Never any extravagances: never any drunkenness. The glimpses one caught of life within the dark curtains conjured up unpleasant comparisons with spectacles that might be seen in the public-houses all over England that same Friday night—the bleak tavern, the unkempt service of beer, ale and porter, the children standing at the door, kept silent by occasional gifts of synthetic potato chips or halfpennies with which to buy bad boiled sweets. Perhaps one should not draw too firm impressions from the appearance of the streets of a city. It is a stock argument. But sometimes I wonder what the foreigner in our midst, having overcome his admiration for our policemen, deduces from the drabness and poverty so obvious in the streets of nearly all our great cities.

Berlin, as always, impressed one with its cleanliness, its thoroughness. The orderliness of buildings and public places are a reflection of the inhabitants. Likewise the scrubbed whiteness of the universal deal-topped tables in the beer-houses and wine restaurants. Likewise for each glass either a cardboard mat or a paper serviette fitting round the stem of a wine cup to prevent unnecessary mess and spilling. Small things, these last named, may be, but so characteristic of the great city, so greatly crying out for imitation elsewhere.

Life in the capital had not changed, except that places were more patronised than previously. In Habel's famous wine-shop, the same close-cropped Prussians of the officer and junker type still sipped the best sherry to be obtained in Berlin with traditional solemnity and occasional grunts. In the Heidelburg in the Friedrichstrasse those up from the country for the day wandered open-mouthed from one fake provincial restaurant to another, and in the Taverna, once the rendezvous of Anglo-American newspaper correspondents, the more arty of the young German Bohemian set strove artlessly to enjoy flasks of Chianti and Orvieto. The night resorts in the Kurfürstendam still pursued their dreary, over-illuminated way. The same cabarets persisted, except that the girls had put on a little lingerie to make themselves look attractive to men of taste, and the homosexuals who were such a feature of the Republican régime no longer sat in women's clothes at the long bars or in the vestibules outside. In the arcades of the Linden one encountered here and there a furtive beggar who waited on obvious foreigners to regale them with stories of Nazi persecution (somehow a profitable source of income for down-and-outs) in exchange for a mark or two. Round the corner the same harlots as of old—middle-aged *frauen* made up to look their own naïve conception of a Champs Élysées *demi monde*, but never getting farther than the Palais Royal or perhaps the rue de Malte. The great yellow omnibuses crunched along unceasingly and taxis darted about like green wasps. In the automats one saw through the wide-open doors young workers from the labour camps, mechanics in overalls, or newly-uniformed conscripts of the Reichswehr, buying glasses of beer and sardines on toast for their young women and then devouring them together while they confided their innermost feelings and told the story which young people the world over will never grow tired of.

One has read of the spirit of fear and terror which prevails in Berlin and other great German centres. Ordinary observation produces no evidence of this. Of course when one attempts to impose British ideas of liberty and procedure on the Nazi plan, one encounters unpleasant shocks. An Anglo-Saxon visitor still finds it difficult to understand the party persecution of the Jews, however much he may agree that the Jews had worked their way into professions and industries to a degree that was out of proportion to their numbers.

The pornography of Der Stürmer is nauseating and the fact that Jewish lawyers must display on their nameplates that they are not permitted to act as counsel is more than petty. The obsession of race purity may be a little absurd and quite impractical of realisation. But the Anglo-Saxon should remember that the vast majority of Germans accept this segregation of the Jews as a bounden duty, a first instinct of patriotism. One might go on indefinitely. There is no doubt that certain opponents of the régime exist both inside and outside the concentration camps. They are well aware of the rules of the political game as played in Germany. If they make any obvious moves against the régime then they are asking for persecution and suppression. One evening I sat down in a café in the Saarlanderstrasse. On the opposite side of the table were a man and his wife. They proved to be Jews in a fairly comfortable position. Their point of view was interesting. I convinced them that I was an Englishman, and when I mentioned the Gestapo they laughed. The man added, " Certainly our lot is not quite so easy as it was. But we keep quiet, obey the regulations, go about our business and no one interferes with us. The fact that we cannot leave Germany is no hardship, for in this respect we are like all other Germans under the *devisen* laws and, after all, in my case I am a German and must agree with what my country wants whether I like it or not. So many Jews and all communists forget their duty to their own country."

During my subsequent stay in Berlin I talked with people in all walks of life, from members of the ministry to the humblest worker. Although there were a few who found the strict regulations of the new régime occasionally irksome, all were unanimous on one thing —that Germany must never return to the political chaos of pre-revolution days.

The general tenor of conversation was, " At least we can now make some arrangements for the future with some degree of certainty. Before, no one in Germany knew what the morning would bring forth."

It was a general feeling of newly-found security and stability which left a lasting impression on my mind. And it was emphasised over and over again during my stay in Germany and in the course of hundreds of miles of travel. It was also made immediately apparent that the average German was proud of the revolution, and what it had done in restoring law and order. Moreover, the stranger was welcome in their midst, the Englishman especially. For the English the Germans of the Nazi Revolution have a very deep respect which they would like to see developed into cordial mutual friendship, into that understanding of common interests which to my mind is the most important factor in modern politics and which persuaded me to take up the task of writing this book.

An immediate result of nearly all national revolutions is an impetus to building. The Nazi Revolution is no exception. Not only in Berlin but in all parts of the country there is feverish building activity —housing, public works, bridges, harbours, railways, motor roads. Plans made in the days of the Republic are now being developed on a colossal scale, and it may fairly be said that whole areas of many cities will be rebuilt in a matter of a few years. On the outskirts of Berlin new suburbs are springing up like mushrooms, but they are not suburbs of smug, semi-detached villas like those which have made the approach to London so dreary and uninspiring: they are widespread settlements of houses and cottages designed for the artisan and labourer. This development is part of a scheme organised by the German Labour Front to provide homes for 5,000,000 workers, where the ordinary factory hand can not only have his own house built in accordance with his means and requirements, but also own a tract of land big enough to grow his annual supply of potatoes and cabbages. Germany is a very big country and it is possible to indulge in such ambitious experiments. Outside Berlin there are enormous tracts of land available for such developments of workman-cum-peasant proprietorship. Similar conditions do not apply in the immediate vicinity of Manchester and Glasgow and it would be impossible to undertake similar schemes here at home. But in Germany it is possible, and already there have been some remarkable changes in the housing of the working man.

Perhaps a difference of mentality enters into this

question of housing. The German worker has never been thoroughly wedded to the city. In the great mining districts of Upper Silesia and the Ruhr the miner at the pit-face leaves the shaft to go back to his potato patch. In the Saar territory many workers cycle ten miles to their work so that they can live in the country and grow their own vegetables. The same applies to tens of thousands of the labouring classes, and I was not surprised to find a similar eagerness on the part of the Berliner now that facilities are being provided. I visited many of these new settlements, some of them only just being developed, others half completed, others already inhabited. There was one especially interesting new workman's suburb far beyond Coepenick, famous for its cobbler who became a captain for a day. True, it was no show-place: there was nothing of the trim, monotonous red brick cottage streets about this new village: on the contrary every house differed from its neighbour, often startlingly so. Occasionally indeed one felt that individuality had been permitted too loose a rein: but, after all, these were working men's dwellings and the working man was entitled to live in a house which he found convenient and attractive to himself. In any case, after he had paid the requisite monthly instalments from his pay-roll, the property would be his own.

This particular settlement was roughly built round a huge open space in a clearance of a wood. It was approached by a road specially connecting with the electric railway station that served the factory in Berlin, where most of the workers were employed. As I have said there was no attempt at uniformity of design. Some of the cottages had two storeys: others were extensive bungalows. But each had a plot of land and each its own decorative garden gate. In some of the homes the more enterprising workers had installed central heating. Each owner having put down a small sum of money, and being advanced the remainder by the equivalent of a building society, is entitled to do what he likes with his land. And some of the results were at least surprising. At one home I visited, the owner had a veritable menagerie. He had enclosed a large area with wire meshing and within these lived a medley of poultry, ducks, geese and tame rabbits—the last named grown for both food and pelts. The labourer insisted on showing me his cellar. There, in huge bins, were a ton of potatoes and half a ton of turnips. In a second room was his wife. She was busy bottling gherkins. This same man had grown five hundredweights under glass ! The German loves gherkins but I am still wondering how this simple man and his wife could contrive to eat five hundredweights. Another house had a series of pens containing ewes which were kept for milk. The flower gardens were invariably exquisite. Some houses had large rose-beds. In others young apple and pear trees were bearing their first fruit. In their spare time—how they find it after tending their enormous plots is a mystery—they help transform the open space of their settlement into a large green suitable for a children's playground in the middle of which they one day hope to erect a fountain !

Such rural settlements for town workers are now becoming quite frequent. In most cases they are being built on the principle of self-help. If the workman can assist in the building, he is encouraged to do so, for by such means he can reduce the ultimate cost. In this particular settlement several of the houses were completely built by their owners from materials provided through public funds on the same principle of partial payments as if the house was erected by a contractor. In the course of my visit I could not help but be struck by the splendid independent spirit of these workers. Nearly all of them had previously lived in the slum areas of the capital. None of them were earning much more than thirty shillings a week after their State insurance and other contributions had been deducted. But each one had a decent house and a garden that could really be called a garden, and not a back-yard. In such circumstances it was not surprising that they were enthusiasts for a revolution that had brought about such an agreeable change in their environment. And it may be added that scarcely one of these working men belonged to the National Socialist party in the days before 1933 and many indeed may have been its bitter opponents.

There are less happy aspects of the social life of modern Germany so far as the working classes are concerned. Germany is a great industrial country, eighty per cent of the population of which are still crowded in the big cities. In a community of 70,000,000 left beaten in the Great War and impoverished by reparations payments and the inflation of the mark, a certain distress must be anticipated. In fact, even in the most prosperous times it is doubtful if unemployment can ever wholly be eliminated and a certain amount of hardship, due to old age, infirmity, disease and accident, is inevitable. Although through the development of the munitions industry and the absorption of hundreds of thousands of young men in the compulsory labour camps and in the ranks of the army, the sum total of unemployed has been miraculously reduced, Germany faced the winter of

1936–7 with more than a million out of work. Besides this there were many more who, although employed, were far too near the bread line to do without help from outside. To alleviate national distress became a pressing necessity just as it had been in previous years, and indeed before Hitler came into power. But it is very much to be doubted whether there has ever been organised in the history of the world such an elaborate charity as what is known as the "W.H.W."—Winter Hilf Werke, or Winter Help Work—that exists in modern Germany.

Although I encountered many instances of the ramifications of this great organisation during my travels in Germany, I found evidence of its greatest usefulness during my stay in Berlin. For it was in Berlin that I was witness of really striking acts of State generosity of a kind that ought to command both the attention and admiration of the most ardent Socialist as well as those who organise balls at West End hotels, spending several thousand pounds on amusement in order to give a few hundreds to charity.

Now if the new régime in Germany suffers from one besetting sin, it is the sin of over-organisation. There have been instances of such an addiction to bureaucratic methods as to leave certain districts short of food and give abundance to other areas simply because the requisite forms have not been filled up. Bureaucracy is an inheritance of modern civilisation, something from which the world may never be quite free. I encountered something of this new despotism in the headquarters of the Winter Help Work. It is situated in a former factory in the outskirts of Berlin—an enormous building of offices and passages, but chiefly passages. At the entrance gates stand the appropriate guardians and in a panelled chamber—presumably the former directors' waiting-room—there sit a number of officials who regard the visitor either with indifference or meticulous courtesy. It would be difficult to gather from first impressions that here is the entry to the great office that is the aid and hope of millions. But the right introduction and the appropriate salute on the part of your companion, will introduce you to one of the most amazing organisations of the modern world.

It was my privilege to meet Herr Hilgenfeld, the chief director of the Winter Help Work. He is a handsome man, tall, slightly bald, clean shaven and even cleaner skinned. He began life as a professional statistician and later graduated in the world of industry. He has been known for many years as one of the best organisers in Germany, and his choice as director of this great relief work was singularly fortunate and happy. He received me in his office and instead of entering into pæans of praise concerning the achievements of this elaborate state charity in the past, was much more concerned in emphasising its difficulties in the future. He was essentially realist. He knew that the world situation made money scarce and that of all the activities of mankind, that which took the most persuasion to accomplish was charity.

Herr Hilgenfeld told me that in 1933 he was asked by Herr Hitler to organise social relief for 17,000,000 destitute or near destitute German people.

"We had to start from nothing, but we had to succeed because it was the wish of our Führer," he said simply. "He had given the order that in the first winter of his power no German citizen should go hungry, be without fire and shelter.

"There was only one source of supply of money—the people and their industries. We worked on the basis that those who have most should give most. It is surely fair. We managed to get an organisation together and provided food for the 17,000,000. In the following year we had an easier task for conditions in Germany had improved. Only 14,000,000 came on the books of the Winter Help Fund. By this time we had had time to look into the workings of our nation-wide organisation and it was gratifying to discover that administration expenses were only one per cent of the total money raised for public relief.

"The staple diet of the German is the potato, and we concentrated on the supply and distribution of this vegetable. If the worst came to the worst, adequate potatoes would work wonders for they could be supplemented by provisions purchased by the unemployed worker from the money he received out of state insurance—the equivalent of what you call the dole, only on a much more modest scale.

"In the winter of 1934–5 we distributed 60,000 railway wagon loads of potatoes, or approximately a million tons. How enormous was the task may be judged from the fact that we sent 700 trucks every day to Berlin for more than a fortnight and in distant places like Breslau everyone received one pound of potatoes a day at the very least. The tastes and habits of the German provinces had to be taken into consideration. In the east the people eat far more potato than they do in Bavaria. Also Bavaria and Silesia have sufficient local supplies, but even in normal times potatoes have to be transported in bulk to Berlin, Rhenish Westphalia, the Grand Duchy of Baden and parts of Wurtemburg. Believe me, it took all my statisticians and economists all their time in working up accurate lists, and perhaps with the best will in the world we occasionally made mistakes: for we are only human.

"After potatoes came coal. We required 170,000 trucks. The coal had to be purchased as cheaply as possible, and so I appointed local committees all over the country. Matters have been so arranged that each local centre fixes a price for coal with its own coal merchants. The distribution is so arranged that those in need receive tickets on the basis of one ticket for every hundredweight. The coal merchant assembles his tickets and forwards them to the pits when he has enough for a truck-load. He gets vouchers from the wholesalers and these vouchers are paid by cheque at once by the central authority. Thus for the ordinary retailer the transaction is just a matter of ordinary business except that he is selling to our organisation instead of to a private individual.

"We have worked it out that a family with two children consumes 900 lb. of coal during the cold winter months. In the coal-mining districts a similar poor family is given 2,200 lb. for here they have always been accustomed to burning large quantities of coal in more prosperous times. It is not our desire ever to emphasise poverty or changed circumstances.

"Generally speaking the quantity of coal supplied suffices to keep at least one room heated throughout the whole winter. The amounts given are increased according to the number of children in the family. A family of three or four children cannot live in one room and so coal for other rooms must be provided. You can guess how much coal we require from the fact that the total quantity would keep the whole of the Saar coalfield at work for three full months.

"Last year we gave away enough boots for the

whole population of the major part of Wurtemburg and the whole of Baden. The amount of material purchased for making clothes was more than 5,000 miles. And yet the enemies of our organisation say that most of the money we raise in the name of winter charity goes in the manufacture of war armaments. It is just another scandal. Germany is becoming accustomed to being misunderstood and maligned."

Herr Hilgenfeld went on to describe the various methods of raising money—by the sale of tokens, by the " one pot luncheon " on the first Sunday in the month. I had not yet experienced this grim form of self-denial. In fact, on the Sunday in question I went into a restaurant and calmly ordered a satisfying meal. The head waiter politely informed me that all I could have was a bowl of soup and an apple ! In Germany one becomes accustomed to the unexpected and I did not complain, I just awaited my soup. The Germans often make good soup, but this soup was in the nature of an ordeal. In a mass of lentil beans and dirty gravy there floated a piece of greasy bacon. The bowl became an object of horror and disgust and I quickly ordered my apple, preferring to starve until evening rather than spend the rest of the day in agony of indigestion—or perhaps something worse. I was charged two marks and fifty pfennig for this collation, the greater part of which went into the charity box. I reflected afterwards, however, how admirably contrived was this compulsory rationing. It was a sort of Friday fast day brought up to date and made effective. And in the long run it must prove good for the middle-aged Germans' stomach !

The amount collected last winter for the funds was approximately 212,945,000 rentenmarks. In addition there were gifts of goods, and produce purchased at reduced values of 154,480,000 rentenmarks. The total figure thus reaches the formidable height of nearly 370,000,000 rentenmarks. Of this, soup-Sundays produced a total of 29,000,000 rentenmarks—which goes to show what can be done for charity when a nation goes without a meal in the interests not only of its own health but also of the less-fortunate members of the community.

Herr Hilgenfeld also showed me that in Berlin alone over 8,000 foreigners and 13,000 Jews had been assisted in some way or another by the organisation. Incidentally of the first-named category sixty-one were British subjects. Poles required most assistance. There were 2,008 on the unemployed and indigent list.

"I would like to emphasise," concluded Herr Hilgenfeld, "that the German Winter Relief Organisation assists those in need regardless of creed and political feelings."

And I was able later to prove the truth of his words for as I shall describe I had a meal with the down-and-outs at Cologne for the token sum of twenty pfennig—a meal provided by the Winter Help Work which was the equal for the actual fare of that provided in any restaurant in the city.

The moment I left the presence of this broad-minded, intelligent organiser, I was almost overwhelmed in a cloud of charts and diagrams. I was taken from room to room and shown elaborate graphs and maps, that must have taken expert cartographers weeks to prepare. Some of them were marvels of the draughtsman's art. I learned—or I ought to have learned—all about the distribution of foodstuffs in the Reich—animal, fish, food, and vegetable. I found out that there had in the past been much waste of surplus fish which was now being distributed by the winter help organisation—aided by fast trains—throughout Germany. An official declared that they were making Breslau " fish minded ". Another chart—a supreme work—indicated the distribution of the essential potato cultivation in the country. I discovered that the Germans ate three kinds of potatoes—yellow, red and white. It did not follow that the people who grew red potatoes liked to eat red potatoes. More often they preferred white potatoes and the people who grew white potatoes ate red potatoes for choice. It was all very paradoxical and was made even more so by an indication that Berliners with Catholic taste liked all three varieties—yellow, white and red. From potatoes we went on to coal, both hard and soft. Fierce-looking coal-trains sped across the map carrying coal from Gleiwitz to East Prussia and Saarbrucken to Pomerania. I learned that the man who can prove his need could obtain a hundredweight of coal periodically on the production of 15 pfennig. This charge is made in order to give the impoverished individual the feeling that he is at least paying something, and is not falling into the ignominious position of the man who, condescendingly, is given a present for nothing—which is the way of too many charities. Even so this lesson in practical knowledge of Germany's interior economy as demonstrated by charts and statistics might have continued indefinitely without materially adding to my knowledge apart from theory of the Winter Help Organisation, if I had not suggested very meekly that I would like to see the organisation actually at work. My request took these worthy civil servants completely by surprise. I realised how entertaining and helpful they thought they were being and felt quite embarrassed. But having made my request I felt I must go on with it. And in the end I had my way.

Now it is often said that visitors to Germany are only shown those things which the Nazis think it is good for them to see. If one would believe report there are certain show-places which are earmarked for the visitor who intends to write about what he sees on his return home. I can fairly say that this was not my experience. Wherever I went I was always asked what interested me and what I would like to see. On many occasions plans were changed at the last minute to suit my personal convenience. Only on one occasion was my request refused and that was when I expressed a desire to see the model village built for the Olympic athletes in the Grunewald forest. The village was ultimately intended as an officer's training school and it was already occupied by young cadets. It was not possible for me to visit it. But on second thoughts I do not suppose that the Officer Commanding the Royal Academy at Woolwich would open up the " shop " for the inspection of an itinerant German journalist who wanted by chance to see exactly how our future gunners and engineers live and have their being.

In due course a car was found, and I was taken through the east end of Berlin to that part which is known as the Horst Wessel Platz, named after the poet who was killed by Communists and became the Nazi hero. We entered a courtyard through a crazy tumble-down wooden door over an ill-tiled pavement. In front rose a gloomy, shabby building and by the side of a small flight of steps leading to the entrance were piles of broken packing-cases and bundles of waste paper. It was all very forlorn. Inside a bleak passage were seated a number of old women who rose at our approach and gave the Nazi salute. They were the neighbouring poor who had come to obtain food from the Winter Help Organisation. We climbed some rickety stairs to the upper rooms. They were filled with files recording in the minutest detail the amount of foodstuffs which had been given away to each individual. The local director was very proud of his records which I dare bet will never be looked at. He was an extremely intelligent Berliner of the middle classes and was almost the only paid official in the centre, the remainder being volunteer workers. He explained that he was operating in one of the poorest quarters of the capital and that his area contained 43,000 people. Last year he was called on to help 11,000 men, women, and children. Conditions had greatly improved and this particular winter he did not think there would be more than 5,000 on the distressed list. However, perhaps I would like to see the distribution of food?

Down on the lower floor I found a miniature Covent Garden. The surplus supplies from the central market had come in and were being sorted. There were enormous piles of cauliflowers, red cabbages (much eaten in Germany), egg plants, turnips, and parsnips. The potato store was next door. In another room were shelves piled high with groceries of all kinds, including a special section devoted to tinned milk. The display of good things to eat in these shabby old rooms belied the dismal appearance of the house. But, as the director said, it had been difficult to obtain adequate premises for both food *and* files and this old house cost practically nothing in rent and so left money to be spent on more foodstuffs. I learned that each family who desired relief applied in person and each case was personally investigated by the volunteer workers. They were given special vouchers setting out what they were entitled to, and on presentation were given the amounts of bread, vegetables, and groceries set out on their forms. At this particular depot the foodstuffs were in charge of an old soldier who had lost a leg on the Russian front during the war. As each old woman came up he had a cheery word and all seemed to go away contented. Certainly the quality of the food handed out was equal to that displayed in the best shops of the centre of the capital.

The Winter Help Work, however, is not confined to the distribution of food and coal. The necessity for warm clothing in the severe weather of January and February in North Germany is fully recognised. Furthermore, Hitler's insistence on the necessity for a bigger population and the protection of young mothers in childbirth is reflected in the distribution of *layettes* and cradles to those who have need of them but no money with which to buy them.

The clothing department of the W.H.W. in Berlin is an amazing institution. It is situated in a modern building that was once a fruit store for the markets close to the famous Bourse railway station, a station that often figured in the street riots previous to 1933. In it is contained storey after storey packed with clothing of all kinds. In fact, it looks for all the world like a wholesale manufacturer's warehouse, with thousands of overcoats hanging on rails: piles of shirts, underwear (for both sexes), stockings, socks, and even hats and caps. An endeavour is made to distribute the various patterns of garments as much as possible to the depots in all the big cities so that a poor person cannot be picked out as wearing obviously charity clothes. It must be said that in the Third Reich every effort is made to remove the stigma of charity and poverty. It is for that reason that only a few examples of a stock model are distributed in each city. This immense store of garments is purchased by the control fund and distributed according to the reports of the official investigators.

Apart from the ordinary routine distribution, two incidents recur to me of my visit to the clothing depot—one was the equipment of a number of German refugees from Spain: the other was the provision of a *layette* for an expectant mother. The refugees had arrived in Berlin from Bilbao in a state of destitution. I saw their miserable rags and heelless shoes. They were indeed a sorry sight—a man, his wife, a Spanish woman, a boy of about fourteen, and a pretty dark-haired girl of eleven. While I was there in the depot they were completely reclothed. Everything was provided from ties for the husband to cotton gloves for the girl. Each was given an overcoat, an extra pair of shoes, and a parcel of under-linen. The whole operation did not take long. The man and his boy were taken to a changing room in the male department. The woman and her daughter disappeared through some curtains to emerge twenty minutes later as well-dressed members of the Berlin bourgeoisie.

The incident of the young expectant mother was even more touching. She was a young girl—hardly twenty I should imagine—and was obviously due to give birth to a child in the course of the very near future. I learned from her papers that she was the bride of a clerk who was only earning a small salary and could not afford to provide the necessary linen and garments for his first baby. The girl had come to obtain a *layette*, sheets, blankets, and warm clothes for herself. The linen that was given—there were huge quantities available—was no cheap material. On the contrary. Moreover, the *layette* was generous in the number of articles provided. Sheets, blankets and baby clothes were made into a huge bundle and then handed to a volunteer worker to take to the young woman's home. It would be difficult to imagine a more complete organisation. And of the good work it does, I have not the least doubt.

Investigation of unemployment problems is always a matter of difficulty, and whatever one concludes is bound to be disputed by one school of thought or the other. In Germany an attempt has been made to absorb the workless on elaborate schemes of public works. The construction of the great motor roads has taken more than a quarter of a million labourers from the streets. Then again there is the enormous total of young men in the compulsory labour camps and the young conscripts required to bring up to strength the thirty-six divisions of the regular army brought into existence by Hitler. The subject of unemployment has always been controversial since the Nazis came into power and in England many of my friends assured me that workless men were scattered in millions all over the country. This fact I proved by my own observation and inquiries to be completely untrue. Let me say here and now that there is no obvious distress in Germany. I often went out on my own in search of slum areas and could not find them. In Dusseldorf, in Essen, in Breslau, all manufacturing centres, there are no dismal congeries of tumbledown insanitary houses like those which disgrace many boroughs in the East End of London or those terrible shambles which pass for miners' homes in the Rhondda Valley or Ton-y-Pandy. Even if the wages of the German worker are low and he has to work longer hours in factory or at pit-face, at least he has a decent place to sleep in at nights.

Now it is a fact beyond denial that at the time of the triumphant elections of 1933 Germany was in the throes of the most appalling unemployment. I can well believe the Government officials when they say there were 6,000,000 able-bodied men out of work. I myself saw signs of desperate misery in those days —in Munich, in Stuttgart, and in Berlin—and it was a misery made all the more poignant by the tense uncertainty of the hour. I would go so far as to say that in Berlin at that time the number of beggars on the Linden was quite as deplorable as that which haunted the main station of Naples in the hey-day of *lazzaroni* before the coming of the Duce. It was impossible to walk alone in the Tiergarten without danger of molestation and threats of subsequent blackmail by perverts and degenerates, unless you gave freely and quickly. It was pathetic to watch the shivering, starving unemployed hanging round the famous beer-houses of the Neuhauserstrasse of Munich, and to enter the pepper-pot-towered cathedral on a weekday was made as difficult by the press of beggars as entry into the Madaleine or the Église St. Roch in Paris on a Sunday when mendicancy receives the blessing of sanctity and religion. Bearing those memories in mind, it was impossible not to be impressed by the conditions which prevailed in the same cities a little more than three years later.

Whether Hitler has solved the unemployment problem in the Reich is a matter for conjecture. The question is already the stalking-horse—or shall we say the hobby-horse—of economists who rarely arrive at correct conclusions in any case. But it is certain that Hitler has removed the more obvious signs of distress and given the needy a system of state relief which make free, and voluntarily organised, midnight coffee stalls under the shadow of Admiralty Arch and the cold comfort of a neighbouring church as a dormitory for down-and-outs, seem just a little unworthy of the great traditions of English rightmindedness which our Prime Ministers, and especially our Primates, are so fond of preaching about.

When I visited the offices of the unemployment organisation I encountered an atmosphere of realism, of a kind appropriate to an office which had to do with stark matter of fact instead of picturesque phrase and faery legend. The head of the bureau reminded me that unemployment and its happier counterpart, employment, were matters of fluctuation. " We are not miracle men," he said. " All we know is that at the moment unemployment in Germany is less than it has been for many years."

It was his contention that on January 30, '33—the great day in Nazi history—there were 6,014,000 unemployed completely dependent on public charity or else starving in attic or gutter. In the autumn of 1936 that figure had been reduced to 1,035,000. He added :

" It may be said that in a great country like Germany one million unemployed is an irreducible minimum. I do not know. Unemployment is no new problem in the world. Our records show that in December, 1895, there were 500,000 out of work in the Reich. To-day our population, in spite of the Peace Treaty, is much bigger. We have tried to get at an accurate figure and our million includes the unemployable, the criminal classes, the habitual inebriates, the permanently sick and infirm, and, most important of all, the always fluctuating factor of the thousands of men moving from place to place and job to job."

The unemployed in Germany receive benefit in accordance with the monies they have paid into State insurance. Moreover, if work is available they either take it or benefit ceased. It is a case of work to eat if there is work to be had. Even if wages are below the bread-line the worker must labour for there are always the relief funds to eke out his pittance. Germany has not encouraged our pernicious example of allowing its unemployed or needy workers to prop up street-corner posts for ten or twelve years in the hallowed name of individual liberty—and the dole.

The method of distributing monetary relief to the unemployed in Germany is very complicated and is honeycombed with the committees and boards and regulations so dear to the bureaucratic mentality of the official classes. It would appear however that a worker who, in the ordinary way, earns 30 marks a week, can obtain 10 marks or so while he is out of work.

At the time of my visit to Germany the industries most seriously affected by the economic crisis were the coal and textile industries. There was a certain amount of unemployment in the Saar, in Saxony, parts of the Rhineland and in Silesia. But at the same time it was maintained there was no unemployment in Bavaria, Wurtemburg, Baden, most of Pomerania, and East Prussia.

The evening I left Berlin for Cologne in my search of Germany I sat at a round wooden table in the Weinstube of the Furstenhof in the Potsdamerplatz and ate an early dinner of roast pheasant and a quarter of a litre of red wine. The bill came to something well under two shillings. All around me men and women were enjoying excellent fare at equally modest prices. In the extensive restaurant a door or two away it was possible to eat at even cheaper rates, and the food was of equal quality and everything agreeable save that you had to help yourself from a machine—a proccss I learned to dislike on Broadway nearly twenty years ago. As I went back to my hotel I made my way through presses of thousands of people all talking aloud, and experience has taught me that only glum crowds are drearily-minded crowds. It occurred to me that in his mass production of outward content Hitler had been eminently successful and that at least was no mean achievement in a world of doubt and apprehension. When the porter at the Friedrichstrasse station had placed my luggage in the vestibule of the flying train for the Rhineland and given me the dual farewell, "Guter Reise. Heil Hitler," I felt that his cheery salutation was a real Godspeed from a man who had come to think that may be this was not such a bad world after all.

CHAPTER II

SEVEN HOUSES IN COLOGNE

ROUND about seven o'clock the hooter of the Diesel engine gave a low moan and imperceptibly the four coaches of the " train " glided from the platform into the darkness, quietly leaving the throbbing life of the heart of the city for the leisurely stillness of the suburbs before bidding Spandau a swift farewell and leaping across the Havel. The flying trains are not the least remarkable innovations of this new Germany. For hour after hour we sped along at an average of 160 kilometres—one hundred miles—an hour, the dial of a speedometer indicating what can only be described as the train's velocity. In one of the coaches was a snack-bar, but uniformed attendants brought trays of food to those who preferred to remain seated. There was a gentle, swaying motion that lulled the mind to a sense of forgetfulness of the swift crack of death that must accompany any defect of mechanism or the presence of obstacles on the track. It seemed as if one had scarcely time to settle down and read the opening pages of one's book, before the train had stopped and through the windows one read the word " Hanover ". Three times more we stopped—at Dortmund, Essen, and Dusseldorf. At each station passengers got off—mostly businessmen and commercial travellers—and by the time we reached Cologne, after five hours and a few minutes, the four coaches were almost deserted.

As the snake-like train had rushed its way through the Ruhr one caught frequent glimpses of glaring blast furnaces and factories with a thousand lighted windows. At Dusseldorf huge arc-lamps picked out the high white walls of a city which is at once a tourist centre and the hub of great industry. At Cologne the train came gently to a standstill in the railway station dominated by the two lofty steeples of the cathedral, eternal stone sentinels keeping their watch on the Rhine. It was just past midnight when I emerged on the great square, but there were lights everywhere and the yellow trams, so familiar to tens of thousands of British war-time soldiers, were growling along in all directions with all the noise and fuss synonymous with tramways on the Continent. The well-kept streets, the big hotels and still bigger public offices, the characteristic pile of the railway station impressed one with a feeling of outward solidity and strength. Here was indeed an ancient city, the birthplace of Agrippina, daughter of Germanicus ; and its towers looked down on two thousand years of authentic history.

Cologne, the true metropolis of the Rhineland, in spite of the jealousy of neighbouring Dusseldorf, is a manufacturing city of about 650,000 people. In such a vast community distress and unemployment have been inevitable during the last twenty years. Since the evacuation of the Rhine by the British army, the economic crisis has laid a heavy hand on the city. But even so, thanks to many schemes of relief work, it would be difficult to find a city in Europe with a more contented population or one with such a sense of *esprit de ville*.

On the morning after my arrival in Cologne I had one of the best simple lunches—and certainly the cheapest —I have ever eaten. It cost me twenty pfennig.

I had come to Cologne expressly to see the Nazi system of self-help, public relief and public works as evidenced in a great provincial city and, as a Hansa town, a city of traditional independence of spirit and individuality of character.

As I have already remarked, in times of world crisis and distress one of the most difficult problems of State has been the question of alleviation of the hardships of those who find themselves without adequate means of sustenance. It is not enough to speak only in terms of the unemployed. In our own country we have, for far too long, thought of the economic crisis in terms of manual labourers who have been actually out of work. And we have only trifled even with this major issue. We have impoverished the earning classes by enforcing heavy taxation to provide for the dole. We have demoralised the unfortunate unemployed artisan by making him conscious that he is in receipt of public charity (although this was not the intention of public health insurance and unemployment benefit relief) and we have made the lot of many deserving poor almost intolerable by the imposition of an arbitrary examination, glibly and dishonestly described as the " means test ". Our approach to the unemployment situation has done more to undermine the mental and physical health of the nation since the war than many of our more spectacular governmental mistakes.

No one will deny that the welfare of the labouring classes is one of the most important and vital interests of the organised state. It is the duty of any government worthy of the name to see that its manual workers have the wherewithal to live. The incidence of the system we have developed since the war has in many cases almost denied that right to the unfortunate out-of-work. In any case it has tended to demoralise him by the pernicious system of the queue and the labour exchange and the callous disregard by officialdom of the pride of the individual who is forced to attend at a counter to receive something which he is made to feel he is getting for nothing. At the same time the tragedy of the blackcoated worker who legally has no entitlement even to these doubtful privileges of charity has been almost completely ignored. Indeed, it is almost expected of the elderly clerk that he shall remain obscure in his garret when he can no longer keep in the race with younger competitors. And at the other end of the scale there is always the stigma of poor relief and that barbaric survival, the poor law institution.

In Germany every effort is made to disassociate the act of public relief from the almost inevitable demoralisation which seems inherent in state charity. At the same time the worker in actual employment, whether he be a manual labourer or an *employé* in an office, if he does not earn quite enough to keep him in the absolute necessities of life, is not forgotten. I came across some very vivid examples of this national eleemosynary work during my visit to Cologne.

On the morning of my arrival in the city, as I have said, I had one of the best simple lunches—in the strangest circumstances—I have ever eaten. It cost me twenty rentenpfennig—or shall we say, twopence farthing. It happened in this wise. I lunched with the poor folk of Cologne in the house of the Overstolz.

As became a rich merchant city, Cologne, the Hansa town, was, in the Middle Ages, the home of great traders. Just as at Bourges in France and Genoa in Italy, these traders built for themselves princely dwelling places in which to entertain their rivals and establish the tradition of their families. Such a house was the mansion of the Overstolz, a tall gabled building conceived in exquisite taste, standing in the Rheingasse. To-day its famous banquetting hall still fulfils its original purpose except that instead of being the scene of extravagant bourgeois luxury, it is the eating-place daily of hundreds of poor people. The house of the Overstolz is one of a group of seven buildings in various parts of Cologne set aside as clubs and restaurants for the working classes who cannot afford adequate meals at home nor buy wood and coal to heat their own flats and tenements. In the seven houses are served more than seven thousand meals daily.

I entered the Overstolz mansion through a lofty carved door. On either side of the vestibule were recesses containing the coats of arms of the merchants who had lived here for generations. Heraldic devices were picked out by the morning sun in the stained-glass windows. At the rear of the house was a charming walled garden, with ancient trees, arbours, and terraces. A century-old vine twined up to the second storey. Within the house there was tremendous activity, for the luncheon hour was near. In the banquetting hall about two hundred workmen, smoking pipes or cheap cigars, and reading newspapers, were waiting for the midday meal. In the long passage-way leading to the kitchen were an almost equal number of women and children come with receptacles of all kinds to fetch meals to be consumed in their own homes. The vessels were of an infinite variety—aluminium hot plates, plain pudding basins, even wash-pails. Each one had the merit of being scrupulously clean. In fact, if it had been otherwise the applicant would have been refused when he went to ask for food. Inside the kitchen were enormous boilers containing soup, boiled beef, brown sauce, potatoes, and sauerkraut. About thirty men and women were putting the last-minute touches to the day's luncheon. Most of them, I learned, were voluntary workers, directed by a permanent staff of cooks and caretakers. At a given signal a number of small doors were opened through which the people waiting outside handed in their empty vessels and printed slips valued at twenty pfennig. According to the number of slips, so the number of portions. The charge of twenty pfennig is made in order to give the poor person a feeling that he is at least contributing something towards his meal. Here is another way in which this new Germany endeavours to get over that demoralisation difficulty. I could not but agree with a German friend who was with me. "We are sincerely trying," he said, "to give all Germans a sense of self-respect. We do not wish to let anybody think that he is committing a crime because he happens to be poor." My friend was young and an ardent National Socialist. He spoke with a mixture of emotion and pride and added, "The German workman has very small wages for the Reich is poor. But he is helped in the spending of those wages. He is given opportunity and encouragement to economise but at the same time live decently. This is just one method. The food costs infinitely more than twenty pfennig, but even so the charge is made because we think it is good that he should make some contribution."

Indeed, the food was worth considerably more than twenty pfennig. It was admirably cooked. The portions were sufficient to stave off the most ravenous appetite. Beer could be had for a penny a glass and fresh milk for the same sum. In the dining-hall crockery and cutlery were provided and everyone was waited on by volunteer helpers. As I sat at table I counted two hundred workmen of all types—some in rough working clothes, some in fitters' overalls, some in ordinary lounge suits. In this hall anyone can sit down and eat, no matter who he is, provided he pays his two-pence farthing. There is no scrutiny as to the man's means. It is left to his personal honour that he abuse not the city's charity. In an adjacent room sat about fifty women, eating from plates and dishes of a rather better quality because in Cologne women are still thought to have more delicate tastes than men.

The catering side of the house of the Overstolz by no means monopolises its mission of kindness and good-will. In the upper rooms are to be found all kinds of facilities for rest, recreation, and labour. There are many workmen's constitutional clubs up and down the country which might well envy the appointments and amenities of this home for unemployed and the near-poor in the Overstolz. On the first floor are reading, writing, and recreation-rooms. Germany is a country of broadsheets and newspapers (the suppression of hundreds of publications would appear to have made little difference to the mass production of diurnal literature). The reading-room was piled high with newspapers and magazines of all kinds, and scores of men were sitting around the big stoves engrossed in one sheet or another. Next door were groups standing round chessboards and in a far corner a volunteer teacher was teaching the rudiments of the game to eager workers. In this same room on certain evenings of the week professors attend to give free lessons in French and English to those desirous of learning. The old music-room of the house continues to fulfil its original purpose and is equipped with pianos, violins, and brass instruments, for each house has its own orchestra. Moreover, they make competitive records which are broadcast to the other six houses in other parts of the city from a private studio occupying the topmost gable. But apart from these facilities for creature comforts, there are provided workshops where men who are temporarily unemployed can continue to work at their trade for their own benefit. Thus upholsterers, carpenters, metal workers, carpet makers are provided with tools with which they can repair their own furniture. A special section is reserved for women, containing sewing-machines, cottons, and materials for the making of garments. A very definite community spirit has been aroused and craftsmen assist one another at their various trades. I stayed in the house of the Overstolz for some hours. I still retain memories of a really happy atmosphere among men and women who through no fault of their own have been thrown into what might have been the miseries of hopeless idleness.

During my stay in this part of the Rhineland, I visited another remarkable State charity institution—the *Mutererholingshein*, or Mother Home, of Hirschen in the hills above Bonn. Here is an experiment which could be developed with profit in every industrial country. It is a home for giving mothers a rest from the labour of bringing up children and running a home in the poorer quarters. You reach it by motor-car from Cologne. The road traverses a wooded plain before crossing the Rhine at Bonn, the birthplace of Beethoven and the seat of one of Germany's most famous universities. After that the countryside becomes undulating, the ground rising to fair-sized hills, covered with forests and intersected by rushing white and blue streams. Each mile brings some new and unexpected beauty. The once formidable robber baron's castle of Siegberg momentarily appears on its high rock on the horizon. Suddenly at a hairpin bend the road climbs hurriedly to a detached wood and ends in the enclosed space of the Mother Home. It is all very unexpected, as unexpected as the home itself.

Here are two low yellow and brown houses, very new but designed to fit the countryside in Rhenish style. They form the living and sleeping accommodation of the mothers who require a few weeks in the country to restore their health. At this particular home there are beds for forty-two women and each one stays in the hills for twenty-six days. It is a place of charity but it might be a professional sanatorium.

The head of the establishment, Sister Frieda, greeted me on arrival. She was dressed in the traditional garb of a matron, but under her starched cap smiled one of the kindest and most gracious faces it has been my fortune to see. Throughout my visit I was conscious of her mission in life of genuine charity. She explained that the home had been founded to give overworked mothers a chance to recuperate their health. They need not necessarily be mothers who had recently given birth to children. On the contrary very few such mothers came to this home. Most of the women were of middle age, women who had had large families but who had never been able to afford a proper holiday. They were selected by doctors as being in need of a change in the country and so they came to Hirschen.

The two houses were almost identical except that one had an elaborate sun verandah overlooking a deep valley. Each had its requisite dormitories and bathrooms. The dormitories were all decorated in pale beige and the furniture was enamelled ivory colour or *eau de nil.* Some rooms contained four beds, others three. There were those reserved for the very sick which had but one cot. But in each case there was a separate single bed, a bedside table with independent light and an individual wardrobe. Furthermore, each mother had her porcelain wash-basin served with hot and cold water. The floors were of parquet and were strewn with rugs. In these rooms the mothers sleep, retiring to bed at nine and rising at a quarter past seven in the morning.

Practically no discipline is required from them while they are in the home. They may not leave the extensive grounds. They must be at table when meals are served. They are also expected to do twenty minutes' physical exercise every day provided their health and hearts permit. Otherwise they can do precisely as they like. There are writing and reading-rooms. Germany is cursed by radio far more than Great Britain and the United States. There is one room in which a loud-speaker shrieks all day. But in the other house there is a sitting-room where no radio is allowed. The women sit at long tables at dinner which is served from an adjacent kitchen. The cooks and maids are all women and girls who have lived in these hills all their lives. Some of them even worked on this very farmland before it became the site of the Hirschen Mother Home. The food is adequate and decently served. On the day I was at the home there appeared on the sideboard a huge haunch of venison.

Sister Frieda explained to me that each mother, some of whom came to the home desperately poor, was given the sum of three marks with which to buy postage stamps. Stamps in fact were all she could buy for everything else was provided. The women were brought from their homes in the Rhineland and the Ruhr at the expense of the State and transported back again after their stay in the hills. We sat on the terrace and had tea in the afternoon sunshine, real tea, with slices of white bread, piles of dairy butter (made on the farm) and pots of raspberry jam. One might have been at an English country nursing home as a guest, except that the food was infinitely better. In front of us was the valley, deep in trees, with the skyline filled by a great bluff of hillside. One could discern the blue waters of the River Sieger through the branches of the orchard just below. Some workmen were clearing a plot of ground which very soon will be an open-air swimming bath for the mothers and staff of the home. Behind us builders in picturesque smocks were constructing an outhouse that is intended for the bachelor farm labourers working on the estate. Cows lowed as they were being driven to their byres. There was a formidable quacking of ducks and a confused murmuring of hens. Occasionally pigs in an open compound grunted with satisfaction. Inside the dining-room forty women were making a tremendous noise as they gabbled and gossiped over their tea. One felt that here was a place which liked to be visited. It is certainly a hard place to leave.

One of the features of the Nazi régime has been the care bestowed on public health. Germany has always been renowned for her medical schools and the skill of her physicians and surgeons. And in both Imperial and Republican times great attention was paid to hospital services. The Nazi régime, with its consequent centralisation, has developed such services to the utmost. It is their boast that the scheme for training nurses in the Third Reich has no equal in the world. This may be so. Certainly one cannot fail but be impressed by the efficiency of the training schools and hospitals which exist all over the country.

I visited the nurses' home attached to the well-known Lindenburg hospital at Cologne. A very extensive private house has been converted for the purpose of providing a dormitory for the nurses undergoing training at the hospital about a quarter of a mile away. Like everything else in official Germany, it is spotlessly clean. In fact, it was difficult to believe that the house was inhabited by forty young girls, so neat and tidy was every room. No personal belongings, apart from a clock or a Bible or a copy of *Mein Kampf*, were to be seen by any of the beds. In its severe order, the only indication of a woman's hand was the presence of large bowls of flowers and ferns in every room and on every landing. The recreation-room was just as severe as the rest of the house. The head sister seemed stern and unbending and in her attitude betrayed her conviction that her girls must be brought up as good Nazis not only for their own benefit but also for the salvation of their souls. I was not in the least surprised to find the most prominent object of the common-room a large illustrated map of Germany. On it were carefully delineated the pre-war frontiers. The restoration of the Saargebiets was revealed with an enormous coloured flourish. A star marked the fortress of Landsberg where Hitler was imprisoned after the abortive Munich Putsch. Every event in the Nazi struggle for power was duly indicated. A cross marked the place where Schlateger was captured by the French in the Ruhr before his execution. Nuremberg with its party arenas had come in for special attention by the designer of this colossal map dedicated to the Führer and the Germany of the future.

After hearing full details of the economic and financial side of the training of nurses in the Third Reich, I went across to the Lindenburg hospital. I had been made aware of the fact that hospital instruction, together with the requisite accommodation in hostel and asylum, cost but a matter of 340 rentenmarks over a period of two years. During that period the young girl is moulded into a nurse with very high qualifications. It was a machine-made plan. It was therefore expected to work. In the extensive grounds of the hospital, nursing-nuns, in black robes and white linen, walked from building to building under the trees, along the alleyways. There were others in trailing robes of white. Each sister bore round her neck a rosary and a crucifix. I came to the office of the hospital to which I was admitted by a nun of the Augustine order. I explained my business. I had come to visit the matron of the hospital. "I will telephone for her," came the reply. We sat in a severely furnished office. After having spoken down the telephone the nun said no word. I interested myself in the various portraits of Hitler hanging on the walls in company with the interiors of clinics and the outsides of sanatoriums. Here and there were enormous files and ponderous ledgers. The room might well have been that of a successful manufacturer instead of the private office of a hospital matron. It was all so very, very efficient.

After an interval the matron appeared. She was dressed in a skirt and bodice of plain brown cloth. Prominently displayed on her bosom was the swastika of the Nazi party. She greeted me with the courtesy of a German greeting a stranger. We talked for a long time about hospitals and the prevention of disease. She spoke of the training school. Her voice rang with pride as she entered into details of the wonderful facilities that were accorded to young girls in these days, and there was just a faint note of regret that such conditions did not apply when she was being trained in those long years ago before the war. Throughout our conversation the nun, in her black and white robes, sat still in her chair in the corner of the room. It was by pure chance that I heard her story. I put a question concerning lay sisters and the religious. The nun asked permission to speak and here is her amazing story.

"To-day is the last day on which I shall wear the robe of a religious," she said.

The remark in itself was amazing enough. The girl was unabashed, and, after a slight pause, continued:

"I remain a good Catholic. I shall always be a good Catholic. But I feel that I must also be a good German."

In a calm clear voice, she told the story of her life. She came from a Bavarian noble family in which it had been a tradition for generations for some of the daughters to take the veil. "I have been a nun for ten years," she said very quietly.

She proceeded that she had come to the conclusion that she never had a vocation. It had all been a matter of circumstance, perhaps of upbringing. Since the revolution she had begun to realise that her primary duty was owed to Germany and not to the vows she had taken as a girl. It was an alarming revelation. It was made all the more alarming by the fact that this girl spoke with such deep conviction.

She added, "I have communed with myself for a long time. I felt that I was becoming a hypocrite, that I was ceasing to be even a good Catholic. I have decided to abandon my vows and to-morrow I shall wear the dress of a Nazi nurse in this hospital. I shall not abandon my faith in the Catholic Church, but I feel that I can be a better Catholic by taking the step I propose taking."

There was not a little real drama in the scene. There was no hypocrisy of sentiment. The girl looked up and there was something of ecstasy in her face. For her the new Germany represented a belief and a faith. It had come to be her first allegiance.

During previous visits to Germany I had come across instances of ecstatic devotion on the part of girls and women to the person of the Führer. I shall not easily forget the spectacle at Coblenz during the historic visit of Hitler to Ehrenbreitstein to make his speech on the Saar when young girls swarmed up the gangway of a Rhine steamer in an endeavour to kiss the leader's boots. I have seen women swarm round Hitler in Berlin with an enthusiasm bordering on fanaticism. Such scenes might well be explained away on the score of pure emotionalism. Mob hysteria still defies definition even on the part of the most learned psychologists. But the case of this Augustinian nun was in a different category. Here was a girl of noble family and careful upbringing, who had made a very grave and personal decision.

From time to time during our conversation she insisted that her decision had been made of her own volition.

" I am persuaded in the step I take by my own convictions. No one has persuaded me. One has duties to one's country as well as to one's religion. Germany has suffered so much. She needs the utmost service of us all. The Führer has given new life to Germany and brought back greatness to us."

I would not presume to pass judgment on the decision of this beautiful girl who spoke with such sincerity and conviction. I remember at the moment that I felt that here was possibly a path, freshly discovered, to an individual's aspirations and objects in life. After all, great suffering alone has given rise to the profoundest beliefs in the human race and no one will deny the sufferings of modern Germany. Perhaps it was the edict of Tertullian all over again. I am still a little mystified and awed by that strange interview at the Lindenburg hospital.

Vivid recollections of the Augustinian nun came to my mind much later when I was lunching with some of the leading citizens of Hamburg at one of the famous restaurants of that northern port. The conversation turned on the question of Church and State and the Nazi viewpoint in regard to religion. The previous evening there had been an international lecture at which some Englishmen had spoken. In the course of the discussion one of the speakers had expressed himself very forcibly on the subject of religious persecutions and the doubtful position in which profession Catholics find themselves. In the end there had been agreement to disagree. At luncheon two of the guests returned to the subject. One was a prominent merchant. The other had been burgomaster of the city at one time. The education and culture of both men were above question. They said in effect:

"In the new Germany the State must come first. The Church ought to be the servant of the State, an educating and not ruling force. In the Third Reich the Government of Germany must always be first and foremost and any religion which questions that authority must be opposed."

With disconcerting directness, the former burgomaster mentioned that in England although there was an Established Church, the head of that church was His Majesty the King.

I mention the two incidents because in their own way they indicate the intense sense of nationalism which is the guiding instinct of the new Germany. Discussion of religious questions is always a delicate matter. I do not wish to enter into controversy. The future of the

Church in Germany is just as much a matter for the Germans to decide as was the equally drastic issue in England at the time of the Reformation. At the same time I would like to add that throughout my visit to Germany I did not once encounter any obvious expression of impiety or absence of religious feeling. Certainly the churches, whether they were Roman Catholic or Lutheran, were infinitely better attended than our parish churches or nonconformist chapels in England. Because a change is taking place in the relations between Church and State, it by no means follows that there is a corresponding falling-off in religious belief. It may fairly be said that the Nazi régime in preserving Germany from the red menace saved Germany for Christendom. How the teachings of Christendom are to be interpreted is a matter for the Germans to decide. In any case pontifical criticism is hardly justified from the English hierarchy who, although they may command a wide public in the press, have yet to find a means of inducing the general public to pray in their cathedrals.

As I look back many impressions of modern Cologne come vividly to mind. There is something eternal about the silhouette of the city seen from Dietz on the right bank of the Rhine—the tall steeples of the Dom, the squat tower of the Rathaus, the outline of the church of St. Martin, the gigantic steel frame of the Hohenzollern Bridge. It is a city which once visited cries to be re-visited. The returned soldier looks instinctively for the sentry in khaki keeping sentinel outside the old-time headquarters, but when he discovers he is no longer there, can recapture old-time memories in the gay and hurried life of the Hohestrasse with its myriad of neon lights, a narrow version of the Great White Way but so much more genuine. The old beer-houses are still there with the familiar smocked waiters serving city-brewed beer and that local snack known as " half a chicken "—a chunk of Swiss cheese, a pat of butter and half a roll.

One need not be in Germany for more than a few hours to realise that here is a people that has moved with the times and has become air-minded. It is not a question of military sense. For the German of to-day the conquest of the air is a matter of common sense. Wherever one travels, throughout the length and breadth of the Reich, one comes across magnificent airfields. I have landed on many aerodromes in Germany but with the possible exception of Frankfurt, which I shall speak of in my next chapter, there is surely no more striking airfield in all Germany than that at Cologne. It is not far from the centre of the city—a quarter of an hour's journey by car on a brand new road. In war-time this broad open space had been used as a base for Zeppelins, and from here many of the dirigibles departed on journeys to England and the North Sea from which they were doomed never to return. To-day the once modest flying-ground has been transformed into a spacious air base which is used every hour of day and night by most of the important civil flying companies in Europe and Great Britain. The administration buildings have been constructed by design and not by accident as may be said of Croydon and Le Bourget. The facilities for the comfort, transit and temporary accommodation of passengers are most admirable and the bars do not close perversely just as a machine has arrived after a rough journey as sometimes happens in our own land of exaggerated liberty. There are spacious promenades both under cover and in the model gardens approaching the concrete taking-off ground. The low white stretch of buildings look out on to a mile-wide sweep of grass plain. The whole field is laid out on a vast scale in anticipation of the inevitable progress of flying as a universal means of travel and transport. As the passenger emerges from the aerodrome buildings to enter the waiting omnibus there stretches before him a broad highway, the end of which is filled in with the distant spires of the great cathedral.

I met a Nazi youth in the city. He was indirectly attached to one of the official tourist offices and he volunteered to show me certain objects of interest. I was specially interested in re-visiting the Rathaus, the famous city hall of Cologne, which occupies the site of a Roman building. As we walked across the Domplatz, I remarked on the imposing architecture of the cathedral. My companion was not greatly impressed. " It is a Roman Catholic cathedral," he said. " The whole of this neighbourhood is very black. I should say there are ninety per cent Catholics and only ten per cent Protestant. But, of course, you can tell."

I looked at him a little startled, and I may add that I make record of a walk through the city with him because the few things he said were indicative of an outlook which was strange but absolutely sincere.

" Yes," he said again, " you can always tell. If you look at a group of Cologne people you will see that nine out of ten of them are dark and short in stature. The tenth man is blonde and has blue eyes. You see the real Nordics only came to Cologne after the Reformation."

The youth looked up at the stately towers of the cathedral with something akin to contempt in his gaze.

We went to the Rathaus, that gem of municipal architecture, and admired doors, and pictures, windows, and ceilings. In the council hall is the world-famous screen with the nine effigies of the Christian, Jewish, and Pagan creeds. The three Jews occupy the middle niches but they were hidden from view by a huge swastika banner, the end of which draped a bust of Hitler. I said it was a pity even in an excess of patriotism, that a work of art of such beauty should be partially obscured even by so honourable a flag. My youthful companion was equal to the occasion.

He said, " But it only covers the Jews. It was fortunate that they should have occupied the middle of the screen. No one wants to see them any more."

Later, we went to the ancient quarter of Cologne down by the banks of the Rhine, that confusion of picturesque houses and narrow streets that have long delighted the antiquarian.

They were condemned some time ago as dangerous for further habitation, but the city fathers, realising their great beauty and knowing them to be one of the glories of the Hansa town, decreed that while new houses for the working people should be created in courtyards and open spaces the façades of the older buildings should remain. And by a miracle of engineering and restoration the decree is being carried out, brand new houses are being built behind the ancient brick and half-timbered frontages. The feat did not impress my companion who had no interest in the past and thought the action of the city fathers old-fashioned and unprogressive. He almost growled:

" It would be far better to put up some real buildings instead of tinkering with a lot of old bricks that my generation considers ugly anyway."

Before we got back to the Domplatz we had to climb through the narrow street of the red lantern known as the Stafelgasse. Two or three hawkers were slowly pushing barrows laden with black grapes and red cabbage (of all things) in front of the half-open doors. Although it was broad daylight, an occasional inmate could be seen through the doorways or between the tawdry curtains of the windows of the numerous small houses. At the end of the street a fat blonde girl with enormous hips and legs in proportion, wearing attenuated red silk knickers and showing a broad expanse of thigh, stepped out to purchase a red cabbage. It was indeed an astonishing spectacle. It was so incongruous at midday as to be almost ridiculous. But the youth at my side boiled with anger.

He glowered:

" This Cologne is so loose in its morals, so Catholic. We must sweep it all away. In the fulfilment of the Nazi Socialist state such things and such conduct are impossible."

As I said good-bye under the spires of the cathedral he despised so much, I wondered as to the faith of the boy who believed that a political creed could change the animal instincts of men where the Ten Commandments and the Sermon on the Mount had failed.

CHAPTER III

"JUDEN NICHT ERWÜNSCHT"

FRANKFURT AM MAIN has always struck me as a cold forbidding city. There is something aloof about it, like Berne, something even sinister, like Basel. Perhaps my aversion dates from the unhappy days when the French occupied the city as a punitive measure for some breach of the outlandish Reparations clauses of the Treaty. But for me, at any rate, Frankfurt will never have the attraction of other German cities. It has none of the glamour of Dresden. It lacks the vigour of Cologne.

It was in Frankfurt, however, that the house of Rothschild flourished, and the city still remains one of the great banking centres of the country. Furthermore it has always had a considerable Jewish population and their presence gave rise to movements of anti-semitism which are often to be found when Jews live in masses in close proximity to Gentiles. Anti-Jewish feeling in Frankfurt am Main is no new thing. One need not be long in the city to discover that.

I arrived at night and made my way through the big cumbersome station to the great open space that gives on to the city. I walked across to an hotel and signed the register. Taking the customary slip, containing room-number and price, up to my apartment, I discovered on the writing-table two or three green cards, one of which I still preserve. It announced that the place I had chosen to stay at was a Jew-free hotel. This was the legend printed on the card:

Schon mehr
40 Jahre ist der
als
Kolner Hof
in Frankfurt a.M.
das erste
Judenfreie Hotel
in unserem deutschen
Vaterlande.
Und ist auch heute noch;
" Judenfrei "

Which is interpreted that for forty years the Kolner Hotel in Frankfurt am Main has not permitted Jews to sleep under its roof and that it was the first hotel in all Germany to forbid the entry of Jews as guests.

In other days Jews were always prominent in the streets of the banking city but on this occasion I saw none. There were none in the few night bars, there were none in the cabarets. Nor in the waking hours did I see but half a dozen Jews in the course of a whole day. They seem to have disappeared from the city.

It was pleasant to revisit the birthplace of Goethe and note with what loving care the ancient house is being maintained. In places the furnishings and hangings are so much to the period that one would not be surprised if they had been really genuine possessions of the Goethe family. In the actual birth-room stands the white monument of the great poet and on the day of my visit there was propped up against the foot of the pedestal a huge wreath of laurels sent from Stratford-on-Avon with a riband dated August 28, 1749—the birthday of Goethe. I am told that a similar wreath is sent to the house every year from the same source.

Those who condemn the Nazi movement for its ruthless modernism should know of the interest which the party leaders take in the monuments of the past. I found evidences of such a hankering after tradition and history everywhere I went. Certainly the house of Goethe has never been better looked after than since the revolution. And perhaps for good reason, seeing it is one of the most interesting buildings in Europe. Here one can get a vivid picture of domestic life in a well-to-do Frankfurt family in the eighteenth century. There is the narrow window specially built out from the walls of old Father Goethe's study so that he could see if his son was making mischief in the street below. There is the big stone-walled kitchen with the huge open kitchen range on which could be prepared banquets for scores of guests. Furthermore, in the kitchen was a private pump drawing water from the private well. That in itself was a sign of the wealth of the Goethe household. In those days only two other families had private pumps for water. One was the house of Bethmann and the other, significantly enough, was the house of Amstel Rothschild. The night lanterns had sockets for two candles. Ordinary people when they walked abroad had to carry lanterns with only one candle. It was a subtle way of indicating class and wealth.

My visit to Frankfurt necessarily included an inspection of the giant dirigible Hindenburg, one of the most wonderful creations of modern times, a miracle of silk, aluminium, and human ingenuity. Nowadays to go to Frankfurt is to go to see the " Hindenburg ", if her great envelope happens to be in her hangar at the moment. The visit to the airship was also an introduction to the great new motor roads, for I spent the remainder of the afternoon travelling at breakneck speed along the most

BUILDING A CROSSING BRIDGE ON THE BERLIN—STETTIN MOTOR ROAD

[face p. 60

perfect motor tracks I have ever seen outside Italy and certain parts of the eastern states of America. I also was enabled to explore the workings of the new roads as they make their way across the face of Germany, and to recapture memories of two of the most delectable places in all Europe, Bad Homburg and Bad Nauheim. During a drive of some two hundred kilometres I saw a great deal of the new Germany which is being superimposed on the old ; it was a vivid experience of contrast between a world of yesterday and the world of to-morrow.

Herr Hitler has announced that he intends in the future to open six hundred miles of new motor roads every year. The elaborate plan, which aims at giving Germany the most up-to-date system in the world, involves the construction of about 4,300 miles of highway. At the moment of writing only about 400 miles are ready for use and, by process of arithmetic, the German people know that the whole system will be available in six and a half years time. It will be so, because Hitler has said so. Hitler has a reputation for getting things done at home as well as abroad.

Now of all the public works undertaken by the Third Reich the most important is the new motor road scheme. Carping critics declare in a superior way that the motor roads are the only really new thing introduced into Germany by the Nazis. Everything else—the labour camps, the winter help work, town planning, harbour works—all were there in embryo under the Republic, and Hitler has merely carried on. This assertion is only a half-truth, but that is by the way. When it comes to the motor roads, however, it is admitted that they are a new thing and that the whole scheme is magnificently conceived. Even this concession to Nazi achievement is modified by the hint that they are merely being made for military purposes. How absurd this contention is I will discuss later.

Just after the war—in the days, let us say, before ribbon development—our victorious Government embarked on a road-making scheme which, under the heading of " arterial ", was to make Britain a country in which both the motoring and the non-motoring communities had equal chance of surviving. Who of us, with ordinary memories, can forget the spectacular gesture of the first " by-pass ", that potential death-trap, which was regarded as the apotheosis of the new-fangled doctrine of " safety-first " ? At the same time who could have anticipated the dead hand of the speculative builder, or the fact that almost within a decade a prominent member of Parliament would publicly demand the closing of one of the most important by-pass roads serving the metropolis, as a menace to human life ? Whichever way we look at our own road problem, it must be confessed that we lag behind in the matter of inter-communication. The number of motor vehicles increases enormously every year ; the problem of traffic and transport has become a major domestic issue and its importance is recognised by the admission of the Minister responsible into the select circle of the Cabinet : even so there is a persistent reluctance to tackle the question of roads on a national basis. One is forced to agree with a contemporary commentator that in ten years from now Britain will awake to the necessity of universal motor roads when so much sporadic building and town planning have spread over our limited countryside as to make their construction an economic impossibility.

The tremendous achievement up to date of the Reichsautobahnen is indicative of the determination of the Third Reich to make Germany the most up-to-the-minute country in Europe. It is a reflection of the new spirit that puts public convenience first in the interests of national prosperity. It is an example which we might follow with profit.

The vast system of Reichsautobahnen is still in its beginning. But already the network that will cover the whole of Germany is laid out and the plan to connect Berlin with the Baltic, the Elbe, the Rhine and Munich and the Bavarian Alps is proceeding slowly but surely to its final accomplishment. The construction of the motor roads is such a significant gesture of German self-help that I think it necessary to append a few details concerning the amount of men and material involved before proceeding to a more personal narrative of experiences while travelling on the roads themselves.

In other days the control of the roads in Germany was in charge of State and local authorities. There was inherent in the system all the disadvantages that result so often from our own system of local government, with various bodies refusing to shoulder responsibilities that ought to be national and not parochial affairs. There was no uniform scheme of construction or maintenance of public highways. The establishment of the Government of the Third Reich introduced centralisation, and the launching of the scheme to build more than 4,000 miles of new roads necessitated a uniformity of control which Germany, land of small states, had never known before. Incidentally the fact that Hitler was able to make such a drastic move was a proof of the universal approbation of Germany for the German Government in contrast with previous local patriotism. Hitler, like a Roman Cæsar, realised the fundamental importance of roads and from the beginning took a great personal interest in their construction. At the present moment he has direct ministerial responsibility for the Reichsautobahnen. He has always maintained that Germany had very bad roads. He had come to that conclusion during his long tedious electioneering journeys before he was forced to take to the air as the only sure way of getting to his destination on time.

The Nazis had not been long in power before Hitler put his long-cherished road plan into execution. It was on June 27, 1933, that the Reichsautobahnen Company was formed as a subsidiary unit of the national railways with a capital of only fifty million marks. The company was given the monopoly of constructing the new motor roads. At its head, immediately under the Führer, was appointed an Inspector-General who was to be technically responsible for lay-out and general design. It was found practical to allot the work in the various provinces to private companies, but in any question concerning the diversion of existing tramways or the construction of important bridges the last word rests with the Inspector-General.

Germany has wide areas and is a perfect heaven for the ambitious road engineer with unlimited resources at his disposal. But even so the road works with their embankments and sweeping approaches occupied vast areas of territory and that territory had to be paid for. A system of compulsory purchase was organised, and compensation made to owners. The system is still in operation and now that the complete plan of the final road scheme is known, alternative land is being found for farmers whose acres are being completely absorbed or rendered useless by the coming of the motor road. In some cases, as I saw near Heidelburg, adjacent land has been specially cleared and irrigated in order to compensate the local farmer for the loss of his broad acres now covered by the great white highway. At the same time special attention is paid to co-operation with the existing railway system. Both road and rail belong to the State and the new roads are made to serve the railways as much as possible in exchange for the inevitable transference of much merchandise transport by motor-car and heavy lorry.

One begins to obtain an idea of the enormous money and energy involved by the study of a few outstanding figures. There are a quarter of a million men engaged altogether. Something like 2,500 high-powered miniature steam engines have been built to drag 50,000 wagons on the narrow gauge railways. More than 2,000 miles of rail-track were manufactured in the Ruhr factories for use in the roads, not to mention 700 concrete-mixers and 300 power-shovels.

The absorption of so many workers in this new work has meant drastic reduction in unemployment figures. At the same time the amount of money saved in State relief has indirectly helped to provide funds for the great road scheme. In fact, it has been estimated that of the total cost of the roads completed and under construction 35 per cent would have been paid out in alleviating the distress of the workless. The amount of floating capital required has been raised through loans and in the years to come when the road system is completed motorists will be obliged to pay a small daily fee for the advantage of using them—money which will go towards defraying their initial cost and future upkeep! All kinds of schemes to make the road service the most perfect in the world have been inaugurated. At set intervals are the most elaborate filling and repair stations, each one fitted with the most modern gadgets and each one either standing in a garden or else backed by a plantation of trees. The roads are also constantly being patrolled by special relief and first-aid lorries which contain petrol, breakdown apparatus, and medical chests. If a car should break down on the highway the driver has merely to wait for a while in the certain knowledge that an official lorry will be along in due course.

There were grim reminders of the demoralising effects of long years of unemployment among the German workers when the great road plan was got under way in the summer of 1933. One hundred thousand labourers and technicians had to be found at once and they were obtained from the great unemployed market. In a great number of cases it was weeks before the workmen became efficient, so evil had been the effects of idleness and bad nourishment and housing over a period, in some cases, of ten years. Very many of them had forgotten how to work and the technicians had lost the benefit of previous experience in the intervening period. They were so badly clothed that special clothing centres had to be formed at which the men could buy new garments at cut prices on the instalment plan. And as the work developed and the roads stretched for miles into the distant country so special labour camps had to be built. It is interesting to note that Hitler himself made the layout plans of these settlements. They are composed of huts built round a grass compound. Each one takes 216 men, 18 beds being provided in 12 different huts. Each workman has an equal amount of furniture and his own chair in the common dining-hall. Very great care is taken of health and cleanliness, and each man has his own hot and cold water basin in an adjacent hut. In most cases lodging is provided free, but I did come across cases where camps had cost larger amounts on account of land and other difficulties and here the labourer paid about a shilling a week. Everything is arranged with the precision so characteristic of the German nation. The actual personal happiness of the men is looked after by a worker known as the " Senior ". He lives in the camp and does not go to work on the roads. He is responsible for the catering, the laundry, the radio, the games provided in the social hall, the supply of magazines and newspapers. That vast organisation known as the " Kraft durch Freude " (K.d.F.) or " Strength through Joy " also touches on the road-making camps in the visit at intervals of lorries containing talking films and sound apparatus. This same organisation arranges week-end excursions, hiking parties, and other amusements.

Quite a number of the German motor roads have already been made available for traffic. The two most important now operating are those between Berlin and Stettin and Frankfurt–Mannheim–Heidelburg. I have travelled over both of them and their general design is the same. In fact, uniformity is one of the ambitions of the road engineers, for it is hoped eventually to have a fool-proof system with all signs, bridges and approaches exactly alike so that there will be no confusion for motorists whether they are travelling in the distant parts of East Prussia or the congested areas of Essen. The day will come when a broad highway will run from the frontier at Aachen almost directly to Berlin where the various roads will branch off from a huge ring surrounding the capital at a distance of about twenty kilometres from the Brandenburg Gate. Another great road will link up Berlin and the Austrian frontier at Salzburg by way of Halle-Leipzig, Nuremberg, and Munich. A third great artery will follow the Rhine valley from Dusseldorf to Stuttgart and on to Ulm. And there will be many more.

The most hardened motorist must thrill when his car

leaves the secondary road to make the approach to the great highway. For my part I shall never forget my feelings as we travelled near the town of Bernau on the road to Stettin from Berlin. It was impossible not to enjoy speeding, and one regretted that the swift-moving Mercedes-Benz car could not tear along at even greater rate although the speedometer needle hovered round the 120 kilometre mark all the time we were on the road. There was no pulling up. Cars continued on their way without interruption on the one-way track, the slower vehicles being overtaken by the faster with an exultant roar.

The Stettin road was completed and the workers had gone elsewhere. But in the neighbourhood of Frankfurt I was enabled to see a completed road and also one under construction. It was an instructive experience and the fact that I also was privileged to clamber over the passengers' quarters of the great "Hindenburg" airship made the day even more memorable.

As at Cologne, the aerodrome at Frankfurt is immense, and it has the additional advantage of being situated in the middle of woods, so that the low white buildings of the administration offices and the aeroplane sheds have a picturesque sylvan background. The airship's hangar is quite distinct from the rest of the buildings and is reached by a special tarmac road quite two miles in length that encircles one-half of the flying-field. It is a huge steel structure, the doors of which swing on large rails operated by a stationary engine. The presence of the airship has also brought into existence a special restaurant, open-air tea-garden and a beer-hall. On the day of my visit hundreds of German boys and girls were clamouring to buy postcards and souvenirs of the airship, but they were not permitted to visit the interior, the authorities contending that an exterior view is quite sufficient to impress the ordinary visitor. Greater facilities, however, were granted to myself and my friends for we were shown all over the giant ship, and our guide had himself been in command of a Zeppelin during the war.

He was a man of travel and great good humour. "I have been to most parts of the world," he said in perfect English. "I have seen a lot of the world from upstairs. In fact, I know the way to London at night. I have been there so often with only a flicker of light on your Thames to help me. You will forgive an old airman, won't you? But I dropped bombs on London. It was just obeying orders."

The huge silver envelope of the airship towered above us in the tall hangar. The nose of the ship was attached to an enormous mooring mast and the vessel was held in place by means of steel hawsers, to which were attached dozens of bags filled with earth and stones. As we walked along under the envelope we could not but feel puny, for the machine was enormous and seen at such close quarters seemed to fill the whole earth. High above were propellers, looking small and ridiculous. The control tower in the forepart looked like an exaggerated pigeon pen. Presently we came to the passenger quarters. There was a hole in the bottom of the envelope reached by a ladder. It was to climb this ladder that travellers paid hundreds of dollars at Lakehurst, New Jersey, before being permitted to make the trans-Atlantic journey and so qualify for the now historic enamel Zeppelin badge given to all travellers who have made the journey high in the air across the Western ocean.

The ship was in darkness for the electricity system had been temporarily disconnected, and in consequence we had to make our way by means of torches, for uncovered lights were absolutely forbidden except in the skilfully contrived smoke-room where everything is made of asbestos or metal. It was a strange experience to set foot on the aluminium floors that creaked under your tread. Everything was so very slender and fragile and the handrail seemed to be about to give way under your grip. But I was told by the former Zeppelin captain, who never once ceased talking, that everything was as strong as if it were made of steel. Once aboard the ship in the passengers' quarters it was very like being in the saloon of a passenger liner except that the accommodation was more cramped. The berths were arranged on the two-bunk system to save space, but there were adequate washing facilities and the baths could accommodate a heavy individual like myself. The dining-room was futuristic in style, and the walls were covered with dim cartoons that might have meant something to the artist but which conveyed nothing to me. In the smoking-room I sat down in one of the armchairs. When I wanted to move back a little I discovered with some alarm that the chair only weighed about fifteen ounces altogether, although it looked a solid steel and canvas affair of the kind which nowadays passes for furniture. It was the same with all the equipment on board. All the kitchen utensils were of aluminium: the glass ware was most fragile; the crockery was made from a special kind of china clay. Everything had been calculated to save weight.

Close to the smoking-room was the narrow space which the ex-captain facetiously described as "our promenade deck". There was another handrail; like every other it creaked as you leaned on it. Below was a window and through it you could see the concrete floor of the airship shed. It is from this rail that passengers look down on the earth and the waters of the earth when the ship is in flight. But there is no sense of vertigo or dizziness, I am told, because the view is uninterrupted. It is said to be like looking down on the floor, except that the floor is the size of a continent. The "Hindenburg" is no ship in which the robust can find opportunities for violent physical exercise. One must be content to walk from dining-room to lounge, unless one cares to make the tortuous passage through the interior of the ship along a narrow strip of metal not more than six inches in width and which you have to negotiate by foot-over-foot methods, relying for your balance on the stays, very much in the manner of the rope bridges which are to be found across the ravines of Northern India. This narrow path is the only means of walking from one end of the ship to the other—an immensely long journey which must require a great deal of skill to accomplish during stormy weather, for one false step means a fall through the fabric of the outer envelope to swift death some thousands of feet below.

After we had spent a long time in the ship, we descended the ladder to the firm ground below and conversation fell to the question of the future of the airship. The ex-captain remarked that he thought the airship by far the safest and most comfortable means of travel in existence. He added:

"This big ship here will be looked on rather like a flea a few years from now. She will be small and old-fashioned. We are learning every day, and this "Hindenburg" has taught us much. She will teach us much more.

"Why do you English not think of airships? I think I know. One of your ships came down. It was a shocking disaster. Then you scrap your other one. In Germany we did not lose heart because we lost thirty-one Zeppelins during the war. We went on with our experiments and we will go on. You got cold feet because you lost one or two. It seems strange to me."

He told me of plans to build more airships next year both on the lake of Constance and at Frankfurt. "We shall soon be wanting half a dozen hangars like this one," he said, "for German Zeppelins will soon be travelling round the world as regularly as tramcars in Frankfurt. You mark my words."

As we drove away, the airfield was filled with aeroplanes of all kinds. Machines, in descending, almost skimmed the top of the trees and swept impudently in front of our advancing car. On all sides were evidences of activity and the air-mindedness of the German people.

The road south from Frankfurt skirts the important city of Darmstadt, for none of the new roads actually enters either town or village. All human habitation is avoided as far as possible so that the roads can never be hampered by local pedestrian traffic or the horror of the built-up areas which render arterial highways something like suicide clubs. In fact, no pedestrian or cyclist is allowed on the road, which is made entirely for fast-moving motor-cars. We sped on our way over undulating country, flashing past signs and petrol stations. Sometimes the road would cross a valley by means of a long viaduct. A moment later we would be in the middle of a great cutting with the green banks rising forty to fifty feet on either side. It did not require the eye of a road engineer to see with what skill and exactitude the roads had been laid out—the gradual curves that did not necessitate any slowing down or braking; uniform grades and consequent visibility were maintained for miles at a stretch; the erection of bridges of such heights as not to interfere with the line of sight. In places one could look back and see the road sweeping across the countryside—two long streaks of white in the green fields. Those who declare that the roads are merely another indication of German militarism ought to bear in mind the fact they are the most prominent features of the landscape. Nothing could possibly be more visible from the air: the white ways simply invite attack. Then, again, the large number of bridges make them vulnerable. There is one viaduct outside Berlin built of welded steel at a cost of seven million rentenmarks that could be so badly damaged by one well-aimed bomb from an aeroplane as to destroy communication completely. So much for their military aspect.

Now a road, as such, is hardly a beautiful thing. In fact, too often, bleak arterial roads are a disturbing feature in a picturesque landscape. It must fairly be said that in Germany these new roads have been made as pleasing in appearance as is humanly possible. On the way to Mannheim we travelled alongside an endless garden of lawn, flowers, and shrubs—for the *terrain* in between the two tracks has been planted according to a definite plan. Furthermore, before a road is constructed special attention is paid to the lay of the land so that the highway interferes as little as possible with natural scenic amenities. It is intended that the motorist should both enjoy the landscape as well as traverse it. Expert gardeners and botanists have been called in to give advice as to the planting of gardens and arrangements of new woods and spinnies. Only such vegetation as would ordinarily thrive in a particular area is cultivated, for it must be recalled that Germany is a vast country with extremes of climate and a flora which varies considerably from the Baltic Sea to the Bavarian Alps. I was also greatly impressed by the frequent parking-places. They are none of them very extensive but they are very numerous. Furthermore each area was chosen with an eye to the landscape—either near the banks of a river or else in the path of shady trees. It is thus hoped to make the new motor roads a means of inducing people to go into the German countryside, for in practically every case there is a pleasant walk or some corner in which to picnic within a very short distance of the parking-ground.

The manner in which the new roads are being made is just as remarkable as the finished product. While I was in Hesse work was being pushed forward on the road to Cassel and Hanover. When it is finished the highway will link up such famous resorts as Bad Homburg and Bad Nauheim which I have already mentioned. Our motor-car travelled to the north through wooded country of great beauty. We saw the two watering-places in the closed season, and it was difficult to imagine that these streets of shuttered windows and sepulchral hotels and *kurhauses* in the appropriate season throb with fashionable life. We motored to the famous hill-restaurant above Bad Nauheim, the restaurant with the terrace that can only be reached by a corkscrew road. There was not a soul in the place. It was not the season. It seemed strange, for there was lovely autumn sunshine and the great panorama of woods, and valleys apread out like an uneven and multi-coloured carpet hundreds of feet below could never have been lovelier. But fashion all the world over thinks nothing of these things. One goes to a place at a certain time, and no other. And so the hillside restaurant was deserted and we drank our *steins* of beer in almost funereal silence.

When we reached the workings of the new motor road I fancied I had happened on the aftermath of an earthquake. Holes gaped in the earth : the whole of a hillside had been torn away by terrifying, dragon-like mechanical scoops. Rivers and streams were being diverted. Great masses of half-completed masonry—bridges, dykes, parapets—rose in the air. The whole a glorious medley, a grand confusion. It was all so unexpected for a few minutes before our car had been travelling through a countryside that was truly rural. The villages—and the roads for that matter—are genuine survivals of the Thirty Years' War. Of that there is not the least doubt. It was the harvesting season and in every field men and women were bending over turnips and parsnips, and making them into enormous piles. At the end of the furrows were huge carts, and old bullocks waited patiently in the yokes. Sometimes one saw a pair-horse wagon, but that was unusual. The crops seemed abundant. Never have I seen so many root vegetables in one place. We had to cross a side line of railway which seemed to come from nowhere and was looking where to go. A train crawled along—a train of forty-five enormous open trucks : each one was piled high with the parsnips collected from the adjoining land ! Then a little later the chauffeur had to brake heavily in order to avoid a massacre of geese which were being driven along the road by a boy with a short stick—the old-time gozzard surviving in modern Germany ! In places the villages were primitive and sanitation non-existent. Huge midden heaps obtruded into the roadway and gave off their own peculiar odours. The last flowers of autumn were blooming in the little front gardens, and the sunflowers, so greatly loved by the German peasant, were drooping sadly on their tree-like stalks. Everything seemed so peaceful and far away, a picture by Old Crome come to life.

And then the hand of man disturbing the earth with the vigour of a Titan. Apparently a hill was in the way of the new motor road and so that hill must be taken away. And it was half gone when I made my way with difficulty over the soft sandy soil, dodging the ubiquitous miniature railway engines dragging trucks of earth to a place appointed. There were about a score of instruments of all kinds, grunting fiercely as they savagely ate their way into mother earth. It was all so thorough, so matter-of-fact. One felt that the horizon was disappearing under one's very eyes. The sand torn from the hillside was being transported many miles away to form the basis of a new embankment. I went also to see this remarkable work—a mountain taken from one place and deposited in another. The little trucks came along at regular intervals, spilled another half-ton on to the pile, and then hurried away behind a busybody puffing locomotive to fetch some more. Not far away engineers were building a bridge which will carry an approach road to the main highway. It was just a mould of concrete, and the moist material was being mixed on the spot and carried to the rough troughs by means of a most ingenious system of cranes and buckets. While I was watching the wall of one side of the bridge progressed a matter of six inches. I was told that within a fortnight the bridge and its two embankments would be ready and that the plant would then go straight to Cassel to start work on another!

For miles into the distance virgin soil was being

prepared and shaped for the final concrete surface of the subsequent motor road. The first sections of the newly-laid face were still covered in straw matting to ensure perfect setting. As I progressed along the work I came across vast machines travelling on broad rails which were making the various sections of the road on top of embankments or at the bottom of cuttings. It would require the pen of an expert on engineering to make plain the various processes which led to the final making of the road. It was all being worked out according to plan. It was like the advance of an army, an army with limitless resources that was consolidating its progress by leaving behind perfect communication.

The time came when we had perforce to leave these triumphs of road engineering and make our way back to Frankfurt am Main by means of dirt and gravel tracks where passing bullock wagons in the dusk was a matter of driver's skill and where deep gullies on each side invited unpleasant accident or worse.

CHAPTER IV

IRON VIRGIN

IN a grim loft in the ancient citadel of Nuremburg is preserved the notorious "iron virgin". It is fair to say that no instrument of torture has enjoyed a longer or more vicious reputation. On a previous visit to this most beautiful of all German cities, the castle was closed to the public for renovation, and I was unable to obtain admission to the celebrated collection of weapons and racks and thumbscrews which are preserved there. I mentioned to my guide that I would like to see this strange assembly of instruments devised by less civilised generations for the suffering of fellow-men. Especially was I curious to look at the "Iron Virgin of Nuremburg". He looked surprised, and then alarmed. "The Iron Virgin?" Of course, the horrible thing existed but he believed it was no longer available for public view. Historians had proved beyond doubt that it had never been put to its intended purpose. It had merely been built to threaten and frighten malcontents and heretics. The German people had never been quite so cruel as to shut men up in living death in the confined iron skirts and bodice of the iron virgin. He was convinced that the instruments had been hidden away somewhere, for the authorities did not wish visitors to obtain a false impression of the true character of Germans in the past.

His point of view intrigued me. It was the first

time that I had encountered such a material censorship of established historical evidence. Furthermore, his assumption that Germans could never have been so cruel as to resort to death by such *peine forte et dure* was yet another indication of the fathomlesss faith which the latter-day German has in his nature. The very doubts he expressed as to the history of the iron virgin and its present whereabouts were eloquent of a pride and faith of nationality which was something more than a religion or belief.

Nevertheless, we made the steep ascent of the hill over the cobblestones to the ancient castle. It was like an excursion into medieval legend. Nothing seems to have changed for centuries. As we passed the house of Durer, I would not have been in the least surprised to have seen the creator of the immortal " Knight and Death " standing at his own front door. The red brick houses and their pointed gables made the background for a fairy-tale. Fountains plashed gently in the morning sunshine. Slender trees were shedding golden leaves. The music of young laughter came to the ear. About two-score children were dancing round an aged beggar, barely covered in the most picturesque rags. Like a ghost who had escaped from a medieval legend, he was playing on a reed whistle and the children of the side streets were cavorting to his shrill melody and, in the agelong spirit of mischief, mocking his crazy gestures.

For the payment of a mark or two one gains access to the most terrifying museum in the world. A few minutes spent within the galleries of this display of instruments of torture are sufficient to convince one of man's humanity to man. And the " iron virgin " is still to be seen!

This is no place to describe the *macabre*, sinister

museum of the castle of Nuremburg. I have referred to it only because of the remark of the ardent Nazi who was my cicerone while I was in the city. We entered a long narrow passage, the walls of which were covered with gruesome contemporary prints of torture in the sixteenth and seventeenth centuries. In adjoining cases were rows of thumbscrews, pincers, whips, scourges, and the like. In a corner was a huge wooden " throne ", every inch of which was covered with sharp iron spikes. Then there were specimens of the wheel on which criminals were broken, and the round knives which aided the work of the executioner in smashing the unhappy victims' limbs to pieces. When eventually we reached the " iron virgin ", we were prepared for anything. Strangely enough the most famous of all the torture instruments must have been a comparatively mild form of punishment compared with half an hour sitting on the throne of five thousand spikes. It is a huge iron effigy of a young woman in the costume of the period of Tilly and Wallenstein and made of cast iron. The front divides in the middle and the two sides swing on hinges. It was inside the ample space of the " body " that the heretic was supposed to be shut up. The iron virgin stands in solitary state in the middle of an ancient room in the pentagonal tower of the *Schloss.* It has not been taken away from public gaze even though learned historians have proved it was never used for its intended purpose. Very sensibly the guardians of the castle realise its commercial value, for it is the star attraction of this awe-inspiring collection and each day in the summer months draws hundreds of travellers—and marks—to the museum. I am informed by my knowledge of history that at one time the interior of the iron virgin had had intestines of spikes. But to-day they are practically non-existent!

The city of Nuremburg plays a very considerable part in the organisation of the National Socialist movement. It is here that the annual party congress is held. It is here that Julius Streicher publishes Der Stürmer, the organ of anti-Semiticism. It is in Nuremburg and the immediate neighbourhood that the stranger comes across outward manifestation of anti-Jewish feeling. In most cities of Germany there are no obvious signs of persecution of the Jews. In Berlin Jews still frequent the important cafés and beer-halls in the Kurfürstendam as well as the Alexanderplatz. They may not be permitted to act as advocates, and the fact is indicated by an appropriate obliteration on their brass doorplates. The synagogues remain open and are extensively attended. Occasionally I encountered immediate signs of the segregation of the Jew, but only occasionally.

In Nuremburg, however, Julius Streicher has whipped the local population into something like a frenzy against Jews and non-Aryans. In the villages dotted about the wooded, sandy plain on which the city is built, streamers wave above the head announcing that Jews are not wanted. There is scarcely a café or restaurant which is without the forbidding notice above the door: " Juden nicht erwünchst " (Jews are not desirable). It is not surprising that one rarely encounters a Jew in public places in the city of Nuremburg. Doubtless they exist somewhere in the city. But they are not visible.

At the other end of the scale is evidence of the new religion inaugurated by General von Ludendorff and his wife. In one of the main streets of the walled part of the city is a shop devoted to the literature of the ancient Teutonic God, supreme above all Gods and such parvenu beliefs as Christianity. Ever since the great German staff officer ceased to take an active interest in politics, he and his wife have devoted themselves to this new pagan faith in which they firmly believe, if nobody else does. A shop window of Nuremburg bears testimony to their fanaticism. Every book derides some form of Christianity. One openly declares that the Bible has deliberately falsified every human value, that it is a literary fake and was the united effort of Jews and early Christians to destroy the ancient Gods. One begins to feel that Ludendorff imagines himself a sort of Nordic Julian. There is no squeamishness about this grotesque propaganda. In the very middle of the window I saw a dust cover in which a naked woman was depicted on the rack, while hooded priests and masked executioners look on in sadistic glee. Actually the picture is taken from an old print preserved in the castle. Ludendorff has added in red letters—" See how the church in the past has shed the blood of honourable German women " !

The Ludendorff bookshop may yet become a rival to the museum of torture instruments in the *Schloss* among those travellers who are looking for the odd and unusual things in life.

The very air of Nuremburg seems to breathe the spirit of Nazism. The German city of tradition, *par excellence*, it has been taken as the background for what is sincerely believed to be the highest expression of the Germanic ideal yet given to the world. Here in Nuremburg is the home of the most famous of all the Mastersingers, those successors of the Minnesingers who began to enrich German poetry and song in the school of Frauenlob of Mainz to find completest expression under the poet-cobbler of Nuremburg, Hans Sachs. The traditional home of Sachs is preserved as a beer-house and in an adjacent room is the alleged window and cobbler's bench, strewn with half-soled shoes and an amazing collection of knives and awls, each looking remarkably new. All that is lacking is the face of Beckmesser at the leaded panes. Wagner's comic masterpiece, "The Mastersingers of Nuremburg", has been adopted as the official opera of the Nazi party. At each annual meeting of the congress there is a special gala performance with Hitler sitting in the best seat. He is genuinely an enthusiast for the genius of Richard Wagner and for him Wagner is the mightiest expression of Germanism in music. I have often thought that the Führer finds some form of symbolism in this great opera which reflects the Nazi movement, and the part he himself played in the restoration of order in Germany. One remembers the glorious riot of music and fancy at the end of the second act. The ineffable Beckmesser had sung his serenade. He had been severely pommelled by the apprentice David, and the historic street brawl had ensued. Neighbour fought neighbour. Friend upbraided friend, and relatives settled their differences with fisticuffs. Hans Sachs forces the half-fainting Eva and the warlike Walter into the safety of his humble shop. The riot proceeds with ever-increasing noise and violence. Then suddenly is heard the noise of the watchman's horn. In a flash the mob disperses and lights in windows disappear in a matter of seconds.

"Hark to what I say, good people,
Eleven strikes from every steeple,
Defend you all from spectre and sprite;
Let no power of ill your souls affright!
Praise the Lord of Heaven."

(Hort ihr Leut, und lasst euch sagen
die Glock' hat Eilfe gaschlagen,
Bewahrt euch vor Gespenstern und Spuck,
das kein boser Geist eur'Seel' beruck!
Lobet Gott den Herrn!)

The watchman sings and as he pursues his lone vigil down the narrow streets his horn sounds again, its harsh note breaking in on the melody of peace and happiness which are the dreams of the eternal lovers, Eva Sachs and Walter von Stolzing.

Having known the confusion of the pre-Nazi régime, every generous mind, unprejudiced by incomprehensible political and ideological theories, may well understand the feelings of Adolf Hitler.

Although the first official congress of the Nazi party is assumed in party records to have taken place in Weimar of unhappy memory, it is to Nuremburg that all Nazis, imbued in the faith and having the confidence of men who have the courage of their convictions or the strength of character to have changed them from something indecisive to something definite, turn when it comes to outward expression of their opinions. Nuremburg in the mind of modern Germany is another Mecca, another Benares, a place where pride of race is also expressed in terms of belief. And this is no exaggeration.

Although Munich may still preen itself as the jumping-off ground of the Nazi movement; although the Brown House, with all its strange, florid decorations, almost as out of keeping with the Bavarian atmosphere as the neighbouring Propylaea, stands facing a broad avenue; it is Nuremburg which is the real focus of the Nazi movement. And to emphasise its importance the party has plans to make the city the most imposing political party capital in the whole world. In seven years' time Nuremburg will have monuments to the Nazi régime on a scale of magnitude and magnificence that might have occurred to Augustus but which could never have been constructed even by Charles the Fifth, himself no mean builder.

The Nazis have often been accused of over-indulgence in the spectacular. Newspaper correspondents who have arrogated to themselves the offices of ambassadors without the requisite letters of credence, have been at pains to emphasise this particular aspect of the Nazi régime. It would appear that what is quite normal on Red Square or in the ancient ceremonial of the few remaining royal families is quite legitimate and justifiable, though the main purpose of both high endeavours is to hoodwink the general public. But if similar ostentation and propaganda is employed on behalf of the National Socialist cause, then it is both reprehensible and dangerous. Actually the main criticism of the Nazi methods of publicising their point of view (a more familiar expression might be putting National Socialism over) is based on the jealousies of political opposition parties who have been by no means as clever. It is a philosophy of sour grapes. If the extremist, subversive parties had been inspired in the way the National Socialist leaders were inspired then they would have prevailed, and it would be the Nazi minority which would now be complaining in their remote asylums of persecution by their own kind.

The party arenas at Nuremburg are laid out in pleasant places. Nuremburg is built on an undulating plain, adequately wooded, unexpectedly attractive in its forest glades and open spaces. The lay of the land in the immediate vicinity lends itself to big ideas of walled fields and grand amphitheatres. A war memorial was erected in a park and this war memorial forms the background of the Luitpold arena, the assembly ground of the Nazi party at the annual conference. Those who attend the conference may be impressed by the organised cacophony and the marching and counter-marching. Such demonstrations arouse intense passions and stir the more obvious emotions. No one can witness the spectacle of a quarter of a million men responding *en masse* to a gesture without being impressed in one form or another. But even with the most meticulous and obedient organisation, there is always the confusion consequent on the assembly of a multitude, and the thousand and one inconveniences which are its immediate heirs. It has often occurred to me that the sight of the empty arena at Nuremburg, seen in the light of an autumn afternoon with the trees beginning to shed their auburn leaves, or on a spring morning with nature re-awakening after a long, cold sleep, is even more imposing and significant than when the Führer is roaring from his tribune and hundreds of thousands of men are swaying in time with the seventy-feet-long banners. The vast empty Luitpold arena, with its well-ordered and proportioned squares of grass and pavement, leaves a real impress on the mind of the ambition and attainment of the Nazi régime.

One approaches this remarkable political and oratorical setting by means of a commonplace macadamised road on which the woods look down with an air of apology. There is nothing to indicate the astonishing scene to come. Through a clump of trees one espies a very ordinary, albeit enormous building which looks exactly what it was originally intended to be—a pavilion in an exhibition. Its ponderous bulk suggests immediately that it once housed an exhibition of engineering, and its very area made it suitable for a grainstore during the war. The motor-car hurries by, for the driver is ashamed that the party should still be forced to occupy an exhibition building when the leaders wish to escape from the rain. There is a rise of ground. The trees divide. The car pulls up sharply on the edge of a grassy slope. A wide open space reveals itself. It is the Luitpold arena.

Here every year assemble the S.S. and S.A. formations in mass formation. They come from every part of Germany, content to pay their own fares and expenses, and live under war-time conditions in huge camps dotted about the countryside. For hours they stand on grass and paving stone while the Führer and members of the Cabinet declaim party policy for the ensuing twelve months.

The tribunes, rostrums and galleries of the Luitpold arena were designed by Adolf Hitler himself. The Führer ever had the ambition to be an architect and although the circumstances of his early life frustrated his hopes, since he has attained power he has been able to gratify his building instincts to the full. There have been those who have decried the architectural designs of the German leader so far as Nuremburg is concerned. Such criticisms, I venture to suggest, are just part of the wiseacre attitude sedulously maintained by far too many correspondents resident in Germany. The Luitpold arena is grandly conceived and the original plans have been admirably carried out. It would probably have more appealed to Hitler's critics if the arena had been arranged like a sports ground instead of an open-air temple. A broad marble way leads to the great stone platform on which is situated the speaker's rostrum. That rostrum overlooks an area of something like 84,000 square yards. Directly in front—it seems as if it were on a far horizon—is the former war memorial. Stone galleries extend to right and left eventually to form a huge rectangle. The centre field itself is traversed by a broad pilgrim's way. Here the Führer slowly marches through tens of thousands of storm troopers to lay a wreath to the memory of the dead.

It must be remembered that the Luitpold arena is essentially a party meeting-place. All the Nazi talent for demonstration and propaganda is brought into play. The space immediately behind the rostrum is reserved for the hundreds of standard bearers, officers without whom no Nazi gathering can be thought of as complete. The high marble wall in this part is surmounted by two bronze emblems of the eagle and swastika, rising to a height of twenty feet and with a wing-span of twenty-one. In between are three tall masts capable of bearing banners seventy-three feet in length and eighteen feet in breadth. On big days the uniformed members stand in the enclosed space to the number of 150,000. The raised galleries on the four sides can accommodate 50,000 privileged sightseers and guests. When the arena is full it may well justify the simile of Walter Scott—a sea of upturned faces. But when it is empty its message is even more telling to the sensitive mind. Here is a formidable expression of human will. The eye wanders across the broad deserted acres. The mind is filled with thoughts of the past, of the lives and achievements of men who have made history in Germany in the last ten years. As the wind rustles the leaves and branches of the belts of trees, one seems to hear the echoes of the voices of a nation.

Less impressive is the neighbouring meeting-hall. It is a comparatively modest affair, for there are only seats and standing-room for a mere 20,000. Even so, every inch of space has been adapted for the purpose of crowding as many people as possible under its roof. The vast floor space is covered with simple straight-backed wooden stalls. The Nazi is no respecter of persons and even on the platform where one of the seats is labelled with the name of Hitler, the space is just as confined and as uncomfortable as that of the most humble storm trooper in the body of the hall. The lofty ceiling is covered with swastika banners, and at the far end is a terrific organ which can indeed make the welkin ring. But the building, after the visit to the open-air arena a few yards away, comes as an anti-climax. It seems so very unworthy.

In a few years' time, however, all will be changed. A new hall is already rising which will be the biggest building of its kind in the world. This hall is emerging from a lake and a marsh. It is quite a fair step from the existing hall and at present one can only form an idea of its potential vastness by taking a look at the pile drivers and huge palisades and dams that stretch out to meet the forest clearance in the far distance. Workers are conveyed to their various occupations by means of miniature railways, so immense is this new building scheme. In other days the good people of Nuremburg of a Sunday afternoon used to walk out to these woods with their children and picnic boxes. There was an ornamental lake among the trees. It was a favoured place, indeed a delectable one, for the waters reflected the blue skies and the trees lent welcome shade on hot summer days. But now that same lake is being moved bodily into the forest in order to form the foreground of the new Nazi congress hall. Here at least is an example of the use of architectural imagination in adapting the countryside to suit a building. Broad stairs will lead down to the water's edge from a hall which will have a frontage almost as long as that of the League of Nations Palace at Ariana. The completed building may fulfil a more concrete purpose than the elongated palace near the lake of Leman, which seems doomed to the fate of the original tower of Babel. Those emerging from the high glass doors will be confronted by a broad stretch of water and a view of a forest of slender trees. They will come from a hall in which 60,000 men can sit down in comfort and in which there is a stage designed to accommodate 5,000 standard bearers and their assistants! The walls of the hall will reach to a height of 250 feet at the highest point. They will extend over a distance of two hundred and fifty yards. The masonry will cover the colossal area of seven and a half acres.

Some distance from this scene of building activity —thousands of workmen are now engaged in preparing foundations and ramming piles into the morass—is the Nazi military parade ground, an arena on an even more imposing scale than that of Luitpold but in my view not so impressive. Exaggeration occasionally fails of its propaganda purpose even in parade grounds.

The Zeppelin field is immense. Within its stone and concrete folds a quarter of a million men and their tanks and tractors can perform appropriate evolutions. But it will never capture the imagination, like the Rushmoor arena which was made by nature. It makes one feel that it is a stage set on a colossal scale for a display of tin soldiers, or, at least, stage soldiers. The German soldier is neither. His mechanical drill and strict conformity to regulation ought never to be allowed to detract from his military qualities. The use of good soldiers for purposes of civilian spectacle has always seemed to me a cheap way of obtaining great effects. The passage of the Guards in their fancy dress has always made me feel a little sad on this account, for one recalls the Mons Retreat and Flanders mud. But it is almost the universally accepted rule that a military parade is a reflection of a nation's glory: ambassadors turn up at the review at Longchamp on the fourth of July just as they send their military attachés to the trooping on Horse Guards parade. It is not therefore surprising that Hitler brings in the Reichswehr on that same account—for making a show.

But the fact remains. The Zeppelin field must rank as the most stupendous military parade ground in the history of the world. The Champ de Mars was never anything but a barrack square by comparison. Here is a field 289 metres by 312 metres. One side is taken up by a colossal gallery made from stone brought from the Jura. There are numberless boxes and *loges* and an enormous rostrum from which alternatively the Führer takes the salute of the army or addresses them as to the traditions of the service, a tradition of which he personally has full right to speak. The flagstaffs are immensely high. The centre gallery rises to some seventy feet, and above it are huge columns erected in the manner of a Greek colonnade. Each column—and there are exactly a gross—is more than twenty-five feet from pedestal to capital. The other three sides of the field are enclosed by embankments rising to about twenty feet and capable of taking 70,000 spectators. And to set off the outline of the arena in these parts against the skyline are thirty-four towers which I thought grotesque but which are locally deemed to have high æsthetic value.

We drove away from it all. The car turned back to the road with a grunt and a roar, for we were returning to Nuremburg by way of a special highway built in connection with the new arenas. We hurried through the woods. Here and there were the clearances of the camps of the storm troopers during the party congress. A pre-war tram growled along slowly and uneasily and came to an abrupt halt close to a point where hundreds of workmen were gathered round enormous machines and steam-rollers. The sharp crack of axes falling on tree-trunks struck the ear. A way was being made through a forest to take the new road that was to lead from the camps to the arenas. It would be several miles in length but it was an absolute necessity for the hundreds of thousands who flock to Nuremburg for the annual congress. It would only be used for one week in the year : it would cost a fortune : but it was all for the glory of the party.

I had been told in Berlin that while in the vicinity of Nuremburg I must on no account omit a visit to the Freemason's house at Erlangen. Now Erlangen is a small town something like twenty miles to the north on the road to Marberg. It is the seat of a university and is the centre of academic learning in Franconia. The approach is delightful, the road traversing woods and fields and occasional picturesque villages. The town itself has the charm of all small German university towns—a restraint reflected in its architecture and in the quiet serenity of its shops and public buildings. It boasts also, by way of contrast, beer-halls and students' wine taverns that might almost be described as gay. It was strange to think that a town so pleasant in appearance and with inhabitants of so mild a nature should house what is now a museum of hate—a masonic lodge, preserved as an emblem of everything a German ought not to be, and shown to the visitor with a fiendish satisfaction that takes no account of the feelings of the visitor himself.

So far as one can discover this particular lodge was seized by force on the very eve of the Nazi triumph in the early part of 1933. It was raided and captured by storm troopers from Nuremburg under the grim leadership of Julius Streicher. It is supposed to stand intact to-day exactly as it was on the day it was seized, a fact which I am not disposed to doubt but which from its intense orderliness and the extraordinary number of show cases, I fancy may be wide of the truth. But in any case it is something which must be visited if one wants to obtain a correct view of the Nazi mentality in its immense common sense and occasional lapses. This is no place to enter into a discussion of Freemasonry. Argument concerning it causes more breaches of friendship than religious controversy. As a brother of an English lodge of nearly twenty years' standing I can fairly say that in all my connections with the craft I have never once heard mention of politics. A meeting of a lodge has always been an occasion of good fellowship and a genuine spirit of charity. It has also been my experience in admittedly only a nodding acquaintance with masonry on the Continent that members of the craft did not exercise their minds in such amicable and wholesome endeavours. I have known instances in which freemasonry has definitely been made a stepping-stone to commercial and political advancement. The Nazis always contended that freemasonry in Germany, in spite of the fact that reigning monarchs and princes held exalted ranks in the craft, was practically a monopoly of the Jews and that each lodge was a sort of political pocket working for its own interests and using the state either as stalking horse or pawn. One of the first tenets of Hitler's creed was the elimination of all forms of secret societies from the Reich, and it is not surprising that Freemasonry was an early victim along with the assuredly harmless fraternities of students at Heidelberg and other universities. When the Nazis began to assert their power, lodge after lodge disappeared and all records and regalia disappeared with them, whither no one knows. At Erlangen it is claimed that the lodge was taken lock, stock, and barrel. To-day that lodge is preserved as a memorial of a monstrous evil from which Germany suffered in the past.

The Freemason's house at Erlangen occupies a detached villa of substantial size with a small front garden and a medium-sized iron railing. There is nothing to distinguish it from a score of other houses along the same road, no outward sign, no hint of a masonic emblem or device. The garden is less well kept than that of the other villas. Inside, the building is bleak, and there is no sign of a dining-room or reception chamber of the kind which warms the heart of an English Mason paying a periodic visit to a Temple. Indeed, in the whole building there is hardly one comfortable seat, and one gathers the impression that Freemasonry as interpreted in Germany in pre-revolution days must have been a severe and dreary business. Upstairs there is the main temple and several minor temples. There are coffins, and skulls, and skeletons; there are swords and daggers, and abundance of sashes and medals. A Bible, blackened with age and opened at the twenty-sixth chapter of Jeremiah, occupies a prominent place on a desk. In another room one is shown a series of questions which the lodge invited a neophyte to answer. They were quite simple questions concerning loyalty to the lodge. The ardent young Nazi who escorted guests round the building pointed to the faded document with a finger of scorn:

"Do you see? It is signed by a Jew of Nuremburg."

I read that this same Israelite had declared his desire to be loyal to the lodge.

"The traitor. Loyal to the lodge. What about loyalty to the state. The cursed Jew and Mason."

Experience has taught me that all argument is useless with fanatical young Nazis of this kind, and so I said nothing. On the wall of one of the passages were displayed in large letters the various past misdeeds of Freemasons. Each enormity had been proved beyond doubt by an examination of the secret archives. Apparently Masons—and Jews—betrayed Prussia to Napoleon at Jena and Auerstadt. (Interesting to think what Marshal Davoust could have said about that.) Apparently they were not quite so successful in the case of the Third Napoleon before Sedan, although they surely tried. And much more of the same *genre*. All over the place were pictures of German princes in Masonic regalia and the young caretaker looked on them with pity. "They could not have known everything," he said by way of apology, the logic of which completely escaped me.

Out in the clear air, away from those hermetically sealed rooms made to look so horrible and menacing,

I breathed deeply and freely. It had been a strange experience; it was all so vulgar, so unconvincing. One felt that the open-minded stranger coming away from this parade of coffins and skeletons, which looked so absurd through the dirt-begrimed windows, must think that here was surely much ado about nothing. If Freemasonry had been such a menace then mankind was easily menaced. For my part I felt that if Freemasonry had been such a subversive political factor in Germany—and I take no sides in the matter—then it would have been better to have announced that the craft was no more and had been suppressed, and left it at that. To maintain this masonic lodge at Erlangen as a museum makes the ordinary observer think that the Nazis have made political capital out of nothing.

CHAPTER V

LAUGHTER IN BAROQUE

I SPENT a week-end in the beautiful city of Dresden, where I had time to marshal my impressions of the many and various things I had seen during the first part of my stay in Nazi Germany.

The journey from Nuremburg by cross-country train was long and tedious and occupied a matter of many hours. I was too weary to sleep when I reached the Saxon capital, and after registering at an hotel suitably near the main station I wandered down the broad boulevards to the historic market-square of the city. Although it was in the region of midnight, there were lights everywhere and the big cafés and restaurants were filled with men and women sitting over plates of sausages and enormous mugs of beer. I understood later. It was a Saturday evening and a day of feasting. On Sundays the people of Dresden put on their Sunday best and wander about the streets in solemn companies of six or seven : and smile not. Only a very limited number of places of entertainment are open before the late hours of the Sabbath afternoon. They even close the museums and picture galleries at midday, and attendance at the beautiful State opera house is looked upon as a cross between a penance and a tribute to music and the local opera company, of which the people of Dresden are inordinately proud. But on Saturday evening there is laughter and rejoicing, and if anyone doubts that laughter and rejoicing are non-existent in latter-day Germany I would recommend him to happen on Dresden by a night train and wander where he will in the middle portion of the city.

Scores of motor-cars and horse cabs were drawn up round the market-square. Neon lights looked down from every coping. Lights shone unexpectedly through the restaurant windows, for generally in Germany heavy curtains are drawn at night and doors are concealed by means of weighty leather hangings. The life of the town responded to the gaiety of the illuminations.

The modern German beer and wine-houses—I speak of those established since the war—are very extensive. Some of them can entertain a thousand people at a time. There was one such place in Dresden which seemed capable of taking twice that number. Life there was not of the night-club variety. It was just an occasion for the bourgeois to extend itself, and extend itself it surely did. As I walked from hall to hall, past decorated pillars and through gay arcades, so the press of people became more and more congested and the music of a very large orchestra was overwhelmed in the concourse of voices and even yodels (the mountains are not far removed) of the good people of Dresden, out to make a real Saturday night of it.

The people of Saxony are said to have very distinct relationships with the people of Great Britain, or, at least, certain parts of Great Britain. Take their Sunday behaviour. It is akin to our own. Everything closes and the faces of the majority become long-drawn. The Roman Catholic minority flock to Mass. The Protestants of the more evangelical kind rush to sit on hard seats and hear still harder words from their plainly-cassocked pastor. The less evangelical look at the church door and pass on and wonder in their minds why the Sistine Madonna is not on view on a Sunday afternoon, just as so many English provincials can never understand why they cannot see Mickey Mouse and the newly-released Hollywood nonsense before six o'clock. It is all so like England without the vulgarity of taste.

For the Dresdener has great taste. He keeps celluloid in its place. Like ourselves the Saxons are people of conflicting loyalties. A dissenting majority continues to tolerate the Church of England. Likewise in Saxony a Protestant population was loyal to the royal house before the revolution, although the reigning monarch was a Roman. The present pretender to the throne in the baroque palace overlooking the Elbe is a Roman Catholic priest, I believe. The members of his family are still provided for by the Saxon people—and provided for very well indeed. They have still a sneaking regard for the picturesque if ineffectual royal house. A story is told of the last king. It was in the days before the revolution and already people were beginning to weary of the Weimar constitution. The King arrived at a certain railway station. Hundreds of good Saxons had gathered to greet him. The Saxon Majesty flung up the window for a moment and shouted, "Damned good republicans, aren't you?" The story, I have always thought, bears not a little relationship to the attitude we ourselves would maintain in similar circumstances. The rest of Germany regards the Saxon as being a stupid person who, by some strange process, gets there in the end no matter what the obstacle. Europe has long thought the same of ourselves. The Saxon is supposed to be perfidious and unreliable. You can never tell where you are with him. The same criticism is applied to the British race by Continentals. And like ourselves, when the Saxon decides to enjoy himself he enjoys himself to the full, however dreary he may be in his outlook at other times.

That sense of wholehearted enjoyment was fully expressed the Saturday evening I wandered about Dresden. And, when the small hours came, the good people abandoned their beer and wine haunts for the more elegant night dens and dancing floors near the station. The party spirit was not allowed to die until the lights finally died out. Which is, of course, exactly what would happen in England if an undiscerning government did not treat the people who keep it in power and pay for its existence exactly like children.

That same night, or rather at about half-past two on the succeeding Sunday morning, I was about to enter my hotel, when the noise of music and folk-singing came floating through the air. There was a light in a window across the way and at the door of the house stood a porter in multi-coloured clothes, presumably the cabaret version of national costume. It was one of those evenings when sleep seemed far away and I decided to prolong my night wanderings.

Inside some four or five rooms, all linked up with each other and heavily decorated with paper festoons and imitation bunches of grapes, about a hundred men and women were singing lustily to the accompaniment of two extremely pretty blonde girls playing a grand piano and a zither. On the tables were flagons of white wine and diminutive glasses of *Steinhager*. From time to time groups of young men would strike up some traditional air, and whether it was the lateness of the hour, or the extraordinary unison of the singing, it seemed to me like the music of the spheres come to earth at last. A spirit of glee pervaded everywhere. There was no sign of horse play, or excessive drinking, or cheap love-making. Now and then, a few boys and girls would rise and go through the steps of a folk-dance, to be followed by a general roundelay. The stranger was forced to join in the general fun through the sheer goodwill of the place. It was well after four o'clock when I crossed the road back to my hotel. My nerves were too highly strung for sleep and I asked the night porter if he had any newspapers from London available. He regretted greatly. He had sold the last about midnight. But if I desired to read an English book he had one by him. He had just finished it. I was quite welcome. It was a Tauchnitz edition of George Bernard Shaw's *Saint Joan* !

Sunday was tame by comparison. The streets were deserted. The trams ran only occasionally. In the morning there were some processions of Hitler youth and I saw a long line of men in naval uniform marching briskly along, men whom I presumed to be drawn from the navy of the Elbe River. Why such a naval demonstration in inland Dresden I was not able to discover. I spent a while idling in the celebrated theatre place in front of the old royal palace, surely one of the most delightful corners of Europe, a laughter in baroque, a complete expression of a taste that is now dead but might well be revived. A few minutes were left to look at the Raphael masterpiece in the art gallery, for the collection is closed at noon on Sunday. Then a glimpse of the royal palace and the stone watering-place where the horses of the Saxon kings were once led down from their stable ramps to refresh themselves before feeding. At luncheon my waiter spoke English with fluency and correctness. He told me he had been in service in an English noble family before the war and had taken the last boat home on the eve of the outbreak of trouble. He had never been back, even for a holiday. He added as he brought my coffee, " I like working in Germany *now* and Dresden is such a beautiful place."

It was with the waiter's avowal in my mind that I left the city for the hillside of Lossnitz. An old friend of mine was undergoing treatment at a clinic there and I had promised to pay a duty call. It is some distance away and the final stages of the journey have to be made by a funicular railway and on foot. The climb is steep indeed, and a steady rain began to fall as I stepped out of the station at the top of the hill. I took shelter under some trees which were doing their best to keep the seat of a convenient bench dry. The waiter had said that he liked working in Germany *now.* The word brought back many other conversations and gave food for thought. Below lay the bend of the Elbe and the hollow of the earth in which Dresden is built. One could see the famous domes and spires of the city—the minaret-like shape on top of the cupola of the cathedral church of Our Lady, the classical façade of the State Opera House, the decorated tower of the Roman Catholic Court Church, the Crown gate of the celebrated Zwinger, and the outline of the Bruhlsche Terrace. Nearer, tug-boats were towing immense barges across the wide waters of the Elbe, close by the newly-reconstructed Konigshufer. All around were the hills of Saxony, full of autumn beauty, a coat of many colours. The grey sky and drizzling rain could not detract from the majesty of the scene, a garden of nature and a city of men. It was a great city of Germany, and Germany was a great country and, in spite of adversity, always had been. Yet the waiter in the hotel had only made up his mind recently that he liked to work in it.

And why?

It summed up in a few words what the non-politically minded German thought of the new régime. At long last he had been able to work in an atmosphere of security. Furthermore, he was encouraged to work. He realised that a good workman was looked on as the best citizen, and that his labour counted for something in the state.

My travels had convinced me that the average German is fond of two things in this world—his home and the well-being that it brings; and the labour or method by which he obtains such advantages. He will fight to the death for his homeland and the homes it contains with a devotion equal to that of any people in the world and far more than most. That exaltation of the Fatherland has too often been put down to an extreme of military arrogance, whereas a not dissimilar motive on the part of the Frenchman is dismissed as just characteristic chauvinism, of only ephemeral significance. The tenacity of purpose of the German people was more than proved by their grim pursuit of the war until empty stomachs brought inevitable capitulation. That they should desire to rehabilitate themselves and resurrect their sense of self-respect has been attributed to base motives for far too long.

As I sat on that bench, high in the hills, beneath the dripping trees, I thought of the many things that had gone to justify the words of the waiter in the Dresden hotel. Before the coming of the Nazis there were about thirty political parties in the Reich and the proceedings of the Reichstag was a cross between a jigsaw puzzle and a dog fight. Because there was such a state of affairs and Parliament, as is the custom of such things, made an undue amount of noise, it was thought that all Germans were intensely interested in political theories as distinct from political and national questions. Nothing is further from the truth. One has become accustomed to the cry of commentators that all Europeans are politically minded, because politicians have such spectacular games with each other. The same old story is constantly repeated about France because there are often three or four Prime Ministers a year and the Parisian concierge, having nothing to do all day except read the papers and pry into his tenants' business, occasionally becomes eloquent on unexpected developments in Senate or Chamber. But in actual fact the ordinary Frenchman is far too interested in the art of living to care much about what happens in the Palais Bourbon, and the great peasant class, ignorant and narrow in outlook, looks on everything connected with city life with something more than suspicion. Too often has it been shown that when France is in a tight corner, it is to the solid peasantry, who know nothing of politics but a lot about *primeurs*, that the peccadilloes of the Chamber turn for support and safeguard. If the peoples of the earth ruled the earth instead of professional politicians history might tell a far different story. Emphatically may this be said of the unhappy German people before the coming of the new régime. For fifteen years they were the victims of political theory as interpreted by thirty parties in the Berlin Parliament; and out of it all they obtained nothing but confusion and misgovernment. Now they are satisfied with political fact, which, though it has often proved uncomfortable and may even be more uncomfortable, at least provides them with a sense of knowing where they are.

In the course of long talks with many and various Germans, from retired Generals to labourers hoeing turnips in Hessian fields, I had learned two things about modern Germany. The first was that nowadays the ordinary German once more believed in the stability of his country and was prepared to defend it against both aggression and criticism. The other was the universal feeling of friendship of the average man towards England and the English.

There was a conversation I had with a German who returned from South Africa just before the final revolution that was very eloquent of the new state of mind. He said:

"When I landed at Hamburg after spending years in Cape Town I looked forward to living in my native land once more. I had heard a lot about the political situation and the conflict between Nazis and Communists. Like most people who have not experienced political strife at first hand, I thought they were very exaggerated. But I had an unpleasant reminder a few hours after I arrived. I was walking across a square in the old town when two bullets whizzed past my ear. During the war I had never had such a narrow escape. Two men fell dead a few yards away and I began to realise that I had walked into a miniature civil war.

"It was the same in every big city in Germany, nothing but trouble and shooting. Nothing was stable. I have never seen such beggary in my life. Thousands of my fellow-Germans had been reduced almost to vermin by the appalling conditions of poverty and unemployment. And things were getting worse every day. I would gladly have returned to South Africa.

" But to-day things are changed. There is a new spirit in the country. Unemployment is disappearing. Workmen have jobs to go to and decent clothes to wear. Germany has her head up and because she has her head up once more she is said to be on the way to war again. The charges are unjust and unfair. I wonder how many other peoples would have come out of the ordeal as well. And again every German is supposed to be an active Nazi. That also is wrong. I have never belonged to the party although I support it. I take no interest in politics but I am tremendously interested in Germany, and I am convinced that the Nazis have the cause of Germany at heart before any other. They are not the political rascals their enemies would have us believe. They just happen to be good Germans."

I fancy that the opinion of this returned exile sums up the point of view of millions of Germans to-day who are heartily weary of political strife and sincerely desire to work for their livings and contribute something useful to the general welfare. It is not everybody who wants to make speeches at the street corner and who thinks himself aggrieved if authority prevents him from making himself a general nuisance by disturbing the tranquillity of others. And if it comes to any question of self-sacrifice on the part of the community for the benefit of the less fortunate—remembering how much this attitude maintains in the teachings of communist elements—one would travel far to find more external evidence of real charity and generosity on the part of the people than in modern Germany. These things are true ; but truth is still akin to Rudyard Kipling's lady who lives at the bottom of a well.

Thoughts of anti-Semiticism and the suppression of Freemasonry and the abolition of trade unions came to mind. Rightly or wrongly the leaders of the Nazi party have set their minds against both Jews and secret societies in their midst. Whether they are wise in their policy one may doubt, however much one may admire the major achievements of the Nazi régime. At the same time one must bear in mind that perhaps the two problems obtruded on public life in a manner far different from which they occur in our own. In the case of the suppression of trade unions one must not be carried away by a false sense of democratic values. Trade unions on the Continent have never had that ambition to improve the status of the working classes that our own have. They have almost always been of an intensely political and party complexion. (English trade unionists do not unanimously vote for Mr. Attlee.) Even in France, which is supposed to be so enlightened, trade unionism has never made great headway and the efforts of M. Jouhaux, himself an international figure, have failed to raise their leaders to a much greater dignity than that of political agitators. And so in Germany trade unions were merely party and vote-catching machines. The improvement in working conditions was to them a secondary consideration. Their disappearance is not greatly missed even by the most extreme German artisan. Something better has taken its place in the German Labour Front, a huge organisation which looks after all those interests which previously trade unions were only too apt to forget. One must never fall into the trap of discussing German labour conditions *vis-à-vis* the trade union movement in terms of our own Trades Union Congress, and the right to strike to obtain reasonable conditions under which to work. It is a very different story.

Nothing is perfect in this worst of all possible

worlds. No one can say with truth that the Nazi régime is perfect. Even the propaganda ministry has never asserted that. But it is certainly a great improvement on what went before it. The spectre of the concentration camp loomed before me. Those tales of horror and bestiality one had read brought a shivering feeling. Then there was the cleansing, so-called, of June 30. It all seemed horrible, sitting there looking over a countryside that appeared so prosperous and so grand. But when the first shudder had gone, came the thought of the destiny of mankind, and the realisation that high endeavour has always been preceded by great human suffering. In Spain both sides were shooting prisoners at sight at the very moment I was sitting there, simply because they happened to be wearing a different uniform. A revolution had degenerated into a civil war and the same might have happened in Germany.

My mind traversed distances of history. I tried to think of a " bloodless revolution " that meant anything. There was that bleak December morning when the Roundheads threw down the head of a king from the gallows of Whitehall for the world to contemplate with horror. There was the massacre of September, the parade of death on the Place de la Concorde, the blood of the revolutionary wars in which the spirit of Europe's nations was born, although we often attempt to disguise the fact from ourselves. The risings of July, the barricades of the Paris commune, none of them bloodless. Garibaldi leading his country to unity over the bodies of his compatriots. And, finally, the mild methods of Lenin and Trotsky, massacres that made the Lubianka smell like a cesspool and look like an abattoir. All these things have happened in the name of liberty in one form or another. That a successful revolution should happen in Germany in the name of what the Germans think is something the equal of liberty, that it should happen when the people were starving and should be accomplished without violence, is surely asking too much from mankind. In fact, I wondered if on the whole less blood had been shed for the accomplishment of so great a change in the manners and outlook of a great people than in any similar upheaval in the history of the world.

I had seen enough of this new Germany to realise how greatly it was changed from the hesitating half-hearted Germany I saw during my stay in Munich and elsewhere at the elections of 1933. Until the very eve of the Nazi assumption of supreme power there was still room in the minds of Germans for doubt: and doubt they did. Hitler came to power and promised much. It is said that even he was doubtful if he could achieve one-quarter of what he promised, but after three years of the new régime he had re-created Germany and once more made her voice felt in the councils of the nations. Previously Germany had only been regarded as a great power on sufferance, because she happened to have a population of some sixty million people. Otherwise she was just the public nuisance of Europe in the eyes of France, Russia and the Little Entente. A few months of the Hitler régime changed all that. The Führer first astounded the world by walking out of the League of Nations one Saturday forenoon because he was weary of the insincerities and shibboleths of Geneva which promised Germany equality with one hand and took it away with the other. The inevitable restoration of the Saar to Germany after the plebiscite enhanced Hitler's reputation among the people. And thence he went from strength to strength. The military clauses of the Versailles settlement were thrown down one by one. The Rhine was reoccupied and in Paris the squealers in the Press wrote about war the next day. But the world public was not greatly interested in the fact that German soldiers were doing sentry-go opposite the Maginot line. In a day or two the whole question was forgotten.

The British Foreign Office recognised the existence of the new German spirit which was prepared to take equality of rights if she were not granted them as promised, and hastened to compromise in a naval understanding which would have been unthinkable five or six years ago. All these things have happened in the matter of thirty-six months. To-day there is no talk of reparations or beaten enemy or anything of the sort. To-day the Germanophobe Press is horrified at the strength which the new Germany has assumed, forgetting that it was external persecution and vendetta which were so largely responsible for the revival of Germany as a strong military power.

That Germany is strong, there is no doubt. That she wishes to make war, I have very grave doubts. I fancy that if Germany were given a square deal and that if the nations instead of pursuing academic discussions about reforming the League Covenant would revise the Treaty of Versailles (a great deal of it remains), then Europe would be able to look forward to a period of peace and prosperity. But as it is most unlikely that the predatory succession states will ever give up their territorial acquisitions to which they have no title, Europe must continue to be a sort of melting-pot and the danger of war must always be just round the corner.

Who knows what would be the outcome of that

struggle ? How would the various lots of enemies line up ? As I sat looking down on the Elbe and Dresden, I thought of the futile war of 1914–18 and wondered what anyone had got out of it that they could be proud of. And I thought that if perhaps the Empire had been on the side of Germany, the sequel would have been very different, or there might never have been a war at all. And I thought again, and still think, that the one safeguard of peace in Europe to-day is a complete reversal of our present policy of Locarno and collective security and the like, and an understanding with Germany. If such an object cannot be obtained then it were best we stayed out of Europe altogether.

There is another aspect of this great issue. The definite feelings of friendship of the ordinary German for England. This is specially to be found in the ranks of ex-servicemen who are ever willing to pay tribute to the tenacity of the British soldier and his dogged resistance in all kinds of circumstances. Every German who has studied the history of the war as well as having fought in it is unanimous that if England had not intervened, the result would have been very different. And they always add the conclusion that it was madness on the part of pre-war German rulers ever to have made a situation by which Great Britain could have been brought into a war with Germany.

I have also had hundreds of conversations with Englishmen in various parts of the country and nowhere have I found hostility towards Germany. The majority of people are filled with admiration for a nation that fought the world for more than four years and nearly won through. Every soldier will agree that the German was a gallant enemy and that he would rather have Jerry on his side next time instead of a Frenchman. These are statements of fact and not the glosses of a foreign minister speaking from the front bench to an audience of Parliamentarians, most of whom must vote as they are told in any case. I have long since come to the conclusion that the only section of the population which adhered to the pro-French viewpoint and were anxious for more commitments on the lines of the dangerous Entente-Cordiale was the influential insidious minority who have come into unlawful possession of the tradition of the landed classes. Nearly all of them have a sentimental attachment for France of an entirely personal nature. They are the types who prefer to shiver on the Riviera in winter rather than spend their holidays in our own resorts. They nearly all of them learned French at school but never learned how to speak the language. The man who came into contact with the French and French methods during the war and during the peace, knows the significance of the phrase " all for the benefit of France ".

On not one occasion had I found any hostility towards England on the part of the German people. In fact, it had been the reverse. The schoolboy endeavoured to show off his knowledge of English at every opportunity. There is a genuine enthusiasm among German boys and girls to acquire something of the English language and so far as youths are concerned, tens of thousands speak our tongue quite well and tens of thousands more can read it with comparative ease. I was told by a Berlin professor who invited me to give a course of lectures in German cities that he could guarantee an audience of five hundred natives who could understand English in each place, and I have also heard it said that a broadcast address in English from a German station could be understood by one million of the population. These figures in themselves are surely an excellent augury for peace and understanding. One only wishes that there was a similar dissemination of knowledge in this country. But that is too much to hope for. The Englishman will never learn foreign languages.

I sat once with a group of ex-service men and the talk turned on the British army and Great Britain in general. One of them spoke English well. He told me he had been taken prisoner in 1916 at the Somme battle and had spent a long time working in the fields of Kent.

" I have every reason to be bitter about the British soldiers," he said, " for I was treated badly. When I was taken prisoner the escorts searched me, took away my cheap watch that had been given me by my mother and tore my wedding-ring from my finger. Now that was not fair, for surely they were personal belongings and ought to be respected, even in the case of a prisoner. But I had fought in the trenches for a long time and I knew that this must be exceptional. There are scallywags in every army. In England I found the British soldier a much kinder person. He had a nasty job, looking after prisoners, and there was not much food. But he did not go out of his way to make us unhappy."

I felt a little hot under the collar when this round-faced German from Swabia told me the story of the British soldier who took his wedding-ring. Who wouldn't? But this German, looking back long after the war, now found nothing but admiration for his late enemy and desired to live at peace with them.

" We must never fight England again," he said later on, " and England must never fight Germany. I don't think either thing could happen. The world is not quite so mad as all that."

I resumed my walk up the hill towards the clinic and fell to wondering whether the world was as mad as that, or not.

CHAPTER VI

YOUTH AT WORK

THOSE who have been persuaded to regard Dr. Josef Goebbels merely as a firebrand propagandist out to exploit any means of publicity in the Nazi interest, may be surprised to learn that from time to time this much-criticised party leader voices observations of great significance and truth. At the recent "World Conference for Leisure Time and Recreation" held at Hamburg (this important aspect of modern German life is discussed elsewhere), Dr. Goebbels said to the gathering of international delegates :

> The stability of a State is based first and last, not on the number of guns which it has, but on the number of hearts which it possesses. The happiness of the citizens of our State is the surest pillar of our nation. Woe betide those statesmen who only possess power and who can only call on power.
>
> Look into the faces of German men and women and you will know what change has taken place in Germany. You do not need to visit any theatres, national highways, sports grounds, and monumental buildings—you only need to look at the people in Germany and you will know that Germany has become finer and happier.

During my visit to Germany I was immensely impressed by the obvious spirit of self-respect and national pride which sat upon all. It was reflected in a new cast of countenance, no longer hang-dog, no longer abject : a cast of countenance put on by a people conscious that at long last something was being done to make the future less uncertain and more pleasant to contemplate. I found evidence of the truth of the Propaganda Minister's words wherever I went. It was never more strongly emphasised than in the much-discussed compulsory labour camps.

In England our politicians, drawing their own conclusions and deeming them the reactions of the community, have, to a very large extent, set their minds against any form of compulsory service. In recent months when the more far-sighted began to take alarm at the decline in physical fitness of the nation and suggested some universal form of physical training of youth, the short-sighted majority came out against any such infringement of the traditional liberty of the subject. Since the war we seem to have developed the idea that discipline can never be an effective servant of liberty. It is perhaps for that reason that the compulsory German labour camps have been bitterly condemned by critics who have never taken the trouble to go and see them at work. I have heard people say that the camps are akin to slave-grounds : that they are places of unmentionable vice : that in the barbed-wire compounds the German youth is deliberately deprived of his personality in order to make him suitable material for the conscript regular army.

Such criticisms are very wide of the mark. The compulsory labour camps have now become an accepted part of the life of German youth. In the six months of hard work—hard work is not necessarily slavery—the boy of nineteen becomes strong and hardened—equipped physically for the increasing difficulties of life ahead. Allegations of vice come easily to all critics of institutions where groups of boys are concentrated in a small space. One seems to

PLATE 3

YOUTH AT WORK

[face p. 116

remember periodic insinuations against our public schools. In the case of the German labour camps such a possibility is avoided by plentiful hard work and frequent holidays. Finally in the labour camps individuality is encouraged and it by no means follows that all the boys when they complete their six months of training are taken into the Reichswehr. The regular army still has so much raw material at its disposal that it can pick and choose. It must further be remembered that it is the ambition of every German boy to serve in the army. I have heard of cases of boys who, after they have left the labour camps and been rejected by the army authorities, have tried to commit suicide because they thought their failure to reach the necessary standard of fitness was a personal disgrace. A spirit of that kind must surely give pause to those who have read of the failure of our own authorities to obtain "sub-standard" recruits for the army to maintain "lines of communication".

And so far as the German Youth Camps are concerned the impartial observer must come away from them feeling that Dr. Goebbels is justified in his view that in the faces of the modern German you discern a finer and happier race.

During my visit to Germany I went to labour camps in all parts of the country. Although there is a regular pattern for the many hundreds that are now in active operation—there are over 1,300—each one has its own individual aspect and, one may even go so far as to say, its own corporate life. In some ways one may compare the camps with the houses of our public schools—all are supposed to be the same but yet so many of the agreeable differences are dependent on the housemaster. The personality of the officer in charge of the camp is all important: he can further be father as well as master of his charges. The analogy only breaks down in the matter of rationing—the authorities insist on adequate food. Otherwise all the advantages and amenities are there—dormitories, sports activities, a keen sense of competition, and the corporate spirit.

Let me describe a typical labour camp. Of the many hundreds in the Reich, I select that near the ancient town of Radgeburg, close by Dresden in the former Kingdom of Saxony. I do so because at the time of my visit the camp itself was deserted—the youths being engaged on some reclamation work some miles away—and I was enabled to spend several hours inspecting its actual equipment and lay-out. Later I will endeavour to give some description of camps in Silesia with the boys at work and at play. Radgeburg is a pleasant Saxon township—built round a square, with low painted houses and cobbled streets—not altogether without similarities to French provincial towns of the Dauphine of the same size and importance. To reach it you take the famous military road built by Augustus the Strong of Saxony. Tall trees line the route from Dresden. Man has dealt kindly with nature in this by-way of the world and the countryside opens on all sides in a marvel of forests and green fields. Presently a glimpse of water is caught through the trees and on the far side of a lake, that is surely a sportsman's idea of heaven, rise the walls of the ancient castle of Moritzburg, the hunting lodge of the Royal house of Saxony and the home of the heirs of the now dispossessed Saxon Kings. The road follows the edge of the lake, keeping the castle in view for several miles before making the open country once more on its way to Radgeburg. Beyond the little town is a wide plain, intersected with streams running at the bottom of ill-kept ditches. Hitherto great sums have been lost annually through the absence of reasonable irrigation and it is to terminate such waste that labour camps have been established in these parts. On the day of my visit the one hundred and fifty youths stationed in the camp were engaged in transforming a weed-ridden ditch into an irrigation channel—work which was a gift from heaven to the local farmer and an endowment of good health for the young labourers.

It was a beautiful sunny morning when I came to Radgeburg. Some old peasants went by with their shirts open at the necks revealing skins tanned dark brown by age and years spent in the open air. It was real farm-land, only moderately developed. An occasional cow strayed on the road and once a pig threatened self-destruction as it grumbled its way out of the path of our motor-car. The camp itself consisted of wooden huts, similar to those used by the British army during the war. They were arranged on three sides of a square with a smaller hut built near the palisade entrance to serve as a guardroom and office. A uniformed official was waiting and, as our car swung through, the youthful sentry came to attention with an almost thunderous click of his heels and brought his spade to the ground with an even sharper ring. I took a close look at him. He was typical of so many thousands. He was approaching six feet in height and wore the grey forage cap and swastika badge of the labour camp uniform. His hair was closely cropped in correct German style. His face was round and well fed and he stood to attention with the rigidity of a trained man. He had a dull grey tunic and trousers and black jack-boots. His equipment was rough as befits those who work in the fields but it was well kept and the hands and face of the youth were scrupulously clean. That appearance of cleanliness is typical of the labour camps of Germany : indeed, it is typical of the whole of modern Germany. As he addressed the officer on duty, I saw two rows of white teeth and I thought of thousands of youths in our own special areas.

There were only about twelve youths on duty in the camp—the remainder were at work miles away. Of half this number six were busy in that most essential institution—the kitchen. It was hither we went at once. Again a clicking of heels and the resounding " Heil Hitler ". Then the *Vormann* came forward and spoke of the rations for the day. The four huge cauldrons supplied from a central furnace were loaded with food—soup, stew with a most alluring smell, green vegetables and, of course, the inevitable potatoes. One of the youths was assembling plates and dishes in readiness for a late afternoon meal. Another was polishing cutlery. I found another in the adjacent store-room checking over a newly-delivered consignment of flour and groceries. It was all tremendously efficient and supplies were there in abundance. Next to the kitchen was a long, low dining-hall, with long, curtained windows. On each table were huge bundles of evergreens and bunches of flowers brought from the camp gardens. The beams were festooned with favours and banners and the walls were hung with the familiar portraits of the Führer, President Hindenburg, and Prince Bismarck. The benches and floors were scrubbed to look like a quarterdeck newly holystoned. Conspicuous at one end of the room was a display of the bugles, drums, and mace of the camp—a vision of metal polish and blanco. The *Vormann* was especially proud of this collection and said, " Our band is considered one of the best in all the camps of Saxony."

The dormitories were to be found in the huts on the other two sides of the compound. They were more or less uniform in size and furnished with the usual double tier iron bedstead which is as inevitable in German ordnance stores as the three planks and " biscuits ", still remembered by many of us who served in wartime. There were straw palliasses about nine inches in depth and the mountainous bolster which the German obstinately believes is better than blankets. On each bed was the name of the occupant. Arbeitsman Then ; Vormann Herne ; and so on. To each of the occupants of the dormitory was assigned a locker and there was a large table round which twenty could sit with ease. It seemed very comfortable except in one respect. It was a sunny day but the central heating was in full blast. An Englishman, no matter how long he lives abroad, will never properly understand why a Continental can never agree that a room is comfortable unless it is at tropical heat and hermetically sealed.

I was struck at the orderliness of everything. Outside each door was a row of highly-burnished spades in an appropriate rack. These were the " Dress " spades used for exercises and ceremonial drill. In the equivalent of the quartermaster's store were piles of spare clothing and equipment and masses of hobnailed boots. There was a canteen containing shelves of cheap German cigarettes, packets of bretzels and the pralines which the German youth regards as special luxuries. The miniature hospital was excellently equipped and the consulting-room contained a modern surgical examination table and cupboards filled with medicinal and first-aid appliances. While I was at Radgeburg a youth was brought in by motor-car. He looked pale and was obviously suffering from a heavy cold. He had been sent back from the irrigation work in the country as unfit. Before I left he was lying in bed in the hospital ward with a doctor in attendance.

An attractive garden had been planted round a cenotaph in the middle of the compound and autumn plants picked out the legend in colour " Alles für Deutschland ". The garden had been made by the boys in their spare time.

I was indebted to Gunther Arndt for facilities to view the work of the youthful labourers at first hand. We spent many long hours in the camps in the vicinity of Breslau in Silesia. Herr Arndt, a war veteran who lost a leg in action and wears the Iron Cross, is formidably described as the *Oberstarbeitsführer*—the head leader of the labour camps in this particular district. Together we travelled long distances over the Silesian countryside exploring those areas of the marshes which had been reclaimed and irrigated by the youths of the labour camps and those still swampy and unsalubrious parts which await agricultural development when the supply of water is regulated by canalised channels.

Silesia is well favoured by nature with woodlands. It is a hunter's delight and every open field as we passed by contained three or four covies of partridges feeding among the stubble. Never have I seen such beautiful tints of autumn foliage. No valley in the Tyrol or glade of the Black Forest has anything to compare in colour and richness with the falling leaf of the Silesian forests. But beauty in nature does not coincide with productivity in soil. For generations farmers in these parts have suffered from indifferent drainage and inadequate forest clearance. Crops have been wooed from the soil where they ought to have been yielded in abundance. But how human endeavour can produce a farmland countryside is forcibly proved in Silesia.

The particular camps I visited were north of Trebnitz, the little town where was born the great Seydlitz, perhaps the most skilful cavalry leader of all time and a name revered in German military tradition. Our car had quickly to leave the high road and proceed by way of cart tracks. The journey was both thrilling and perilous for the country we crossed was more suitable for tanks than a high-powered limousine. In fact, a car containing some members of Herr Arndt's staff broke its back axle before the morning was passed. In a wide wilderness which I was assured was near the village of Deutsches Hammer was a labour camp for some two hundred boys who could be seen at work in the fields about half a mile away. The camp was like the others except for the subtle differences of decoration and amenities. Its particular chief happened to be a great nature lover and ornithologist and he had infected the boys with a love of his particular hobby. The result was that a corner of the compound was occupied by a considerable enclosure containing birds and beasts of all kinds. There were golden pheasants and Minorca hens : ducks and doves were everywhere : and many rabbits. One of the youths informed me that the rabbits had appeared reluctant to make their own warren and so one had been made for them. The flower gardens of this particular camp were a joy to look at and plans were in hand to surround the hutment buildings with high clumps of blossoming shrubs. In addition an attempt had been made to give each dormitory a personality of its own. Each one was dedicated to a battle in the Silesian wars of Frederick the Great. The walls were covered with prints of the various actions. There were portraits of contemporary officers and of course the King himself, and where portraits were unobtainable mural decorations had been made by the more artistically minded among the labour youths. And some of the drawings displayed no mean talent.

In the adjacent fields about 200 boys were completing a ditch designed as a conduit from a canal some distance away. As we made our way with difficulty over the rough ground each group of workers came stiffly to attention. They were engaged on all kinds of tasks: some were hauling turf to make the banks of the channel: others were in waders digging out a passage for the water: some were busy with a theodolite, measures, and other surveying instruments planning the work which had to be carried out the following week. We seemed to walk for miles among the criss-cross of channels, some half completed, some hardly begun, but at length we came to the main stream that had been enclosed in deep embankments by the labour of the boys from Deutsches Hammer. The neat escarpments stretched to the horizon, conducting the waste water in a straight line to a distant river. The channel itself was edged with sawn tree-trunks, cut by the youths from neighbouring spinnies. The whole of this colossal work was their achievement except for the concrete road bridges that had been erected by outside contractors.

Later in the morning near the township of Trachenburg, I witnessed a very remarkable example of the way these German youths are kept in perfect trim. It was in a wooded area on the edge of a big forest. Once more the boys—there were about three hundred altogether—were engaged in making an irrigation trench. It was an even bigger scheme than that of Deutsches Hammer, and in places the water was waist-deep. The whole task was being carried on methodically with gangs engaged in the first heartbreaking work of cutting into the swamp in an endeavour to make a channel to gangs placing turf in place on the completed embankments. The boys were working as if the end of

PLATE 4

BOYS FROM LABOUR CAMP AT DEUTSCHES-HAMMER
MAKING AN IRRIGATION CHANNEL

[*face p.* 124

the world was coming that night. Perhaps they were making an extra special effort because of the presence of Herr Arndt—although I doubt it, for Germans of all ages seem to live for work. As we reached the more primitive end of the working and the waters swirled in opaque, ominous mud at the bottom of the ditch, Herr Arndt ordered a stalwart boy to carry me across the morass. I am no lightweight but he lifted me with ease. No sooner had I been deposited on the far side, than the woods echoed to the screech of a whistle. Looking round I saw the three hundred boys jump out of the mud on to the bank and begin gesticulating in a strange fashion. I thought that everyone had gone crazy until it became evident that they were performing the same gesticulations in complete unison. They were doing physical jerks—on the hands down, touch the toes, and the like. And out there in the open air they continued for ten minutes. Another screech on the distant whistle and they were back with their shovels and picks in the mud.

Herr Arndt, noticing my surprise, said:

" While they are in the fields, these boys have to do a lot of bending. Digging does not exercise all the muscles. It leaves a number unoccupied. That is what makes men feel tired. The boys do physical exercises every hour so that their bodies are completely exercised. The exercises have been scientifically worked out so as to make for the most perfect physical fitness."

It is in such little details that the Nazi régime springs surprises in most unexpected places.

The camp at Trachenburg is situated close to the town. But that makes no difference, for the boys are only permitted out at week-ends when they can cycle wherever they like. The compound is overshadowed by a picturesque windmill and there are large playing-fields. Here again there is individuality in the hutments and dormitories. The last named are devoted to the great German knights of old—Heinrich of Plauen, Heinrich von Salza, and so on. All the lamps are decorated with symbolic figures, and in the dining-room were carvings of great imagination and skill. As we lunched in the canteen of the camp—we ate the same meal as the workers, thick soup, minced-meat balls, potato and cabbage and black bread—a party of the boys came cycling in from the fields in squadron formation. Each party was singing one of the thousand songs with which German folklore is so richly endowed. As each group was dismissed by its particular leader so the bicycles were garaged and the youths tore to their various huts. In a minute or two they were swarming across to the shower-baths, having shorn their working tunics and heavy working boots. A triumph of riotous youthful laughter could be heard emanating from the bath-house. Then more slowly the boys went back to their huts to wait the intervening ten minutes until their dinner would be served.

May good digestion have waited on their appetites. I do not remember seeing so much food consumed by such a limited number of people. But that is what happens to young men when they are taken from the sheltered lives of the city to work for a while on the soil and obtain physical fitness from nature.

German labour camps on a voluntary basis were in existence during the régime of the republic. The present system may only be a development (critics of Hitler always emphasise that he did not invent the Labour Camp) but it is a development on a gigantic scale that may have far-reaching results. Certainly one can fairly say that taking the average youth of nineteen to twenty in the nations of the world in the aggregate, for sheer physical fitness the German is an easy first. Moreover, they develop the instincts picked up in the six months in the camp to continue in a state of physical health. By way of digression at this point, it ought to be borne in mind that similar results could be achieved in England. The astonishing popularity of hiking and week-end bicycling among the youth of the nation in less fortunate circumstances are sufficient evidence of the zeal of young people to obtain fitness and exercise. It is not too much to contend that thousands of the rising generation would welcome an opportunity for organised work like that provided by the German labour camp, and surely similar facilities could be provided on a voluntary basis. Physical fitness may not be the most important factor or aim in life, but it is assuredly one of the most important.

In the course of our conversation at lunch, Herr Arndt spoke of many aspects of the ideal of the labour camps.

" I look to the day when there will be similar camps for girls, for the health of women is of equal moment with that of men. Some organisations do exist but they are not yet universal.

" In regard to boys it is universal and what has been the result ? We have made weedy youths into strapping young men. We are eradicating many of the evil heritages left behind by the war—the heritages of bad food and nervous conditions inherent in all who were born during the war. Surely that in itself is a social service of the first magnitude."

I asked him concerning class conditions. He was very emphatic.

" In the labour camp there are no class distinctions. Such a condition would be a negation of the aims of

National Socialism. All the boys in the camps are equal. Here in Silesia we have boys of all kinds. I know of sons of princes and counts who work in the fields just like the rest. In fact it is these high-born youths who prove to be the most enthusiastic. The one way in which class distinction might creep in is by way of money. The son of a rich father might be expected to have a bigger allowance and he might conceivably be able to buy more beer and cigarettes at the bar over there than his comrades. And so it is restricted. Each boy gets twenty-five pfennig ($2\frac{1}{2}$*d.*) a day pocket money, just about enough to buy one glass of beer and a packet of cheap cigarettes. He is never allowed to receive a present from home of more than five marks (5*s.*)."

I had seen a number of hefty parcels in the guard-room and mentioned the fact.

"They are delivered to each dormitory and the boy is expected to make generous division among his fellows. It has always been my experience that boys who do not do such things in such circumstances are punished—well, you know as well as I do."

And come to think of it, boys in receipt of tuck-boxes at school in England are quickly taught the correct rules of behaviour by their fellows.

During my visits to labour camps and in the course of conversations with boys on leave in the large cities, I was tremendously impressed by the spirit of fellowship and *esprit de corps* which the labour camps have engendered. There were never complaints about conditions or unusual hardships imposed by regulation. True the German is slave to authority, and obedience is part of his belief, but at the same time the German, contrary to accepted opinion, will not tolerate that tyranny which excuses itself on the grounds of discipline (I have met dozens of German ex-service men who were amazed at the rigour of discipline in the British army as opposed to that in the German forces. And during the war we thought it was the other way about !). The youth of the labour camp, although doubtless he finds the life severe at first, comes to revel in his labours because he gradually finds himself equipped with a human frame capable of carrying out his work with ease. There is an indefinable pleasure in the self-knowledge that you have strength and are in good health and are capable of enjoying the benefits of both. The whole system of work and training in the labour camps has been hygienically and scientifically arranged by experts. The officers in charge of the compounds are not the Prussian bullies of tradition (tradition dies so hard). They are men specially chosen for their character and qualities of leadership. They may be compared with well-selected schoolmasters or university tutors except that their office is not quite of such an academic character. It is their duty to make their charges fit men, and at the same time to see they are mentally happy, for in the new German ideal fitness and happiness must be combined. A studious boy is encouraged to read in his hours of recreation. The mechanically minded finds plenty of tools in the camp workshop. For the artist there is an endless field in the decoration of the surroundings. And for them all there is that training, rough may be, which comes of mixing boys of all classes into one community, in surroundings where there are hard and fast rules and regulations and where all are expected to maintain a high standard of honour and labour on the basis of equal achievement.

CHAPTER VII

FRONTIER IN A GARDEN

NEAR the mining town of Gleiwitz in Upper Silesia a poor peasant goes to the bottom of his garden, digs a row of potatoes in Poland and takes them back to cook in his kitchen which happens to be in Germany. He has two passports: his slender purse contains a few marks and a few zlottis: he pays taxes to the Reich and to the Polish Government; one of his daughters lives in Germany and works in Poland: a son cycles into Germany to work and cycles back to Poland to sleep. All are Germans: all were brought up in the peasant's cottage. Even now father and son and daughter all live within a mile of each other. Their strange manner of living was decreed by the boundary commission of 1921 which drew a line through the old man's garden and left one member of his family on the one side and another on the other.

I sat in the old man's kitchen and watched half a dozen of his geese waddle into Poland. My German companions could not legally wander as far as those same geese for they had no Polish *visa* on their passports and just across the road was a shabbily dressed Polish soldier leaning against a sentry box. He was posted there to watch the poor old man's garden. Only those geese which crossed the boundary line made their way back without breaking the laws of contraband.

The case of the old man who grows his vegetables in one country and eats them in another is but one of many hundreds of the curious anomalies left behind by the League of Nations boundary commission in the Upper Silesian coalfield in 1921. Perhaps it was because the commission was made up of delegates from such a mixture of countries as Belgium, Brazil, Spain, and China, whose members had never heard of Silesia, just as Mr. Lloyd George had never heard of Teschen, and cared less. It so happens that in the course of the present year—1937—we may hear a great deal about the Upper Silesian border, for in the month of May and on the fifteenth day of the month there expires the so-called "Geneva Agreement". In order to study the question at first hand I made an extended tour of the whole area and I made many interesting and even alarming discoveries.

Korfanty and the Annaberg? Who remembers the man or the mountain. Hindenburg? The name of a retired Prussian General who became a Field Marshal and died a President. Also, perhaps more important in the long run, the name of a German mining city on a disputed border. Grazbancyski? Obviously a Polish name, but who is the man? He happens to be the astute Polish commissioner who may yet become as much a household word as pronunciation of his name permits. And as for Kattowicz, Gleiwitz, Beuthen—smart children answering geography papers in the Higher Certificate examinations might know what and where they are, but the rest of the world is not interested at the moment for they just do not happen to be "news". That is how the modern world appears to be run.

The fact that there was once a plebiscite in Upper Silesia and that it involved the presence of a few companies of British infantry is dimly remembered, but the circumstances and the untoward results have been forgotten in the turmoil of post-war history. But for the tens of thousands of people on the spot, that dismal period is by no means forgotten. It has bequeathed a future of uncertainty, rancour, and hatred.

Silesia was once described as the " Pearl in the Prussian Crown ". The phrase may have been exaggerated and intended to set the seal on the brilliant campaigns of Frederick the Great. But there is no doubt that Silesia was an integral part of Germany, and that it was German brains and German capital that developed the Silesian coalfields. It is true that the inhabitants of the borderland speak a curious dialect which is called " Wasser Polish " or Water Polish and that they are predominantly Roman Catholic by creed. But they looked on Germany as the Fatherland, and even on the boundary at the time of the plebiscite in spite of intimidation and the presence of a hardly impartial French General staff and its army, voted sixty per cent in favour of adhesion to Germany. That vote was made the occasion to give eighty per cent of the mines to Poland.

There is no need to enter into detail concerning the history of the Silesian provinces. It was much disputed at the time of the Peace Treaty whether Silesia was a Polish area or not. Such discussions had only an academic value, for it was known that as early as 1335 Casimir the Great, King of Poland, renounced all claims to Silesia under the terms of the treaty of Trentschin. For centuries it was the scene of great German immigration, and by the first quarter of the sixteenth century had become an hereditary province of the House of Hapsburg under whose domination it remained until the end of the Seven

Years' War saw its annexation by Prussia under the treaty of Hubertusburg. And as a conquered state of the great king it became very definitely a part of Prussia and until the outbreak of the Great War no one thought of it as anything else. The new-fangled doctrine of self-determination, the only one of the fourteen points of President Wilson to survive the armistice, was seized on by the newly-established republic of Poland to make excessive demands on Silesia. It so happened that the extreme eastern parts of the province were rich in coal seams. Coal was made the excuse for what, if it cannot be called a crime, can at least be described as an injustice.

If it had not been for energetic protests on the part of the German delegates, whole portions of this rich area would have been taken from Germany and annexed to the Polish Republic. Eventually it was decided to hold a plebiscite to find out exactly what the people themselves desired. I think it will be agreed by all impartial observers who were present at the time, that the method of holding the plebiscite was a minor disgrace to honourable dealings between nations, conquering or conquered. Sectional risings were deliberately fostered by the Polish authorities with the connivance of the French Government. There were two important ones before the taking of the vote—the first on August 16, 1919, and the second in August, 1921. The voting took place in March, 1921, and there was a majority of sixty per cent for Germany in spite of everything that had been done. Germany had a right to think that the majority vote had given her back the Silesian coalfield intact. But it was not to be so. Poland had no intention of losing such a valuable acquisition. She encouraged separatist movements and matters came to a head with the rising of the adventurer Korfanty who led a Polish force and claimed to represent the inhabitants of the coalfields. By this time the local Germans began to take a hand in the matter and a free corps was formed which stormed Korfanty's stronghold on the famous Annaberg. There is no doubt that Korfanty and his hirelings would have been swept across the frontier had not the French commander-in-chief in the area sensed the danger and abruptly caused an armistice. The armed forces of both parties had to leave the area by July 5, 1921, and the stage was set for the subsequent jobbery and partition. The League of Nations was politely asked to settle a question which the local inhabitants had decided several months before.

The League had a long series of heart-searching and acrimonious debates, for its task was unenviable and the Geneva institution was so young and fragile as not to be in a position to make mistakes. Even so it made the first blunder of the series which has led to its decline and fall. It agreed to the principle of partition, and then handed over the dirty work to the Conference of Ambassadors who had succeeded to the office of the famous Supreme Council. The Conference took on itself to make a new boundary line, and when its decision was made known it was found that the major portion of the coalfields had been allotted to Poland. Germany had to stomach the loss of 793,500 acres of land and 892,547 inhabitants. This meant the loss of 2,200 square kilometres of the total of 2,800 square kilometres of coal-bearing land—a total loss of 48,830 million tons out of 57,500 million tons. In addition she lost more than half the available zinc and lead-producing land. Of the sixty-seven coal-pits then at work, fifty-three went to Poland and fourteen to Germany. Of the zinc and lead ore mines Poland received ten and Germany five. Poland obtained twenty-two blast furnaces as opposed to Germany's fifteen. According to pre-war figures the area was capable of producing 32,344,037 tons of coal a year and 130,264 tons of iron ore, 425,940 tons of zinc ore and 985,418 tons of coke, apart from numerous by-products of immense value. The coal production made up seventeen per cent of Germany's total coal output, sixty-six per cent of her zinc ore production and fifty-five per cent of her lead ore production. The citation of these figures is surely sufficient to show how great was the loss of Germany and how great was Poland's gain—and all in spite of a plebiscite.

The Conference of Ambassadors was well aware of the enormity of its decision, and made provisions for the exploitation of the territory which would prove acceptable to both sides. These provisions were instrumented in the document that has become known as the "Geneva Agreement" of May 15, 1922. It was the result of negotiations that took place under the chairmanship of M. Calonder, then President of the Swiss Confederation. It laid down terms under which the inhabitants might live in some kind of peace and security. It provided for economic and social relief to safeguard the national, religious and language minorities on each side of the new boundary. The agreement was to last for fifteen years and then some other arrangement was to be made. We are on the eve of that new arrangement whatever it may be.

Now the city of Breslau, the capital of the ancient province of Silesia, has a population of 557,000 inhabitants. It is rather bigger than Sheffield but not so large as Manchester. And it was once the centre of thriving trade and a rich bourgeoisie. Its prosperity, to a very large extent, was dependent on the great coalfield a hundred miles away, that coalfield which was the source of so much wealth and which created so many dependent industries of which Breslau reaped a large benefit. To-day Breslau goes to bed betimes. It is one of the saddest cities in Germany. Shortly after half-past ten when the opera house closes its doors and the talking pictures flicker to an end in the cinemas, the streets are quickly deserted and up go the shutters of most of the cafés and wine restaurants. In Breslau there are many very famous *weinstube* but each one has the same tale to tell of lack of custom and a shortage of money. The rich merchants are no more and the remaining aristocracy keep small house in their mansions on the estates round the city. There are a few night haunts which linger on pathetically, the customary barmaids behind their long counters vainly awaiting customers. A vast community has been deprived of its wealth and gaiety by a treaty.

The city contains a renowned university and substantial public buildings. It has a great cathedral and many churches. Its population is devout to a degree. Those who think that the Nazis have robbed the German people of their faith and hope, should pass a few days in Silesia and witness real evidence of devotion. Never have I seen churches more crowded on a weekday in any Catholic country than I saw in Breslau. I recall one very touching moment. It was in the church of Dorothea, a church with a colossal nave and a choir of commensurate proportions. Incidentally it is one of the most remarkable churches I have ever seen. Its decoration is staggering to the unaccustomed eye, a stupendous confusion of the baroque and rococo. But in spite of the grotesque colours and abundance of gilt, the church was crowded with men and women come to tell their beads and kneel in silent meditation at ten o'clock in the morning. A tiny girl entered. She was pathetically thin and very small. To reach the fount of holy water she had to stand on the stone steps. Then she made her way along the great aisle, oblivious of everybody and walked straight on to the rail of the high altar where she remained for something more than half an hour.

I had long wanted to see at first hand conditions on the frontier of the coalfield and I had my opportunity. I took a motor-car and travelled by way of Oppeln to Beuthen and Gleiwitz. The road, by no means an *autobahn*, travelled almost directly to the south-east through woods and plains. Long fields of stubble edged the highway and each field seemed to contain more covies of partridge than the last. All round Oppeln, the horizon was dotted with limekilns and concrete factories. They seemed incongruous in a countryside made for hunting and shooting. Then once again the pleasant landscape of yellow fields and forests in the full glory of autumn, until the road seemed to end abruptly in front of the first pit shaft of Beuthen. It rose in front like a monster, its great black wheels remorselessly revolving first one direction and then the other as somewhere inside the earth cages were being raised and lowered. Here indeed was a mining village expanded into a considerable town, for on all sides one could see new houses which coal dust had had no time to blacken, built to accommodate the miners and their families who had been driven from the Polish side of the border by lack of work or national persecution. I was not surprised to hear later that the three mining towns of Beuthen, Hindenburg and Gleiwitz had doubled in size since the plebiscite, tens of thousands of people having been forced back into Germany because they could find no employment on the Polish side.

Motoring in the area was painfully instructive. One had immediate evidence of the extent to which racial antipathy can play fast and loose with the lives of men. Quite close to Beuthen there is the village of Rudahammer, a simple settlement of miners' cottages and tumbledown shacks. There is a tramway and a brand-new high road. Outwardly everything looks quite normal except that on one side of a dip in the land there are sentry boxes with soldiers wearing what look like green Red Riding Hood capes, and on the other smart, blue-uniformed police in peaked caps and shiny brass buttons on their long great-coats. For here is the frontier. When the worthy ambassadors set to work in this particular area they arbitrarily made a frontier that cut off two German villages in order to give the intervening space to Poland. Furthermore the miners' hospital at Rudahammer was left on the Polish side. What was the result? The German local authorities had to build a detour road and tramway to link up the district, and the Poles, who did not want the hospital, left it to go derelict. Its ruins can still be seen: also a brand-new hospital for miners on the German side of the border.

Down in the working galleries hundreds of feet below ground there are barriers and gates in which the words "Nach Polska" or "Nach Deutschland" are crudely written on the walls.

While on the way to Hindenburg I came across

another evidence of the stupidity of the demarcation of the frontier. It was at the Delbruck works. Some cartographer drawing up the plans put a pencil mark on a piece of paper which when interpreted into terms of land surveying meant that the pit-head plant was cut in half. Furthermore, although the pit was German in every sense the neighbouring village was given to Poland and a new village had to be erected on the German side. In this neighbourhood in addition both roads and railways had to be rebuilt or else the German pit could not have sent its coal to Germany at all. I saw many such evidences of the working out of the frontier arrangements before we entered Gleiwitz and I am disposed to accept as fact the reported statements of similar enormities in other parts. It is a fact that in the village of Glausche in Lower Silesia, the main farm is separated from the rest of the village by an arbitrary frontier. Again at Reichthaler Landchen in the same district forty-six small holdings belonging to German peasants were broken in half, while the arable land of the former Prussian estate of Skorischau was left intact and handed over to the Polish Government. One may agree that if partition was necessary, then there must have been hardship, but it is difficult to understand why that same hardship should have been accompanied by such obvious stupidity and such a lack of consideration for very poor people. If it were not absolutely true it would sound ridiculous, but there is still a signal-box on the railway on the right bank of the Oder near Beuthen, which during the demarcation was allotted to Poland although the railway was permitted to run in what was marked down as German territory. The box is now a favourite roosting-place for hens.

The town of Gleiwitz does not look like a colliery centre. It has broad streets, big shops, and hotels of the first rank. Moreover, there are gardens in the main streets and the tramway service marches with all the clatter and show of a great centre of population, living in less tense times. Actually one need only remain in Gleiwitz for an hour or two to realise the bitterness of feeling which prevails. It becomes quite obvious that the purpose of the Geneva Agreement has not been fulfilled, and that the six hundred elaborate clauses have failed to engender anything but bitterness between the Poles and Germans in close contact across the boundary. And the fact is not surprising when one remembers that more than eighty per cent of the rich mining land was given to an alien people.

While in Gleiwitz I obtained a great deal of information concerning local conditions. A brief visit to Poland confirmed the general report that the standard of living on the Polish side was rudimentary by comparison with life in Beuthen, Hindenburg, and Gleiwitz, and this in spite of the fact that the unemployment figures for the district are the highest in the whole of the Reich. I discovered very quickly that the people are devout Catholics and that the word of the priest amounts to law. The peculiar conditions under which they have lived through the Geneva Agreement have prevented any great interference by the national government at any time, but nevertheless they were German in every respect. In this way they reminded me very forcibly of the industrial population of the Saar. In addition they spoke the strange half-Polish, half-German dialect, which is incomprehensible to all but natives and requires the efforts of an interpreter even to translate into reasonable German, or alternatively Polish. It soon became evident that Polish agitators had made great play of the so-called " Water Polish ", endeavouring to convince the Silesians who remain on the Polish side of the border that it is pure Polish, a fact which is palpably untrue. A Silesian miner endeavouring to make himself understood in Warsaw would not get very far. At the same time it must be said in all fairness that even as far distant as Oppeln there are many Silesians who understand only " Water Polish " and have no German. The general level of education is very low, for it must be remembered that at Gleiwitz we are penetrating into the east of Europe, into Poland where tens of thousands of men and women still literally live on the husks that the swine do eat. Their simplicity is touching. They live for their work and their religion. And they have one pathetic belief—that in the year 1937 there will be another plebiscite and that this time the whole territory will go back to the Fatherland. In fact, of course, there is absolutely no provision for another vote. Another plebiscite might at least supply an equitable solution. But Poland has no intention even of admitting the suggestion, and it is likely that the two governments will come to an absolute deadlock when the agreement finally expires. For in the present spirit of the Reich, there is no question that Hitler will make very definite demands and Hitler does not like being refused.

Now in the city of Kattowicz, the Polish centre of the minefield and the clearing house for all the coal that is sent northwards by way of the Danzig Corridor to be dumped at cut prices on the Scandinavian market, there is a very able Polish administrator, Grazbancyski, whose mission in life is to make the Polish part of Silesia completely Polish. It is said that he has been offered very large salaries on account of his ability but the Warsaw authorities realise that his presence in Upper Silesia is essential if the Poles are to retain their hold on the territory. It is this same official who has directed Polish propaganda for many years past and it has been his job to squeeze out every German workman he can and to destroy all German vested interests in the workings that were given to Poland under the treaty. His methods are very harsh and direct. If a German falls out of work, he can either elect to be a Polish citizen or else no work is found for him. He must make his way as best he can across the border. And across the border he helps to swell the already considerable army of the workless. Such German capital as remains invested in Poland is the subject of high taxation and there have been many instances of big concerns forced into bankruptcy by the incidence of Polish law. In the course of the fifteen years since the conclusion of the Geneva Agreement, every effort has been made to make the Polish side completely Polish in very much the same way as Germans and German property holdings have been eliminated from the Danzig Corridor. It is the aim of the administration of Kattowicz that by the time of the expiry of the agreement, all German influences shall be eliminated, so that the frontier can be closed with impunity. How dangerous such an unjust measure may be, I leave to the imagination of the reader. In this connection it ought to be borne in mind that German schoolmasters on the Polish side have been either imprisoned or dispossessed for teaching their pupils German folk-songs.

Here is a real cancer on the face of Europe brought into existence by the treaty and allowed to fester through international indifference. But it must be stated without equivocation that on the German side every attempt has been made to put a bold face on a hopeless situation. Although there is widespread unemployment, the local authorities have been at pains to embark on ambitious housing schemes. Under the Imperial régime, the central authorities in Prussia were not over-mindful of the conditions of the working-classes. The coming of peace found the Silesian miners living in deplorable conditions and their lot was not bettered by the anomalous situation of having their native province carved about without regard to individual property. Nevertheless, since the war huge areas have been set apart for housing schemes and some of the model dwellings I visited were in the very first class. And following the custom of German mining areas, large tracts have been set aside for gardens and allotments. The roads in the mining area are new and well made. One can tell the moment one crosses the border for the quality of the road surface on the other side is deplorable. Moreover, the mines taken over by the Poles are not producing anything like the quantity of coal they did when in German hands, and huge sums are being lost through inexpert or uneconomical direction. And as for wages, it is true that both are low enough. The German workman hewing at the pit face receives a monthly pay envelope of 150 marks a month—a matter of £7 10*s.* at par. The Polish workman or his fellow-German working in a Polish pit only receives one-third that amount. There can be no comparison between the standard of living on the two sides of the border and that in itself is the cause of grave discontent among all classes.

Not far from Gleiwitz there is the Annaberg, the Anna Mountain. It is a rise of ground, steep at the one side and sloping across fields at the other. The eminence is crowned by woods and at the summit is a chapel. You can see the bluff from the highway to Oppeln and every Silesian points it out to the stranger as a place of pilgrimage, something holy and sacred. If it had the full blessing of holy church, the Annaberg could not stand for more in the minds of the Silesian peasants and miners, for it was here that Korfanty's men were beaten in the long ago. To its historic height men and women make their way on certain occasions to give rejoicing that the whole of their native countryside was not taken by the Poles. When you talk with Silesians about the Annaberg and what it has come to symbolise you begin to realise something of human bitterness. You also begin to wonder why the Annaberg came to symbolise so much and why a peace treaty could have been so devised as to engender so much future hatred and misunderstanding. One may ask whether a sweet reasonableness of the kind to which we have become unaccustomed through long absence, will prevail when the time comes to revise the terms under which the Upper Silesian coalfield is now being exploited both in materials and men.

In recent months there have been so many distractions in Europe that little attention has been paid to the internal problems of Germany. In fact, the war in Abyssinia, closely followed by the internecine struggle in Spain, have been sufficient to monopolise most of world attention. Occasionally on a Saturday afternoon Herr Hitler has reminded the nations of those sections of the peace settlement which Germany finds impossible of further fulfilment. The abandonment of the military clauses, the introduction of the system of conscription and the occupation of the demilitarised zone in the Rhineland rightly caused alarm and sensation on the particular Saturday afternoons they were announced. In England we were not greatly interested in the abrogation of the clauses concerning the internationalisation of Germany's great rivers. In fact, one may fairly say that the general public was unaware that the waterways commission still existed. The closing of the Kiel Canal to foreign warships announced on a recent Saturday caused livelier comment, for there is still something significant about the town of Kiel and the canal it commands that lingers on in the minds of those who fought in the war. But in actual fact this particular move is not likely to have any important effects, for the canal has rarely been used by foreign battleships, and in the future it will be possible to obtain permission to sail through it by using ordinary diplomatic channels. But if one Saturday afternoon Germany decides that the situation on the Silesian frontier is absolutely intolerable and cannot continue any longer, then a really dangerous condition of affairs may come about.

It its present form, the problem seems incapable of solution. It may quite easily resolve itself into war. At the present time the grievances of the Silesian miners have been largely localised by the terms of the Geneva Agreement and the special application of minority laws. At the same time those minority laws have been roughly overridden on more than one occasion by the Poles. There is no doubt that thousands of Germans on the Polish side have been deliberately driven from their jobs and forced to return to Germany to find work elsewhere: just as in the region of the Danzig Corridor it has been the policy of the Polish Government to eliminate German influences as far as possible. And that policy has caused the gravest resentment in the Reich.

In Berlin I have often heard it said that one day the Germans will occupy the Memel land and present the world with a *fait accompli.* Such a move, although it would have widespread repercussions, would almost certainly not create a first-class international situation of prolonged significance. But if in a moment of exasperation some drastic step was taken in regard to the Silesian coalfield, it would be a very different story.

Those who have visited the coal areas are well aware how delicate is the situation. It will require the greatest tact and patience to avoid trouble on a very serious scale. But one thing is certain, that the present régime cannot be prolonged after the expiry of the Geneva Agreement. Before the end of the year the whole world may have reason to take a very lively interest in the future of the mines and frontiers of the Upper Silesian coalfield.

CHAPTER VIII

TOTAL STATE

MY experiences in Upper Silesia were in the nature of an unpleasant shock. One could not fail to realise that here was a crowning example of human folly which must result in increased bitterness of feeling, and perhaps something even worse as time goes on. It is difficult to see how the new strong Germany in its present frame of mind can permit such a state of affairs to continue indefinitely.

What has been the great contributing factor towards making this new strong Germany? I think it is the combination of economic methods with social service. During my long residence in Geneva I had come into contact with the workings of the International Labour Office and knew the broad humanitarian outlook of that great scholar and friend, Mr. Harold Butler, the head of the organisation. I had in my luggage a copy of his report to the conference for 1936 and I was at pains to read it during the train journey back to Berlin by way of Frankfurt am Oder. Talking of the essential links between economic and social policy and the inseparability of social and economic measures, Mr. Butler says, "The conviction is growing ever stronger that this is not a matter of two different aims, to be achieved in separate ways, but of one single indivisible whole." I bore these words in mind as I remembered the close connection under the new régime between the two aspects of the formidable question of a solution of life for the great mass of the people. In modern Germany there have been so many such measures. Taxation has been regulated according to size of family. Flooding the market and so cheapening goods and causing unemployment has been made illegal. Supplies of raw materials for essential industries have been obtained even at the expense of big subsidies. Handicrafts have not been allowed to die out for the sole reason that they are uneconomical; such craftsmen have been assured of a livelihood until the time of old age. And, above all, there has been the enormous development of the combination of work and pleasure in the leisure hour which was the lifelong dream of the great Albert Thomas, Mr. Butler's predecessor in his distinguished office. In this same report Mr. Butler adds:

> Good social conditions are not possible without a favourable economic situation; this, again, can be lasting only when it is based on a high standard of living for the general mass of the population. The recognition and application of this obvious truth are a condition for introducing a social object to be aimed at in economic and financial policy.

Which, I contend, is precisely what the Nazi régime is aiming at.

It is strange that one should have to adduce an International Labour Office document to illustrate the Nazi point of view. I recall vividly the day the German Government severed their connection with the "I.L.O.", making a clean sweep of their relations with Geneva. I have reason to believe that this drastic step has been regretted in certain official circles in Berlin for a long time, for the International Labour organisation can do more effectively research work for governments on an international basis than the governments themselves. Also it costs so much less. The German Government have put into effect many of the ideas of Mr. Butler and his able staff at Geneva. It has gone out of its way to provide work for workers, to keep up a supply of workers, and to maintain both work and workers. I had seen at first hand the colossal efforts made by the authorities in creating work. The new road plan is but one of many activities in this direction. It is an adoption of a socialistic principle that the resources of the state should be used for the benefit of the state. Even M. Jouhaux, the redoubtable head of the Confédération Générale du Travail, has recognised the efficacy of the German method in reducing unemployment and raising the level of general prosperity, and has pressed M. Blum to adopt a similar scheme to relieve France of the existing state of economic and industrial chaos. In Geneva some two years ago there was still suspicion of the Nazi methods, a suspicion based on political grounds, I rather fancy, for the Geneva outlook does not favour dictatorships. But in this latest report Mr. Butler pays a wholehearted tribute to the success of the German battle against unemployment. He writes:

> Whatever have been the ways and means that have led to this result, it is incontrovertible that the number of unemployed sank from 6,013,600 in January, 1933, to 2,520,000 in January, 1936. (The figures are now about the million mark.) Therein lies undoubtedly the best justification for the measures applied in the new industrial order.

Back in Berlin for a few days I spent my time investigating economic and social conditions especially from the point of view of employment and the welfare of the workers. My inquiries brought me into close contact with the vast German Labour Front that has replaced the former trade unions, the intricate unemployment organisation, and the universal movement known as *Kraft durch Freude* (Strength through Joy)—the last named perhaps the most astonishing of all the outward manifestations of the Nazi spirit.

The economic crisis in Germany after the inflation, as I have noted elsewhere, brought millions of country and small town people flocking to the great centres of population, for in time of trouble men always think there is more bread and work to be had in big cities than on the land. It is a fallacy but it is an historical truth. The presence of this huge new population was a source of embarrassment to city authorities and undoubtedly gave rise to much discontent and a spirit of subversive revolution. A year after the Nazis came into power sixty-five per cent of the unemployed were hovering about the great cities and it became necessary to take drastic measures. To prevent the inflow of the workless from the countryside, local burgomasters and other authorities were given plenary powers by which they could absolutely forbid any further settlement in a city area. Immigration into Greater Berlin, Bremen and Hamburg came under this drastic rule. Following this it was declared illegal for any employer to take into industry in a city any man who had previously worked for two years on the land. At the same time former land-workers were given money to pay their travelling expenses back to the farmlands they had deserted. And to give an extra fillip to this essential "back to the land" movement, a sum of £500,000 was at once allotted to improve rural housing and an almost similar amount for enlarging farm buildings, acquiring new agricultural machinery and purchasing tens of thousands of heads of cattle. By way of illustration it can be noted that in the course of eighteen months 10,000 land-workers and their families were settled in undeveloped parts of East Prussia, each one being given 1,800 marks for the purpose of erecting a cottage. Furthermore, to assist the German worker in his search for employment, there was a systematic combing out of foreigners working as manual labourers. In England our Ministry of Labour has long since set itself against the entry of foreigners into this country for the purpose of engaging in work which might be done by British subjects. The rules are strictly enforced in all grades of work, from blowing into a saxophone to peddling soft fruits. British officialdom can be more drastic than that of any other nation when it comes to the point. But we at home never had to face such a problem of foreign labour as existed in Germany and still exists in parts of France. At one time there were more than a million foreigners working in Germany. That number has now been cut down to about 170,000, and the great majority of these are either of German descent or long resident in the country, or married to German wives.

It was quite obvious from the very first that the accession of the Nazis to power would mean the end of trade union organisations just as it would involve the dispersal of the official communist party. The trade unions most emphatically did disappear and were replaced by the much-vaunted German Labour Front. This Front is supposed to be composed of all actively working Germans, and although it is supposed to be voluntary it pays every worker to join its ranks. That fear which makes men who want to belong to no organisation, not even a union, was one of the less encouraging aspects of the Nazi system I encountered. But in the eyes of the Government the universality of the Labour Front is essential for public safety and welfare. It is necessary and necessity knows no law and precious little humanity. The Labour Front, which Hitler once described as the organisation of all Germans working "with brow and fist", includes both workers and employers. Its object is to establish a community of ideal, a great force working for both national and individual betterment. The Labour Front sets itself the high ideal (I quote the Ordinance of Hitler of October 24, 1934) of "creating among the heads of business an understanding of the rightful claims of their staffs, and among *employés* an understanding of the situation and possibilities of the business in which they are employed". That may sound like meretricious high-mindedness, but in actual fact it is really working out in German industry. I came across many instances of a very wholesome collaboration between the employer and the worker in the course of my travels. It was the same in coal-mine or steel plant, toy factory or department store—in the last named especially. I will quote but one instance—the Teves factory for the manufacture of refrigerators and essential parts of hydraulic brakes. It is a big concern situated on the outskirts of Frankfurt am Main and its proprietor is well known in business circles in England where he has considerable financial and industrial interests. Alfred Teves is the type of the German employer who is working wholeheartedly in co-operation with his workers. His factory is a model of efficiency and order. Every effort is made to make the lot of the worker as easy as possible. I made an extensive tour of the workshops and plant and discovered a factory laid out on ideal lines, very like the more progressive factories in the garden townships of England such as Bournville and Port Sunlight. For one thing, every wall that could be composed of huge glass windows was so composed. In most of them were large window boxes filled with flowers and shrubs—something which seemed strange in large shops where men were wearing masks and spraying enamel paint over half-finished ice boxes! The washing accommodation was like that of a first-class hotel, with hot and cold water serving porcelain basins and showers in tiled bath-houses. Each man and woman had an ample locker, and there were dressing-rooms adjacent, for the worker leaves his working apparel in the factory. He eats his midday meal in the large factory dining-room, a meal served at very low prices, with the extra service of a canteen. Moreover, both Alfred Teves and his fellow-directors eat at a table in this same dining-room and make a point of having exactly the same bill of fare as the most humble *employé*. There was a further illustration of the new spirit in the presence of a remarkably fine piece of statuary, cast in bronze and representing the symbolic union of employer and employed. It stood outside the waiting-room in the main entrance quite close to Herr Teves' small, simple office. Herr Teves assured me that the gift had been made to him quite spontaneously by the workers on the occasion of the jubilee celebrations of the firm.

In every German factory there are facilities for amusement and recreation. In a nation that has become obsessed with the craze for sport and physical fitness, factory gymnasiums and playing-fields are a necessity. I am convinced that the modern German would play football on a cinder heap if nothing else was available. It is like the addiction of the South Wales miner to the oval football of the Rugby Union. But facilities for occupational training and simple recreation do not stop at the provision of a playground.

They extend to every form of amusement from cruising aboard big steamers to the organisation of yodelling choruses.

I can speak from experience of the attitude which the new Germany is taking towards work as part of the daily round of human life. Labour is no longer looked on as a vile necessity, something which degrades, which suffers from the stigma of wage slavery. Every effort is made to make work a social duty into which everybody can put his full strength and good will. And in order to make work agreeable, care is taken to make the leisure hours hours of enjoyment. An attempt is being made to utilise modern invention and science in the interests of pleasure as well as of labour, and very great progress has been made.

The " Strength through Joy " movement was developed from the ideas of Dr. Robert Ley, who set out to provide pleasant occupations in the evenings and at the week-end for workers who had completed a hard day's work in factory or office. Maybe in its initial stages it has suffered a little from the universal Teutonic ideas of *kultur*, but it must be remembered that the movement is still in its infancy. Again it must be borne in mind that the ordinary German is incredibly interested in education and lectures and that a long disquisition in the evening by some learned professor, which we would regard as something of a penance, is looked on by millions of Germans as a riotous entertainment. Not even the uplift movements of the Middle West have created such an appetite for lectures and speeches as exists in latter-day Germany. These lectures contribute to the life of the community by making a contrast between the monotonous working day and relaxation in the evening.

Less forbidding are the enormous schemes for providing travel facilities, hiking camps and holidays both at home and abroad. I was informed by Dr. Ley that it is the ambition of the movement (the officials number 75,000 but only 2,500 are paid) to enable every German worker who cannot afford to travel on his own account to make at least one journey a year to places which he has not seen before. It is a laudable ambition and it is being put into effect. During the year 1936 something like 7,000,000 German workers of both sexes took their holidays under the auspices of " Strength through Joy ". The duration of the holidays varied from three days to a fortnight. Hundreds of thousands saw for the first time the Rhine they had sung so much about. An equal number went to the coast resorts of the Baltic Sea, where the island of Rugen is being transformed into a gigantic lido for the benefit of the workers. And seven ocean-going steamers made regular trips to places as far distant as Madeira. When in Hamburg later I saw one of the pleasure steamers of the K.d.F. She was the *Der Deutsche*, a big ocean-going steamer, with the lines of a large yacht and painted white from stem to stern. She only displaces 11,430 tons and was built in 1924. But other ships were bigger and more modern and included the 32,565-ton liner *Columbus*, the 16,732-ton *St. Louis* and two ships round about 13,500 tons—the *Monte Olivia* and the *Monte Sarmiento*. In the course of the coming summer seven or eight steamers will leave either Hamburg or Bremen every week with their complement of working people travelling under the K.d.F. organisation. Of course such elaborate and expensive forms of travel have to be subsidised in part, but no one may participate unless he has made his small weekly contributions towards the cost. A worker buys what is known as " Travel Saving

Cheques "—purchased weekly rather like contributions to a public-house slate club. He can buy as many as he likes. Moreover, it is becoming quite customary for friends and relatives to give books of these cheques to their uncles and aunts and intimate friends on the occasion of birthdays or at Christmas-time. I have discussed the question of these annual holidays with many leading industrialists and all are unanimous that they have resulted in a better spirit among the workers which has resulted in infinitely better individual work.

Every branch of the tourist and catering industry is expected to co-operate in the "Strength through Joy" travel schemes. The innkeeper or charabanc proprietor is not allowed to charge more than an amount which will meet his working expenses and a small margin of profit. In consequence the actual cost of holidays has been brought down to an absolute minimum. When in Berlin I saw actual returns of costs and numbers, and I discovered that last year a Berlin working man was able to spend a week on the Baltic Sea, including his railway fare and lodging, for something like sixteen marks—less than one pound at par. If such an effort can be maintained I see no reason why Dr. Ley should not eventually attain his ideal and give fourteen million German workers a holiday every year—fourteen million being the figure which is thought to include everyone who could not otherwise afford a real holiday under ordinary conditions. The fact that only people who could not afford a holiday otherwise are permitted to take advantage of the new facilities has not affected ordinary tourist and hotel traffic. On the contrary, it has greatly increased the turnover in both industries.

I am not one of those investigators who considers the statistics drawn up by the various German ministries as part of a great scheme for hoodwinking the world as to the real state of affairs in the country. I have myself tested so many tables and I believe that no such conspiracy has ever existed. In any case, the whole idea is too fantastic for serious consideration. It is just as absurd for critics of Russia to say that men and women die every day from starvation in the streets of Moscow. There have been two great revolutions of two different kinds and both have accomplished wonderful things in accordance with the lights of their directors. I suggest that one should not be tempted into disbelief of every record simply because it does not happen to suit one's personal political inclinations or does not satisfy that clamour of certain sections of the Press which require a sensation every day, whether it bears relation to fact or not, in order to keep up their unwieldy circulations. I do know that the new resort of the island of Rugen will contain 20,000 beds solely at the disposition of the K.d.F. I do know that last year four thousand German working men and women cruised to Madeira and the Azores. And it does not astonish me that men earning only 100 marks a month—five pounds—can spend a week in the Bavarian Alps or in the Thuringian Forest. It is furthermore a fact that the organisation at the present moment is constructing two steamers of 20,000 tons expressly for ocean travel for the workers, with cabins containing two to four berths and the upper part of the ship devoted to as wide deck space as possible. They will be cruising ships for the masses.

As I have said, Germany has gone sport mad. Football and athletics are now part of the national creed, and the gigantic efforts made by the Government to make the Olympiad of 1936 a spectacular success were all part and parcel of the Government scheme to encourage sport. The foreigner who travels to Berlin still gets a little weary of the many emblems, souvenirs, statuettes and books dealing with the last Games, which are to be found in every other shop window. There are so many, it must be years before they are all finally sold or disappear. Nevertheless, we ought to take a certain pride in the great wave of sport which has spread over modern Germany. The German does not hesitate to say that he was encouraged in his effort by the example of England, the country of sportsmen in German eyes. In spite of their own no mean achievements, it is to England that they look for guidance and inspiration in sporting matters. Such international or inter-club fixtures as take place are matters of interest to the whole people. I recall the occasion when many thousands of young Germans came to London to witness a match against an English eleven a year or so ago. There was some question as to their deportment and extra police patrolled the approaches to the ground and the railway station at Victoria. But if the British authorities had understood the spirit of these young Germans, such measures need never have been taken. The German takes his sport very seriously. In fact, he takes it as seriously as life itself. Those young men had come over to watch a football match. They were not interested in politics or even in London. When it was all over they invaded the station buffets and drank their few marks away in unaccustomed English beer until their trains were due to leave. Of the many thousands, I believe only one was too late at the barriers. And so it is that on Saturday evenings in the big cities German youth buys the evening papers, not to read about the latest laws—for there are so many—but to find out what has happened in the English football league. Somehow football has become more important than wearisome *aides mémoire* or diplomatic exchanges.

Figures in German become astronomical on account of the intense organisation. But at the moment of writing there are 3,000,000 athletes in regular training at the seven hundred tracks scattered over the country. Last year about 900,000 German girls and boys passed swimming tests and 380,000 qualified to be gymnastic instructors. In the mountainous regions 80,000 youths learned to ski under official tuition!

Every new factory that is erected in Germany must conform to very strict standards of lighting, sanitation, washing facilities and ventilation for the workers. But in an old-established country like Germany, there are necessarily many ancient and unsatisfactory buildings still being employed as workshops. It is impossible to sweep them all away, but plans are on foot to make every place where men are employed as up to date as possible. Certain manufacturers have insufficient money to provide additional conveniences for their workers without going out of business, and here again the K.d.F. has stepped in. A sum of 200,000,000 rentenmarks has been advanced in order to provide workers with surroundings in factories that are clean and make for industrial well-being. Ten million pounds spent for such a purpose is rightly regarded as money well used. And those who are sometimes depressed by unsightly hoardings on our great arterial roads or who find their enjoyment of the beauties of the French Riviera marred by gigantic advertisements of imitation absinthe or cheap racing cars, can take heart from the fact that no such monstrosities are now allowed to disfigure the German countryside. Advertisers must find a more artistic and less obtrusive method of popularising their commodities.

The theatre remains a luxury in England. Several London theatres still provide bare benches for their staunchest supporters in the gallery. One has to be either very rich or very patient to take advantage of the theatre in the West End of our vast metropolis. But in modern Germany the theatre is not the envied possession of the few. Its doors have been flung wide open to the indigent. It can be safely asserted that before the revolution of 1933 there were millions of German men and women who had never seen the inside of a theatre. Like their political enemies in Soviet Russia, the Nazis realised the cultural mission of the theatre and determined that its message should not go unheard. A census was made of several big industrial concerns, and it was revealed that more than eighty per cent of the workers of both sexes had never heard an opera—and this in a country which is so universally associated with State opera houses and nightly operatic performances. About sixty per cent of the manual workers had never been to the theatre and this in the land of Lessing, Schiller, and Goethe. (Some Nazis would add Shakespeare.) To-day every singer and artiste is expected to give his services to the general public freely on certain days of the year. The organisation of the K.d.F. movement has brought into existence special folk theatres, and in Berlin last year seven big houses were continuously giving performances before audiences who had, I believe, not paid more than fifty pfennig, or sixpence, for a seat. Likewise great conductors like Wilhelm Furtwangler, Hermann Abendroth and Eugen Jochum give regular concerts for working people in the big cities. And while in Germany I saw a special train equipped to carry a model theatre and scenery to distant parts of the country, and, as I mentioned in my chapter dealing with the camps of the motor-road workers, there are twenty-five lorries equipped with film sound and projecting apparatus which are constantly on the move in the country districts. It is estimated that 35,000,000 people saw either film, play or opera in the course of a twelvemonth who would otherwise have not had sufficient money to do so.

The World Congress for Leisure and Recreation which was held at Hamburg this last year attracted considerable attention. It was attended by delegates from Great Britain and countries as far distant as Japan and Chile. On this occasion Dr. Ley reiterated the words of Hitler, " My ideas are not for export." But the worthy doctor added:

> We in Germany, then, take pleasure in our work. We respect the characteristic features of every nation, we know that it is impossible simply to impose rigidly on one nation something which is born out of the depths of the soul of another. We Germans were on the brink of destruction. We were confronted with an empty void, internal strife was in our midst, there was even the possibility of a civil war. A civil war is much more terrible, more frightful than any other war. Our leader has preserved us from this, he has rescued us and given us impetus, energy and powers of which we had no idea before, which were completely new to us and which have proved themselves to be an immense never-failing source of strength. It is my hope that the source of that strength may be put to the service of international conferences in future.

Allowing for characteristic repetition and Nazi enthusiasm, that is as may be. But during the Conference a British delegate of wide experience—Mr. R. J. Mackay, former General Manager of the Research Groups of Great Britain—gave as his opinion:

> From what I have heard of the leisure time activities of the German Labour Front, this immense experiment de-

serves very close study on the part of all persons, in no matter what country, who are on the lookout for ways and means whereby man shall be master of the machine; dangers of the opposite state of affairs are too obvious to need stressing.

The funds of the German Labour Front supply the material resources of the "Strength through Joy" movement, which are not made up by extra contributions on the part of the worker who wishes to avail himself of any particular holiday or advantage. The German Labour Front is responsible for many other things in addition. It has taken over the social welfare work of the old trade unions and increased its activities in other directions. The universality of the dole system does not apply in modern Germany, but there is a very definite system of relief extending over a period of some six months. It is merely an adaptation of the system of State insurance which guarantees assistance to workers temporarily unable through illness or unemployment to earn wages. It provides pensions for the aged and infirm. It contributes money at the time of the marriage of a female worker and defrays expenses at the time of death. The German Labour Front, under its system of leaders, may be said to represent all German manual and small job labour. It is part of the totalitarian state that sublimates the individual to the nation. It is an immense organisation that really does effect remarkable things. It has been bitterly criticised by those who believe in the principle of negotiation between employers and workers, with the strike weapon always available as a last resource. There are still very small strikes in Germany, but they are quite insignificant and are suppressed ruthlessly. It would appear to the ordinary observer that the great mass of the German working-classes has accepted the new order of things. It gives him as much and probably more than he got out of the old trade unions. It certainly does not give less. It has brought about a scheme for annual holidays with pay. Even in agricultural districts where a holiday of three days was regarded as a great favour, labourers now get more than a week. In the metal industries round Berlin, holidays extend to ten days or a fortnight. In the Silesian coalfield, miners get eight days. It would appear to work better than the bad strike system. To-day if there is a wage dispute, the workers approach the leader of the group to which they happen to belong. The dispute is carried successively to the director of the firm and it *has* to be settled amicably round a table, for striking is illegal. Again, wages are State-controlled according to industry, and only with very special authority may an employer pay less wages than those which maintain throughout the country. This is, in any case, a matter for the State trustee. Moreover, many of the old trade unions were insolvent and their administration scandalous in the waste of resources by high officials. The new Labour Front has at least the merit of being national and its prosperity is a national concern.

Can one estimate a nation's happiness and content by the appearance of its people? I think so. In such case the Germans are a happy, contented people, who are working with a will and deriving real pleasures from the achievements of their hands and brains. One of the most distressing aspects of the streets of our big towns is the obvious poverty of many of our fellow-countrymen. One has no need to dilate on the acknowledged squalor of the slums of many industrial areas. It is not encouraging for one who has read in the morning's newspaper that prosperity has returned to find groups of down-at-heel Welsh miners (genuine or not) shouting, " All Through the Night " or the Aberystwyth tune in half a dozen main streets. No one can feel that we live in a happy island when there are so many cases of degrading poverty on view at our street corners and when public squares are used as public dormitories. It is too true that although we are undoubtedly the richest individual nation in the world, we cannot keep beggars from the public highway. Moreover, the shabby genteel walk in our midst in their tens of thousands. The great mass of the people cannot be described as well dressed and hundreds suffer from malnutrition. The state of the nation's teeth is a matter for both regret and remorse.

One does not encounter such conditions in Germany. There is no outward poverty on the scale we know it at home. There are a few beggars. A community of millions could hardly be free from the professional mendicant no matter how stringent the laws. There are no slums in Germany like to those which make a visit to our East End such a grim experience. There are no people in rags. In all Germany men, women and children seem to be well clothed. Poverty does not start up from the pavements to hit the observer in the eye. In spite of the much talked of food restrictions, I saw no scarcity of essential food and the cost of living was very cheap. There may not be enough caviare to go round, but there is enough sausage. The German does not look dejected. He has a pride of work and a sense of self-respect that is reflected in all his gestures. Daily life may not be very vivacious as it is in France. But the German is not a vivacious person. Daily life may be described as stolid and a little monotonous, but the German thinks none the worse of it for that. He has not much money to spend, but he has a little and he is content. In fact, Germany, I venture to say, is a nation of people who accept their lot and are content. And what great strength will come from that mass content, is something known only to the future.

CHAPTER IX

WORLD ARTERY

ONE leaves Berlin for the port of Hamburg by way of a quite unworthy railway station—the Lehrter Bahnof. It looks for all the world like a covered-in goods siding that is only used occasionally. The platforms are almost non-existent : porters are rare : the newspaper kiosks are half filled and the buffets bleak and bare. On the morning I left the capital a long train of dirty passenger coaches with enormous wooden seats and doors in proportion drew up with a prolonged groaning of brakes and jangling of couplings. It was a market train and the broad seats are provided so that peasant farmers bringing their produce to Berlin can sit alongside their vegetable and fruit baskets. There is no danger of losing their precious beetroots and cabbages in a luggage van. The good folk of the countryside streamed out of the station, carrying their enormous baskets and crates as best they could, and in the case of one or two of the women their burdens were bigger than themselves. But all were cheery and all looked robustly healthy as they went their way to bargain in the market-place. A pleasant recollection of a depressing railway station.

By contrast with the local country train drawn by a locomotive that surely did service in the days of the 1870 war, came gliding into the main platform the Hamburg flier—two coaches only, articulated together. Another Diesel motor train ready to cross the landscape

HAMBURG—BERLIN "FLYING TRAIN" PASSING THROUGH THE HISTORIC SACHSEN FOREST
at 160 kilometres per hour

[*face p.* 166

at a hundred miles an hour. Nearly every seat was taken. There was no delay. The two coaches had come two minutes before the scheduled time of departure and in two minutes a whistle had blown and we were on the move.

When I travelled on a flying train to Cologne the journey was made at night-time and it was not possible fully to appreciate the speed at which the train was travelling. But now it was eleven o'clock in the morning and the experience was different. For some miles we seemed to linger on the way, the engine making a deafening noise and the speedometer at the end of the carriage registering a paltry 40 kilometres an hour. Then the engine was finally warmed up and the noise ceased as the train seemed to rush into space. And for two hours, houses, woods, telegraph poles, rivers, bridges and factories whizzed past the windows with a speed that was almost sickening. It was impossible to read the names of wayside stations, so swift was the motion, and I gave up all hope of trying to appreciate the beauty of the landscape, if the flat Northern German plain can be said to have any beauty. Even the historic Sachsen forest, the great estates of the Bismarck family, was passed in a confused whirr and one could never have realised that here was a real hiker's paradise, a place of pilgrimage for tens of thousands of German youths in summer and spring. Almost before one had glanced at the morning newspapers, the train was riding triumphantly into the suburbs of Hamburg, and the eye caught flashes of water, as canals and basins came momentarily into view. Then a sudden calm as the brakes were put on and the two coaches came gently to a standstill at the main platform of the Hauptbahnof.

A high wind was blowing, for it was one of the days

of the great autumn storm, but the sun was shining brightly and Hamburg, most spacious in lay-out of all European seaports, extended a bright welcome to the stranger. In front of the great station was a scene of hustle and activity, and traffic was far more in evidence than in any part of Berlin except the narrow Friedrichstrasse. The city had a definite air. Its buildings, a combination of the very ancient and the ultra-modern, rose in a great solid mass from the turbulent waters of the Elbe. Overhead railways everywhere. A clatter of half a hundred tramcars. Tens of thousands of men and women all in a hurry. The distant hooting of sirens and the nearer shriek of locomotive whistles. All strangely reminiscent of arrival in New York, except that there were no skyscrapers and the population was polite to the stranger in its midst. It was very exhilarating, giving the lie once more to those who imagine that Germany is a land of dismal Jimmies. Nevertheless, it was pleasant to sit down at a window seat in the Atlantic hotel overlooking the glorious Alster basin and eat luncheon in quiet, dignified surroundings that know nothing of the noisy, struggling life of the city.

Those were pleasant days in Hamburg, pleasant because of the innate kindliness of the inhabitants, who have an almost cosmopolitan outlook on life, pleasant because the sight of ships and the small craft of a great port always make an irresistible appeal to me. It is much to be doubted if any port in Europe is so obviously active, so full of such infinite variety in the way of things that float on the surface of water, from huge liners to masses of waste garnered by the tide, or broken piles of huge dimensions, torn away by the perpetual wash. Those who live in London are for the most part unaware they are citizens of the greatest port in the world. The Londoner is not conscious of the sea and the ships that sail it for the very good reason that dockland is inaccessible and situated in some mysterious region beyond the Aldgate Pump. Furthermore even those adventurous enough to go to the East End in search of ships find their passage barred by enormously high dock walls above which they can only see the tops of masts of steamers tied up at wharves somewhere far away. But in Hamburg, as in New York, one has but to walk from one's hotel down a hill or along the road to find ships anchored at the very front door of the city.

Few ports offer so many attractions to the visitor as the port of Hamburg. Apart from the actual waterfront with its seething maritime life by day and the inevitable café life by night, the city presents every contrast of architecture, from the ancient houses rising from canal and channel, to the towering prow (no other word can describe it) of the Chile Building, that looks like a stone ship erected on the land. It has more spacious promenades than many a vaunted watering-place and the suburbs that linger on the shores of the Alster basin, with their prosperous villas set in wooded gardens, are among the most picturesque in Europe. Means of communication are almost as swift and straightforward as those of London. There are admirable theatres and a street composed of nothing but cinemas, beer-halls, and dance-halls. And, above all, in all Germany there are no better restaurants than are to be found in the great seaport. In fact, the inhabitants of Hamburg are almost like the French in their nice appreciation of good food.

In the days of the revolution Hamburg enjoyed an unsavoury reputation as being the most disorderly city in the republic. It had a strong communist element and even at the last election, when it was deemed ill-advised to vote against the Nazis, there was still a small proportion of votes against the Führer. In the narrow streets of the St. Pauli quarter down by the River Elbe, there was some of the bitterest street fighting of that unhappy period and no one knows exactly how many were killed on either side. Here and there one comes across a metal plaque let into the wall of a house, invariably accompanied by a laurel wreath, which marks the spot where a storm trooper was fatally wounded. No such memorials appear to the memory of their rivals in the struggle. Certain it is that there were many quarters in 1932 where no Nazi could walk without danger to his life. The red opposition had its headquarters in the tumbledown quarters near the main quayside and in the equally unsalubrious surroundings of St. Martin's Church. Maybe, for that reason, among others, the whole district is being rapidly cleared and hundreds of ancient houses—some of them most picturesque and interesting in their historic dirt—have been condemned as unfit for further habitation.

Hamburg is an ancient city. It was already a thriving community in 1100 when a settlement arose around the Alster. Membership of the Hanseatic League enabled the port to increase in wealth and importance and many parts of the city date from the closing years of the Middle Ages. There are still long canals from which one-time dwelling-houses of merchants rise even more abruptly than palaces from the waters of Venice. Most of them are now used as warehouses but they do not suit the requirements of modern times and their end is approaching. In a few years very little of the old Hamburg of the waterside will be left. Much that is quaint to look on but insanitary to live in will be no more. And as for the old slum areas, they have nearly gone. During my stay in Germany I looked especially for housing conditions which approximated to the working-class districts of our own great manufacturing towns. In Silesia I found nothing like the hovels of South Wales. In Berlin the poor quarter would have passed muster with a great deal of what is considered lower middle class in England. In Cologne, in Essen, in Dusseldorf, there were no slums that could be called slums in terms of our own derelict factory centres. In Hamburg, however, there are still some grim and grimy alleys that look forbidding by day and sinister at night. There were terribly old houses gazing down forlornly at uneven pavements across uneven squares and courtyards. There were houses with sackcloth-filled window-frames, and houses with gaping holes at top and bottom of crazy, ancient doors. If ever there was a breeding-ground of discontent it could be found in these ill-conditioned dwellings and passages that passed for streets. They were more wretched than the streets that give on to the old port of Marseilles and were probably just as devoid of morals. Although here and there the fine line of an old-world architectural design was discernible, the whole district was so sordid that no one could deplore its passing.

It was like coming up for air after long immersion to walk the few hundred yards to the new tenements that have arisen on the site of slum areas that until a short time ago were just as noisome as the small condemned district that remains. Several of the new blocks of houses for harbour workers are already occupied and a score of others are in course of construction. They are designed on an ambitious and spacious scale and each one rises from its own broad square, a square which in time will be a large lawn with ornamental gardens. They are composed of red brick and each apartment is self-contained. They vary in size according to the requirements of the workman and his family. As is customary on the Continent with housing plans for the working classes great attention is paid to big window space and in some of the flats the whole side wall of a room is a series of glass windows. And of course there is the inevitable boiler somewhere in the basement to send out its waves of suffocating steam heat. I went into several of the workers' flats and found them all spotlessly clean. Although this had once been a very red district, the likeness of the Führer glared down from each wall. Outside, on the open space, children were playing merrily, and as my car started up they stopped to give the universal salute, " Heil Hitler ! "

In recent years the aspect of the centre of the city has also changed, and there have arisen some of the most elaborate and up-to-date office buildings in Europe on the site of the picturesque old merchants' mansions. Here is a riot of modern German architecture ; one can walk for more than half a mile between tall structures rising to twelve floors that are a revelation of timesaving and simplicity of design. Here are to be found buildings that are famous throughout the world of commerce—the Ballin House, the Chile House, the Sprinkenhof Building, the Mohlenhof Building, and the Karstadt Building. In Berlin the eager Berliner, anxious to demonstrate the modernity of the capital, invites the stranger to step along to the enormous Shell House, the last word in office architecture. But the Hamburgers can show the stranger a whole section of the city devoted to such experiments in building. After them it is a shock to walk past the old harbour-master's house, with ancient effigies of former occupants set in the walls. And I, for my part, was almost overpowered by the stern straight walls of the undecorated offices round Ballin House, and found a certain solace in the baroque architecture of the comparatively new Rathhaus, with its florid ornamentation and fantastic pillars and quite unnecessarily large staircase. And, of course, as with all town halls in Germany there was a beer tavern and restaurant in the " cellar " : only in this case the restaurant was really first class like an equally famous one under the town hall of Munich, nor did one feel that one was eating or drinking among the rats, for the town hall restaurant in Germany is always known as the *ratskeller*.

I am told that one of the schemes of public works which Hitler has in mind is the erection of a huge high-level bridge over the Elbe which will permit of the passage of great ships like the *Bremen* and *Europa*. That is a dream of the future. In the meantime one of the principal methods of going from one side to the other of the Elbe is the famous Elbe tunnel, an engineering curiosity of the last century which still serves as a vital link in the communications of the city. Indeed, it is the main gateway—albeit underground and under river—between Hamburg and the great shipyard of Bloehm & Voss across the water.

I refer to the Elbe tunnel because it was while making my way across to the other side that I was able to mingle with dock labourers, shipbuilding hands and stevedores who use the tunnel at every hour of the day. The tunnel is nearly five hundred yards long and at each end are huge lifts that inevitably cause long delays. One is forced to admire the native genius of the German engineer that the tunnel was ever made at all. It dates from 1911 and its design is unique. In the case of our

Thames tunnels there are long approaches, but at Hamburg such approaches were found to be impossible, for on the southern bank rises the steep bluff on which the section of St. Pauli is built and where are to be found the celebrated landing-stages. And on the north side of the river there are docks and basins that come right to the water's edge. Therefore some system of elevators had to be devised and they have become one of the sights of the city. It was necessary to sink two great shafts a depth of some 77 feet, one through marl by means of a concrete coffer-dam and the other through the river banks by means of an immense steel and concrete cylinder driven into the depths by compressed air. The tunnel runs between the two shafts, a depth of eighteen feet below the bottom of the Elbe River. More than seventy thousand workmen use it every day free of charge, and to maintain this enormous traffic six elevators are employed capable of accommodating five hundred workmen and their bicycles.

I learned in the course of conversation with workmen using the bridge that the report of activity in the port was not just optimistic hot air on the part of the authorities. There had been a very definite revival in trade and the shipyards were busy building and repairing. I also found that the Hamburg worker, perhaps by reason of his close contact with the outside world and the passing pageant of cosmopolitan life, still regards himself as being a member of a free city that is only part of the Reich because it is convenient. There still lingers that spirit of independence which forced the original Hagenbeck to establish his zoological garden and menagerie outside the city boundary. I did not come across any great enthusiasm in Hamburg for anything but Hamburg. Here was one of the surviving parts of Germany which still looked on the central government as something that was there to be used in the interests of the great seaport. The workers considered that the Berlin Government was treating Hamburg very well, for trade had revived, the yards were busy again, a good deal of cleaning up was being done and there was money to spend and food to eat in a city where women knew how to cook it. It was an atmosphere so different from that of Munich, Nuremberg, or Frankfurt, that I was a little taken aback. But after all Hamburg is one of the gateways of Europe and her port is established on one of the great arteries of the world. The Elbe barges crawl their way to the heart of the Continent and bring back merchandise almost from the wastershed of the Carpathians. It is the one great German city that in any way approaches cosmopolitanism and ships from all over the world ride the waters of the free harbour every day of the year. Most of the inhabitants have dealings with ships and lading of cargoes, and this class of worker has always been the least amenable to strictness of control. There is little doubt that many Hamburg workers find the severity of living according to the edicts of National Socialism a little trying at times. But that does not prevent them from being intensely German in their outlook. They have a pride of city as well as pride of race and they are all too eager to point out the achievements of German skill.

A great ship towered above a forest of timber in a slipway of Bloehm & Voss's yard.

"There is a fine ship," I was told. "She is a German ship built here in Hamburg. In Hamburg we make the best ships in the world."

An unforgettable dinner at the Burgerhaus that evening. The Burgerhaus, as its name implies, is the house of a member of the bourgeois classes. In this case the famous restaurant is established in an ancient five-storied building of the kind which was once typical of old Hamburg. Some friends and I dined on roast veal that could not have been bettered in Paris. The wine of the house was named generically *Rheinwein*. It was like nectar. Then later to the inevitable Rieberbahn, Hamburg's street of fun at night-time where the music halls are far more undressed in their entertainment than would be tolerated in the latter-day theatres of Berlin. Then to two or three of the characteristic dancing halls with crowds of pretty girls behind the bars inviting customers to drink once more and buy an extra glass for the *Fräulein*. All so typical of the night life of Germany, something that goes on in spite of revolution and change of government. The Nazis are unlike the Fascists, who once prohibited dancing in Rome and sent everybody to bed at ten o'clock, until the Duce realised that the basilica of St. Peter's and the via Sacra were not sufficient in themselves to encourage English and American travellers to linger in the Eternal City. But most entertaining of all, a copy of a Bavarian mountain beer tavern, exaggerated in size out of all proportion to its prototype. On a diminutive stage sat a genuine Bavarian orchestra in traditional costume of open shirts and velvet shorts, with rough woollen stockings and hairy knees. The instruments made noise enough to raise the roof and I am almost convinced that when the players began to yodel the vibration shook the chandeliers. In the big hall were hundreds of Hamburgers out for the evening, consuming enormous quantities of beer, and buying piles of *bretzels* and sweet cakes from waitresses of uncertain age whose black bodices were heavily hung with rows of silver coins in the true tradition of Munich and the Bavarian Alps. It was all very noisy, and sometimes the cat-calls and enthusiasm of the audience bordered on the boisterous. But the laughter and obvious enjoyment were infectious. One simply had to call for another half-litre of beer.

The storm was still raging outside the mouth of the Elbe when I made a tour of the harbour. The surface of the river even in the port was torn into great waves by the force of the wind: the launches, as they made their way into the open, were all but swamped. I was invited to occupy one of the tenders of the harbour-master and even so there were times when the water swept over the bows and threw down sheets of spray into our cabin. A tour of the port of Hamburg takes several hours, for the harbour has some of the largest docks and basins in the world. Before one has completed the itinerary, one begins to get an idea of the greatness of German mercantile marine. After the first half-hour I became weary of counting the number of ships of all kinds, from Atlantic liners to miserably small hookers, we passed as we ploughed our way through the angry waters of the river.

Hamburg is, of course, a free port. By this is meant that ships entering with goods for transit are exempt from the control of the customs authorities. Inside the free port area goods may be stored, cleaned or repacked without any State charges. It also remains the port of Prague, the capital of Czecho-Slovakia, in spite of the denunciation of part twelve of the Peace Treaty. A visit to the port and warehouses of Hamburg constitutes a lesson in essential geography. After a mile-long walk over wharves and through warehouses I was not surprised to learn that on an average 160 ships of various sizes clear the port every week on deep-sea mission and that something like 200 tramp steamers on coastwise traffic come and go. One can believe that in the vast storehouses there is space for two million tons of merchandise. During a long walk after I had left the tender I saw cold storage plants capable of taking a hundred million eggs and a great herring dump in which one hundred thousand barrels of herrings were awaiting treatment in the style so beloved in Central Europe.

In the open river cargo steamers up to six or seven thousand tons lay tied to buoys. But it was impossible to discern the outline of their hulls, so thick was the press of barges and lighters moored alongside.

In the yard of Bloehm & Voss and the neighbouring yard of Vulkan, ships were being built and repaired. The noise of steam-hammers and drills triumphed over the high notes of the wind. Not far away a big American liner was about to sail for New York and tug-boats and sirens were about their usual busy-body fuss. Occasionally our tender passed through huge gates operated by gigantic engines to emerge from the calm of a secluded basin into the turmoil of the river once more. There was a row of small British cargo boats from Hull and London, their red ensigns tearing at full length in the full gale. And presently we saw pile-drivers prodding the depths of the river-bed to prepare the foundations of a wonderful new quay which will enable cargo-carrying liners of the 15,000 class to come alongside with the greatest of ease, even in the inner port. As the great drivers methodically thudded one remembered how stupendous has been the conquest of the encroaching sea by the hand of man from the mouth of the Scheldt to the coast of Schleswig.

CHAPTER X

A QUESTION OF "DEVISEN"

THOSE who visit Germany and have at their disposal a goodly allowance of registered marks have little or no idea of the currency restrictions which are part of the law and custom of the land. Each foreigner is allowed to exchange fifty marks a day at par rates for his hotel bill and incidental expenses. (During the high jinks of the 1936 Olympiad the visitor was allowed one hundred registered marks *per diem.*) The allowance of fifty marks a day is both generous and adequate, for hotel accommodation in Germany is very reasonable in price, excellent meals can be obtained for a shilling or two, beer and wine are cheap and the railways are most accommodating in their special prices for the foreign visitor. The traveller with ordinary tastes for the moderate luxuries and amenities of life finds it hard to exceed the fifty-mark allowance. One might be tempted to believe that there is an immense amount of spare money circulating in the country. This is not the case. In point of fact the great mass of the German population is living very frugally on modest salaries and incomes. Outward extravagance is officially frowned on. If the German seems to derive a great deal of gaiety from life it is because he knows how to spend his money to the best advantage. The comparatively low prices prevailing make his choice of entertainment easier than is the case in most other European countries.

It is not until the visitor is about to leave Germany that the full force of Dr. Schacht's regulations in attempting to safeguard the German currency come forcibly to mind. One is made aware, on entering, of the rules that say you may only take out of the country ten registered marks in addition to the foreign money you actually declare. Failure to declare your foreign currency may quite easily lead to its confiscation, for ignorance of the law does not constitute an excuse. And of course if you happen to be a German subject caught in the act of evading the monetary regulations then the penalties are severe indeed. Quite a number of people who have tried to smuggle money now look forward to the dismal prospect of ten or twelve years in a prison cell.

I had decided to return to England from Hamburg by passenger liner, for stormy weather portended an unpleasant passage by aeroplane. There had been terrific gales, and the previous day the storm had reached such dimensions as to tear up the moorings of the famous light vessel *Elbe the First*, and the ill-fated ship had turned turtle with heavy loss of life, while a British tramp steamer stood by, unable to render any assistance on account of the force of the gale. The disaster had plunged the great port into mourning, for the Hamburgers are a maritime people and, as such, feel disaster at sea more deeply than their fellows. It was not surprising that the Hamburg Amerika Company decided that for two days there would be no music or dancing on board any of their liners at sea as a mark of respect to the dead lightshipmen. It was a gesture typical of the streak of sentiment that pervades the German character. During the two-hour train journey to Cuxhaven I came across a more ruthless trait. And it all devolved on the currency regulations.

In the compartment was an English merchant who was returning to London on business, and a German woman of about sixty years of age, and myself. I had no fear as to the *devisen* regulations, for I had but ten marks. My English friend had a wad of English money—which he had declared on entry—and a handful of German silver, far more than the permitted ten marks. The woman, who was well dressed in a Persian lamb coat, and who was obviously prosperous, carried a large leather bag which bulged with documents. As the train rumbled its way to the north, the officials of the monetary regulations made their appearance and politely asked to see our passports and wallets. My friend held out his handful of silver, but they took only the most scant notice and told him he could keep it to spend on good German wine on the steamer. They were only interested in the woman, concerning whom they must have had previous suspicions. After a lengthy examination of a series of green documents, they remained unsatisfied, and eventually they asked her to accompany them to an empty compartment in another part of the train. The woman got up at once and followed, leaving her valuable fur coat behind, together with her hand luggage.

In due course the train pulled up on the quayside at Cuxhaven and in the distance the black hull of the liner *New York* could be seen towering above one of the famous jetties. The woman had not returned and there were no signs of her. The custom at Cuxhaven is for intending passengers to leave all their baggage in the compartment of the train for collection by the ship's stewards. My English acquaintance and I left the train and made our way to the gangway. There was considerable delay for there was an unusual amount of baggage ; it so happened that the Dresden State Opera Company were travelling on board the steamer preparatory to giving a fortnight's season at Covent Garden. I saw a steward come aboard carrying a fur coat over his arm : it was unmistakably the coat belonging to the woman in the railway train. But there was no sign of the woman. After what seemed like an age the ship sailed slowly away and the passengers descended the companion-way to luncheon. By this time I had grown curious concerning the woman and made inquiries. It appeared that her papers were not in order : moreover, on being searched at Cuxhaven she was found to be secreting a large number of foreign and German banknotes. That was indeed a grave offence and she had been detained in prison at once. She would certainly get several years' imprisonment and the money would be confiscated. The officer who vouchsafed the information was even more preoccupied by the fact that the woman's heavy luggage —apart from her fur coat—had come aboard and that up to the present they had not been able to locate it all. The coat had been sent ashore at the last minute.

A passenger on a German liner leaving a German port cannot buy a drink or a packet of cigarettes or a cigar (I have never seen such excellent Havana cigars sold at so cheap a price) until he has visited the purser. He must purchase " ship money " and obtain a number of fifty-pfennig pieces, small silver coins about the size of a sixpence and representing practically the same value. Such coins are the only currency, apart from five-mark notes issued by the purser's office, which are legal tender on board.

Even if you draw on a letter of credit, you are given ship money and as many fifty-pfennig bits as you ask for. You rattle your pockets and get the impression they are full of farthings! It takes a little time to get accustomed to this strange form of money and when you have, it still serves as a reminder of the artificial and drastic way in which German currency is being managed. Incidentally if you exchange dollar bills or Bank of England notes then you only received the small sums quoted in the fictitious gold rates of the Reichbank. The purser encourages such transaction, for every greenback or paper pound he receives means another addition to the reserve of foreign money that is sedulously being hoarded in Germany.

The members of the Dresden Opera Company were each given ten marks pocket money! They were going to England where they would be paid in pounds and that was good enough. These famous singers and impresarios arrived at Waterloo with scarcely a halfpenny in their purses. They were invited to attend a reception in the famous foyer of the opera house. They reached the buffet, which had been laid out in lavish style with all kinds of native delicacies and rows of bottles of whisky—a drink that is very popular in Germany but nowadays prohibitive in price. The singers cared for none of these things. All they wanted to see was the face of the treasurer so that they might get a little advance of salary on account. The incident, small though it was, was indicative of the financial situation of Germany in regard to what is called *devisen*, or foreign exchange.

No sketch of modern Germany, however short, can ignore the economic aspects of the country. The Nazi experiment has entailed a fiscal as well as a political revolution and although in the case of the latter there have been concrete results, in the case of the former there have also been many expedients. In fact, from a foreign money point of view the whole of German economic structure is an expedient built up on some ambitious scheme of international barter which has not quite come off, and now that the so-called gold *bloc* of France, Italy, Switzerland and Holland have seen the error of their ways and devalued their currencies, seems less likely to materialise than ever. Even so, a great distinction should be made between conditions inside the country and those which affect the outside world. Within the Reich there has been great economic revival in trade and output. That fact cannot be denied. It is obvious to all who take the trouble to make investigation. One ought not to be misled by the reports of drastic rationing of fat foods. In many parts of the country the restrictions will not be noticed at all, for in tens of thousands of poor peasant homes butter has never figured in the daily fare. And in this connection I am reminded of an incident which took place in the office of a leading London weekly newspaper shortly after the new food regulations in Germany were made public. A great heap of letters poured in from the special areas lamenting the fact that small as was the ration permitted to the German working classes even such short measure would be welcomed in those homes affected by the means test in many parts of the country. Whatever one may say about conditions in modern Germany there is no malnutrition of the kind that tears the hearts of those who have walked down the dismal streets of Jarrow-on-Tyne.

In order to understand the present economic position

in the Reich it is important to go back a few years. In 1929, before the beginnings of the world crash, the volume of internal production stood at a level of 104. In 1932 when the world was passing through the valley of the shadow it had sunk to 58. In 1936 it had climbed again to the prosperity level of 104. Moreover, in the last three years employment has increased by fifty per cent, so that according to the latest reliable figures there are eighteen millions at work throughout the country. Unemployment, as I have already stated, has been reduced to a minimum and it is doubtful, in such a huge community with so much floating labour and the presence of the inevitable unemployable, whether the figure can ever fall much below the million mark.

The internal economic recovery has undoubtedly been accomplished at the cost of what we should describe as individual freedom; all private interests are considered as subject to the major interest of the state. Yet the individual German—or at any rate the great mass of individuals—does not chafe at the loss of his liberty of action. He regards German recovery in the peace in much the same way as he looked on sacrifice in the service of the state during the war. It appeals to his essential patriotism: it has even developed into a form of national hysteria. The national effort to raise Germany from despond has given rise to a formidable display of strength and unity. It must be remembered that Germany lived under conditions of practically continuous economic depression for just about fifteen years after the armistice. She lost the war, although the great mass of the people seeing the returning armies did not realise it, and many of her leaders, including the eminent Dr. Sthamer, first ambassador of the Republic in London after the war, were never convinced who exactly won it. Later the whole financial structure of the nation was ruined by the fantastic inflation. What salvation there was came from a daring defiance of economic laws and traditions by Dr. Schacht in introducing the rentenmark; and it is well-known that the eminent President of the Reichbank was more genuinely surprised at the result of his own experiment than anybody else. Moreover, Germany, by the incidence of the Peace Treaty, was sadly handicapped economically. She lost her colonies. The ironfields of Lorraine, so much an economic corollary of the Ruhr mining lands, were taken by France, and the nation was a helpless spectator of the incredible division of the Upper Silesian industrial area. There was the formidable reparations bill, the creation of the artificial Dantzig Corridor, the occupation of Essen and the adjoining towns, the universal atmosphere of suspicion with which she was regarded —a suspicion no doubt skilfully fostered by the now highly technical weapon of international propaganda, and aided by her own natural instinct for making enemies. No one can deny that it was difficult to establish a firm economic basis under such strange and even unprecedented conditions. Moreover, there was her population of between sixty-five and seventy millions packed in an area about the size of California.

After the war Germany faced the world with her own natural problems as well as those inflicted on her by the peace settlement. From a food-producing point of view she was by no means self-supporting; her soil is relatively poor and although a quarter of the population live on the highly-cultivated soil, the resultant crops can never be adequate for national needs. Her mineral products are only coal and potash.

She has thus never been blessed by natural resources in her fight for a place in world production. It is here, however, that her native genius has come to the rescue. Her scientists have elaborated synthetic processes almost to the point of perfection and her large-scale methods, combined with her great inventiveness and tremendous personal industry, have made her second only to the United States with eleven per cent of the total world industrial production. That in itself is surely no mean achievement.

The scaling down of wages has also contributed to the economic recovery of the German people in the face of adversity. It must be remembered that a skilled workman in the Reich feels lucky if he earns twelve pounds a month. A domestic servant, and a first-class servant at that, can be had for less than a pound a week and for that she becomes a vital part of the household. The average labourer and servant is quite content and with meagre earnings manages to make something out of life more than mere drudgery. I found in my personal contacts with the workers a universal goodwill to labour and an individual pride in the national concerted effort which has led to universal employment of one kind or another. Labour has become honoured among men even if it is often badly rewarded. The German, looking around the Reich, has cause for satisfaction and gratitude in the knowledge that great industrial plants are being built, magnificent roads are being laid out (shortage of cars to make use of them, no matter), canals are being dug (cf. the Adolf Hitler canal in Silesia), and the problem of housing is being tackled on a comprehensive plan.

The economic recovery of Germany certainly owes much to the steam-roller methods of the new régime —the method that requires the individual to sublimate himself to the demands of State and system. The effort is nation-wide and it is working out very successfully for the time being. Enormous, even fabulous, sums of money are being expended and it is only reasonable to ask the simple question, " Who is going to foot the bill at the day of reckoning ? " " Is present prosperity being bought at the expense of the future ? " is the query of second thought. One may be tempted to draw comparisons with the spoken word of Louis the Fourteenth and the deluge. But in actual fact the nature and character of the German again give the lie to the accepted laws of economics. The *devisen* regulations are accepted by the population in the way no other nation under heaven would accept them. The interior finance of the country is skilfully managed to make it independent of the outside world, and it is possible to experiment with the nation's internal resources in a manner that would be dangerous anywhere else. It has been rightly said that a strong German population willing to make sacrifices —like the present generation—is capable of achieving incredible things. Pressure is being brought to bear on industries, banks, insurance companies, and wealthy individuals, by which short-term credits to finance the creation of employment are being transferred to long-term securities, thus freeing short-term money for more immediate necessities. Moreover, the employment of foreign credits—even if they were available—is being avoided as far as possible.

The new régime tackled the unemployment question on a basis of common sense. It was necessary to find work for the disgruntled elements and to clear the street corners of idlers. At the same time there must not be any " boondoggling " job-making. The victorious party was well aware that national social

PLATE 6

LABOUR CAMP AT TRACHENBURG, NEAR BRESLAU

[face p. 188

insurance was no new thing. For years the German workman has had one-fifth of his earnings deducted at the source for various insurance and pension schemes to which the employer was compelled to make his contribution. There was a dole system although the amount was small. Nevertheless, there were many who had been unemployed for so long that they had forgotten the discipline of labour and were prepared to struggle just under the bread-line rather than pick up their tools. The day came when the relief officers were empowered to say to men who refused manual labour that there would be no more State aid. That in itself was in the nature of an economic revolution. In regard to skilled mechanics it was found necessary to establish vocational schools in order that expert knowledge could be re-acquired. As I have stated the ingress of people from town to city, which always seems to accompany periods of national distress, was rigidly forbidden and former land-workers who were discovered idling in the streets of large towns were sent back to the agrarian districts whence they came. And almost at once work was begun on great public works all over the country. The importance of agriculture as essential to the State was emphasized by the drastic revision of the laws of landholding and direct encouragement to suburban dwellers to cultivate their gardens on a food-producing basis. Then the day came when armament factories were flooded with orders and a death blow was given to the menace of unemployment. In this connection it is interesting to note the effect on the heavy industries in our own country since the breakdown of the disarmament conference, through no fault of our own, led to the present plans for naval and military rearmament.

There is no doubt of the rearmament of Germany. It was a natural sequence to the story of events both at Geneva and elsewhere. The industrial areas are working night and day to make up the leeway lost in the intervening years. If you travel in Germany you find no apologists for such an attitude. The ordinary German takes the natural standpoint: "The others did not disarm. Why should we remain unarmed and helpless?" And it is difficult to dispute the logic of the argument knowing the attitudes of some of Germany's neighbours. It is equally certain that even the most strenuous efforts of the German people could not have kept them on the road to recovery without the present rearmament. It has affected everything, from the building trade, providing new factories, to textiles and tailoring (fashioning uniforms), with all the heavy industries in between. I have seen shipyards working full time. The sight of workmen emerging from the famous Elbe tunnel at Hamburg is something not easily forgotten. It is the same in the great motor and aeroplane factories. The boom has even affected the breeding of horses. Like the Russian general staff, the German war ministry has not put all its trust in mechanical appliances, and both cavalry and horse-drawn artillery still form a considerable part of the Reichswehr. Germany still has something like three and a half million horses to fall back on. In England it is doubtful whether there are more than a million horses of all classes and breeds. The authorities in Germany have been at pains to advertise the necessity of defence on all occasions and the average German looks on the effort of rearmament as a bounden duty. In this connection the same may be said of every country in Europe. In fact, no matter where you travel on the Continent you cannot enter a cinema without being regaled with pictures of manœuvres, or battle launchings, or aerial acrobatics. They are nearly always of an intensely national character. In our own cinemas we have an almost equal amount of warlike display but it generally has to do with foreign countries. Either a sense of stupidity or an assessment of false values seem to guide the authorities in avoiding films of our own efforts to rearm as much as possible. In the case of Germany such films serve to stimulate national feeling and help the individual to overcome the inferiority complex feelings left behind after the war. There are also some who think that such pictures are necessary to instruct Germany's circle of hostile neighbours that a state of preparedness has been brought into existence.

The production of war munitions requires the import of raw materials from abroad, and the elaborate plans for complete rearmament cannot take place under present conditions. The lack of raw material and the necessity of providing synthetic substitutes, was the forerunner of the Four Year Plan now being sponsored by General Goering. It also accounts for the much advertised rationing which, in actual fact, is not so severe as report would have the world believe. The German Government has decided that money must be found for munitions, and to provide the necessary foreign exchange, food supplies must be cut down. How long even the proverbial patience of the long-suffering German will support such a policy is a matter for conjecture, but it will probably be for a long time to come. No one, as yet, has gone hungry for the benefit of cannons and bombs.

Food shortage in the Reich is confined to grains, fodders, and fats. In 1929—an average year—something like 4,500 million rentenmarks' worth of foreign produce was imported. This has been drastically cut down. In 1935, for example, only 2,900 millions' worth came into the country, showing that already local produce was increasing in bulk and restrictions were already being unobtrusively applied. Even so this figure represents something like fifteen to twenty per cent of the total national consumption of foodstuffs.

One must remember that increased employment means increased consumption of food, and that there is an ever-increasing population, the extra million or so babies requiring increased quantity of milk and sugar. The food margin is very narrow and likely so to remain, and that explains why modern Germany is so dependent on the amount of the annual crop. A failure of the potato crop in the autumn and winter of 1936–7 would have been a national disaster. As it was, the yield was up to normal and officials in the Wilhelmstrasse breathed again. The Nazi régime has increased the supply of grain for bread so that there is not likely to be a scarcity, but there is a dangerous shortage of cattle fodder. Grain and fodder kept in storage are being exhausted very rapidly and next year the Finance Ministry will have to find more than £12,000,000 to make up inroads on the reserves. Germany has in any case to find £15,000,000 for her supplies of tea, coffee, cocoa, and raw tobacco, and this item is constantly brought forward in the continuous agitation for a return of the colonies. As for fats, she requires annually 800,000 tons in addition to her home supplies and the rearmament plans are absorbing millions of marks' worth every week and each ton has to be paid for in cash! It had been hoped to avoid any personal restrictions on supplies, but the shortage of money became even too difficult for the wizard Schacht to manipulate, and so supplies were restricted. In the same way during the winter stocks of pork and beef were withheld at intervals to permit of an equitable distribution over the whole country. Such restrictions caused grumbling and a little inconvenience, but nothing more, for by some strange economic fate the cost of living did not rise —and be it remembered there has never been a dictatorship yet which survived for long the menace of dear food. In spite of everything the index was only 125 during the last winter as compared with 100 in 1913. It will have been noticed there have been recurrent appeals to national patriotism, and the people have been told that this difficult period in the rehabilitation of the State must be looked on with the same stoical philosophy as wartime. The people have responded with anticipated obedience.

The extraordinary state of German foreign exchange must not be laid to the account of the Nazis. When they came into power, they found an empty treasury as part of their heritage. The uncertain political situation in Germany had its disturbing effect in international financial circles. Foreign credits were withdrawn from Germany during the last months of the republic, and by the time the Nazis reached office and enlisted the services of Dr. Schacht the cupboard was wellnigh bare. And for one cause or another, it has never been replenished. The reason for thc *devisen* regulations and import control must always be considered in this light if a true perspective of the present German position is to be obtained. When economic recovery began in Germany under the rule of the Third Reich, requirements for raw materials and essential foodstuffs increased enormously. The previous export surplus on the general turnover of trade which amounted to 668 million rentenmarks in 1933 had been converted to an import surplus of 284 rentenmarks in 1934—a turnover of 952 rentenmarks in the course of a twelvemonth. Imports could no longer be paid for in the ordinary way and so came about the present system of drastic exchange control. Under this system Germany has built up a small export surplus but nothing like her requirements if she is to continue to buy raw materials from abroad on a big scale. It must also be borne in mind that Germany has external debts to an amount estimated at 13,000 million rentenmarks, and on this considerable debt service has to be paid in money—an item which still further complicates the international monetary situation. If it had not been for the devaluation of foreign currencies this amount would be still greater when translated into marks, but even allowing for this the German people have through their industry repaid about 10,000 million marks' worth of debt through cash payments and the proceeds of export trade. I base my figures on most reliable information, but at the same time will agree with possible critics that it is impossible to reach an absolutely accurate estimate of the foreign debt situation while the present strict secrecy is maintained by Dr. Schacht and his colleagues. I venture to state, however, from my knowledge of the Finance Ministry, that the situation is nothing like so unfavourable as rumour would have the world believe. Germany has been the victim of inspired malicious rumour, so far as international financial transactions are concerned, ever since the Nazis came into power.

There is no doubt that the Jewish boycott on German foreign trade has had a very great effect. This has been specially notable in the case of the

United States and South Africa, where Jewish influences have enormous power over immediate trade. But it must be remembered that boycotts always cut both ways. The great difficulty the Nazi Germans encountered in striking an equitable export and import bargain on a kind of barter basis has had the effect of depriving the United States of a valuable market. This was in great part due to the Jewish boycott. It has been found possible to make arrangements with South American countries on an equality of import and export basis. The result is that Germany is now importing cotton from those regions, and the cotton grower of the southern states has been deprived of a market—probably for ever. It was quite an economic education to wander through the miles of sheds and warehouses on the quays at Hamburg and see the mountains of merchandise of all kinds, with each box or bale stencilled in black paint with some destination in the South American Continent.

Those who have not travelled in Germany and who are content to base their arguments on academic principles of political economy, must at once remark that the whole question of Germany's financial situation could be solved by devaluation of the mark, the alignment of German currency along with that of other countries, including the erstwhile gold *bloc*. Everyone will agree that the present nominal rate of exchange in relation to sterling of something like twelve to the pound is quite absurd. The fact is recognised by the Germans themselves in issuing the so-called registered marks at practically par rates (I believe 400 million were issued in 1935 to the tourist traffic alone). Moreover, anybody who attempts to exchange marks into a foreign currency gets only a fraction of the nominal value. Banks will not buy large quantities for they cannot use them in ordinary business transactions. Possession of more than a few marks in foreign countries is in itself sufficient to give rise to the liveliest suspicion. These facts are plain to all.

But there is an even more important fact which anyone who knows Germany realises is a fundamental one —the psychological issue. The temper of the German people is such that they will not tolerate another experiment in inflation. The sufferings and miseries of the last one continue to haunt the nation like a bad dream. In many cases its consequences of hardship were more poignant than actual bereavement in the war. That dread period is looked back to with horror by the vast majority of the German people, who are persuaded in their confirmed anger and bitterness that many foreigners and native Jews took advantage of the national misery to pile up enormous fortunes. The bankers know that if the mark was decontrolled its exchange value might conceivably melt away immediately and Germany would once more be thrown to the mercy of the financial wolves. This national fear was very early recognised by the Nazi leaders who solemnly averred that on no account would any devaluation of the mark be tolerated while they were in office ; and it is safe to assert that if any such attempt were made only a miracle would save the present Government, all-powerful though it is. In fact, I have heard it said by men whose opinion is of international repute that only two things will ever shift the Nazis from power in Germany—one is if Germany is the unsuccessful protagonist in another world war : the other is if there was devaluation of the mark.

The German furthermore belongs to a stay-at-home people. He is not wildly excited in what goes on outside his own frontier. (I speak of the *petit-bourgeoisie* and the average working man who prefers his lathe or bench to political theorising.) He sees the internal market more or less solid and prosperous. He is aware that he cannot leave his native land except in special circumstances, on account of the currency regulations, and he is quite reconciled to the fact. He knows that in his own country his mark is worth a mark and he is prepared to leave it at that. In this respect he is not unlike his English counterpart. When Great Britain went off the gold standard the Government in their foreign propaganda quite rightly made much of the fact that in England a pound was worth a pound however much it was worth elsewhere. The Englishman living abroad and exchanging his impoverished pounds read such announcements with mixed feelings. But at home the Englishman did not care how many (or alas, how few) Swiss francs went to make up twenty shillings and cared much less, for he was not going abroad in any case for patriotic reasons. Had, however, the pound in England ceased to buy what the Englishman at home thought was a pound's worth, the career of the National Government in Westminster might have had a more troubled history in its first years than it did. And the analogy can, with certain modifications, be applied to Germany in the year 1937.

Not all Germans are satisfied with the present situation. Merchants and businessmen who have contacts with the outside world, and many that don't, chafe and writhe under Dr. Schacht's elaborate edicts. There is one particularly unpopular levy of one per cent called the export levy. It is universal and imposed on all manufacturers whether they export ten pfennigs' worth of goods or not. It is a legitimate grievance for some great businesses. Furthermore, the machinery for arranging barter deals on balance of imports and exports is necessarily cumbersome and long delays frequently result in loss of business. It is a fact that the business of export and import in the ports of Bremen and Hamburg has become a science requiring the services of experts who spend one-half of the day in their maritime offices and the other besieging the doors of ministries in Berlin to make sure their transactions are within the law, or to find out what subsidy will be forthcoming from the Government so that the exporter may know how low a price he can bid. It is difficult to see how trade could flourish at all if it was not for the two-hour flying train between the Lehrter Bahnof of Berlin and the Hauptbahnof in Hamburg. No one finds the existing system more distasteful than Dr. Schacht, its sponsor, but the great financier knows it is absolutely necessary if Germany is to have any trade at all and while foreign countries continue to organise a financial campaign of no confidence against the Reich. Indeed, I have it on reliable authority that he has often asked the Führer for permission to resign from his post because he can see no end to a situation made impossible by the wealthy nations of the world : but each time Hitler has entreated him to stay in office as the one man whose service is indispensable for the financial future of the Reich.

During the recent winter Germany was faced with serious industrial raw-material shortage, at a time when increasing employment and the armament orders demanded an increase in such commodities. The armament problem was the crux of the situation. Countries with far greater facilities showed no signs of slackening in their plans for re-arming and Germany could not slacken her efforts in consequence. All suggestions as to letting the heavy industries work on shorter time so that the amount of production was curtailed, thus reducing the sum total of imports paid in cash and spreading the work over a longer period, had to be dismissed. Germany kept her place in the race for defence and security, still well behind it is true: but then Germany was not at the starting-gate when the race began.

But a truce to all these figures. The whole world is fundamentally in a state of economic chaos, only Germany happens to be rather worse off than most from an international point of view. The prosperity of many other nations if largely a matter of accident and great financial security is so often at the mercy of senseless speculation. Happily for mankind high financial considerations are the playthings of governments and not individuals, and while we read—and we have read so often—that such and such a state is verging on bankruptcy, it is no longer a matter of astonishment to read in the next paragraph that daily life goes on in very much the same way. So it is with Germany. Economists become gloomy in their studies, but the German completes his day's labour and relaxes over his beer and wine in the evening entirely oblivious of his dread fate—always assuming that the economist will prove to be right at last. Nowadays nations have a habit of playing fast and loose with figures and theories and emerging unscathed at the end.

The liner *New York* glided away from the quay at Cuxhaven and presently the crowds of people on shore became little black dots before disappearing altogether from view. As I have already said there were on board a number of Germans from the Dresden Opera Company—singers, scene shifters, stage carpenters, fiddlers, and conductors—who had only ten marks each, but they did not seem to mind, for beer was only threepence a glass and the journey to Southampton only lasted about twenty-four hours. At dinner a beautiful woman in modest evening dress took her place at table. A diamond the size of a hazel nut adorned one finger and round her neck was a rope of pearls as big as field peas. The wine steward placed the *weinkarte* before her. She looked confused and handed it back. A German-American who occupied the adjacent place noticed her predicament and said very graciously—on board ship introduction is not always deemed essential to good manners—that he hoped madame would take wine at his expense. He understood how difficult it was but he had American dollars and he would be honoured to buy champagne, even the German variety. Before dinner was over he had given the wine steward ship notes for thirty marks—the allowance of three Germans *en voyage* even if they were as beautiful as this beautiful singer from Dresden, who looked as dainty and delicate as any of the porcelain shepherdesses one sees in the shop by the royal castle, not a stone's throw from the opera house where she had established an international reputation.

CHAPTER XI

PRELUDE TO TRAGEDY

SINCE my return to England I have thought long and carefully concerning the great power that is asserting itself beyond the Rhine, and I have come to the conclusion that the domestic affairs of the German people ought to be regarded as their own private business. We do not hear of the Führer entering on a crusading campaign to bring the whole world into the folds of the true faith of National Socialism. He is no proselytiser. There is nothing evangelical about the Nazi movement. No Internationale has been devised to preach the gospel abroad, and in this respect it is unlike the rival faith of Moscow which admittedly is aiming at world revolution. Loose thinking has led a great number of people to believe that all forms of the authoritative state are Fascist. Few take the trouble to define Fascism or remember that the very name is derived from a group of Italian ex-service men who formed a party under Mussolini to combat growing disorder in the city of Milan. Fascism as interpreted in modern Rome bears no resemblance to the National Socialism of Berlin, with the reservation that in both countries personal authority has replaced Parliamentary dilatoriness. Although many may sneer when I say it, I maintain that Germany is rapidly arriving at a form of Socialist state that is really capable of being worked and which is bringing security and content to tens of millions. The dictionary definition of socialism states that it is a doctrine in which the political and economic organisation of society should be based on the subordination of the individual to the interests of the community, involving the collective ownership of the resources and instruments of production. If any such movement is taking place anywhere it is taking place in Germany.

The inherent clumsiness of the German people when they feel they are strong has again created a bad impression. It happens so often. It is the most unhappy characteristic of a great people. It is a state of clumsiness which has made the abbreviation Nazi into a synonym, alternatively of suspicion and of hatred, and has distracted the world into mistaking a domestic issue for an international one. Hitler has asserted time and time again that National Socialism is not for export. It is merely the balm that is to cure the open wounds of Germany's national life and it ought to be regarded as such. It is not our affair, surely, to interfere in any way with the internal politics of Germany any more than it is the business of any other country to question the machinery of our own form of Government.

One fact emerges from this confused situation and that is that Germany has again become a first-class power. The way in which she is overcoming the formidable economic difficulties in her way is proof of her strength. And how is that strength to be used—for peace or war ? It is the mighty question of the day. Another world war might end Western civilisation for ever. It is unthinkable. It must be avoided. And in my opinion the only way in which such a catastrophe can be averted is on the basis of an Anglo-German understanding. Such an understanding the Germans themselves sincerely wish for. Such an understanding would make an impregnable combination and provide security for Europe, including France. Such an understanding would keep in check the present mad race for armaments which each day brings us nearer disaster. Such an understanding would transcend party or sectional politics.

But although a solution is at hand, we are drifting back to the bad old balance of power of a Franco-British alliance, with France openly attached to Communist Russia. We are turning the clock back. In France there is open rejoicing that British policy is once more becoming Francophile. The hate against Germany is being fanned into flame and the old ugly situation develops once again. It is forgotten that Germany has been our friend for a thousand years. Our politicians would have us believe that one cannot come to terms with Germans because they support a Nazi administration, a view which has about as much logic in it as the statement that Germany could not approach England because we have a National Government at St. Stephen's. Surely a golden opportunity is being missed? The world cries out for peace and peace can be assured by a re-alignment of our foreign policy. Are we going to turn our faces against the kindred race beyond the Rhine in the interests of political and diplomatic jobbery? Are we going to break with historical tradition once again, with the fatal results of 1914? Historical tradition? Let us go back a little and see what lesson history has to teach us.

A shot fired in the unknown town of Serajevo at the end of June, 1914, disturbed the tranquillity of an outwardly happy and prosperous world. Its significance was only remotely recognised at the time. In our own country the assassination of the heir of the Hapsburgs was treated as yet another of those characteristic and unhappy events which disturb the Balkans from time to time. In fact, the greater mass of the population was preparing to go on its August holidays when it was abruptly called to face the greatest crisis in its history. On August 4, the people of Great Britain and the Empire declared war on the Teutonic peoples for the first time in our long island story. They fought for four and a quarter years until the enemy was forced to surrender by reason largely of empty stomachs and only secondarily by force of arms. In the stress of circumstance the armistice that brought end to hell on earth was regarded as signal victory and the subsequent so-called Versailles settlement was hailed as the end of a period of storm and stress and the harbinger of peace and plenty.

The unlucky war generation now begin to realise that the sacrifices made in the hopeless, insensate struggle of 1914–18 were almost devoid of purpose : that the war, for whatever reason it was fought, was fought in vain : that the post-war state of peace, as the politicians made it, is fertile with grotesque and gruesome possibilities of another and more disastrous war. There are men now grown to manhood who were infants in arms when the war broke out. They have grown up in two short decades of great human achievement. They have seen the ether tapped to bring their compatriots in Cape Town almost to within calling terms of neighbours. They have seen the internal combustion engine propel aeroplanes through the air at more than three hundred miles an hour and make the motor-car at once the advantage and menace of millions. They have watched mass production bring within the range of all luxuries which were once the envied privilege of the few. If perhaps their mental and spiritual outlook has been deteriorated by the primitive values of Hollywood, at least they have been able to enjoy the material comforts of life in a way which was impossible to their forbears. At the same time there has been a tragic reverse to the gilded medal of our modern civilisation. Before the war the idea of political crisis or international complication was the intellectual pursuit or occupation of the few. Until the war descended suddenly on the world with all its horrors the average man took very little interest in what happened outside his immediate local interests. The wider field of national or international affairs was universally considered as the proper province of Member of Parliament or member of Cabinet. Those who ventured to speak of the wrath to come were regarded either as cranks or public nuisances. One can no longer live in such an atmosphere of sweet forgetfulness or ignorance. The menace to each individual life from the forces bred in our latter-day international turmoil is known indeed, is significant to all. In spite of all the advantages which scientific culture has brought in the last twenty years, there is a universal uncertainty. We may enjoy our many extra luxuries and facilities, but behind that enjoyment there is always a fear that by this time to-morrow forces, over which we have no apparent control, may precipitate us into a war which will make the last one seem like a garden party. There was never a period in the world's history when so many amenities were to hand for the joy of living : it is a tragic thought that simultaneously there have never been so many reasons for dread of to-morrow. The generation that is passing has grown old in its grim realisation of one crisis after another : the new generation, even if it has made spectacular efforts to escape thought of ultimate responsibility, has always been subconscious of living in a world which eludes one crisis only to find itself in the throes of another. When

King Edward the Eighth at the unveiling of the Canadian memorial at Vimy Ridge made mention of "our unhappy human story" he brought to the minds of all an image of vivid reality.

In every corner of the world there is discontent. One is forced to ask every morning for news of the latest revolution for fear of missing one. Nineteen years after the termination of the war to end war our munition factories are working overtime. There is revolution here and political upheaval there. The discontents of the alleged peace settlement have already resulted in a mortality which approximates to active warfare. The new millennium, which was promised after the universal sacrifice of 1914–18, is still to come. Instead of peace and goodwill we have in Europe such tragic reminders of a sick outlook on international affairs as desecrated churches and political concentration camps. The whole world of men seems to lack direction. That temple of hope conceived in ideas and built with speeches called the League of Nations has rightly become an object of derision. Mankind has ceased to attach any importance to the bickerings of Geneva and political high purpose deceives the thinking individual no longer. At the same time the ordinary British subject, sparing a moment from his more immediate pursuits, ought to take stock of the world in general and wonder what has happened to that tradition of British leadership which had an almost Biblical significance when he was taught the elements of European history at school. It is my contention that the absence of thoughtful leadership in Great Britain to-day is a contributory cause to world doubt and to the continuation of our unhappy human story. British foreign policy has become a kind of weathervane instead of being a signpost.

After eighteen years of crying peace when there is no peace we are still drifting. The Prime Minister quite gratuitously announces that our frontier is on the Rhine and our Foreign Minister addresses a questionnaire to the Nazi Government worthy of the ignoble Treaty of Versailles. The fact that the first statement was resented by the German Government and misunderstood by the French and that the Wilhelmstrasse refused to make full reply to Mr. Eden's catechism was not lost on a great part of the British public, seems to be unknown to the superior people in Whitehall who are ostensibly in charge of the direction of our foreign policy. This one fundamental fact ought surely not to be lost sight of, that in this changing world routine ought to give place to realism. The great mass of the British people is well aware there is something rotten in the state of world affairs and is beginning to wonder whether in our support of France and our hesitation in recognising the immense potential force of modern Germany, we are not in danger of falling between two stools. Splendid isolation is a grand ideal, but like most ideals impossible of fulfilment. The principle of collective security is equally a pretty dream from which one awakes in the cold realisation of disillusionment. The whole of Europe is once again feeling its way towards some expression of the old-time balance of power. In the Foreign Office there have been tendencies since the beginning of the century to associate our policy with that of France, and one of our ex-Foreign Ministers has openly said that he loves France as a lover. There are not wanting indications in the great gaunt building overlooking St. James's Park that Germany is still regarded as the essential enemy.

There is still a tendency in certain quarters to regard

the Treaty of Versailles as the permanent basis of a peace settlement in regard to Germany. There is a strange lapse of memory in those same quarters concerning the treachery of Soviet Russia in the Great War and a tacit admission of the reasonableness, and even legality of the Franco-Soviet Pact, in regard to our external relations with Europe. To put it plainly Great Britain is in fair way of being used once more as an instrument for the benefit of France.

The question arises whether the British people exist for the benefit of France and whether the guarantee of French security is a real guarantee of peace in Europe. In spite of what is said in the confusion of Westminster there are millions of British people who feel that our close official relations with the unstable French Republic are positively dangerous and that our continued belief in the disintegrating League of Nations quite absurd. There are many who believe that the time is ripe for a new alignment in our foreign policy. Instead of thinking so much of French security the time has come to think of British security. Whenever the British Government begins to think of the British people at the expense of the French, the French press rises in fury and accuses us of the basest treachery. At the same time the French Government, since the war, has rarely gone out of its way to think of British security, and even the mutual assistance pact in the Mediterranean during the unhappy period of sanctions was only agreed to with the greatest reluctance. Contemporaneously, when the Germans denounced the last of the military clauses of Versailles and occupied the demilitarised zone, French statesmen came posthaste to London to demand with great heat what Great Britain was going to do about it.

Our relations with France since the war have always

been arranged in the French interest, and the mildest approach towards an understanding with Germany has invariably resurrected the screech of " Perfide Albion ". When Hitler declared after the Saar plebiscite that Germany had no territorial designs against France and wished to live at peace with his neighbour across the Rhine, Prime Minister Pierre Laval was derided by his countrymen for the crime of believing anything a German said, however sincere it might be. The age-long animosity between France and Germany continues to be sedulously fostered by the French authorities, and now that the Socialists have come into power under M. Blum, the fact that the Nazis reign in Germany is proof of German intransigeance. Perhaps if Germany was still suffering from Socialist misrule and the inflation of the mark, official French socialism might think differently of Germany's future intentions. But I doubt it. And side by side with this fantastic vendetta there has never been since the war any outward sign of aggressive intentions on the part of Germany towards France.

For ten years after the armistice the once great German Empire was reduced to a state of impotence and indigence unparalleled in the history of the modern world. The Treaty of Versailles prevailed in all its injustice and inhumanity, and there were millions of Frenchmen who thought that such a state of affairs could, and should, continue for ever. When Germany began to show belated signs of a revival of national self-respect she automatically became a menace to French security once more. It is always forgotten in Paris that French antagonism to Germany at this period was an important contributory factor to the final triumph of Hitlerism. The time came when France's ill-assorted allies in the Little Entente and her *rapprochement* with

Poland were not deemed a sufficient guarantee for her eternal security. There was always Locarno, of course, but that was incidental. A more material guarantee must be found and it was found in the Franco-Soviet understanding, that agreement which Germany deemed almost an act of hostility and which Great Britain was invited to accept with all its implications, presumably because it was for the benefit of France. It meant the end of the Locarno Pact in its original form, and Locarno was always looked on by the Quai d'Orsay as an essential instrument for the continuance of the security of France, already sitting pretty safe behind her two hundred miles of frontier fortifications.

It is my contention that the majority of the British people are quite weary of that interpretation of the Locarno Pact which makes it a treaty to guarantee French security. Equally are they averse from any attempts, like that of Stresa, to align a row of powers against a Germany that is attempting to throw off the more humiliating incidences of the Versailles Treaty. Our national sense of fair play enters into the thoughts of all at this crisis in world history. There are those of us who remember the Germans as men who fought a splendid fight against practically the massed forces of the world. There are many who contend that the Germans were unlucky losers of the war. It is known to all that the German army capitulated while still encamped on foreign soil and that the imposition of a military armistice in Berlin would have involved months of further warfare and the loss of hundreds of thousands of lives. Whatever our feelings of vengeance and chauvinism may have been in the summer of 1919 with the memories of war still unpleasantly near, there are few Englishmen who to-day are not secretly ashamed of the disgraceful severity of the Peace Treaty, with its Olympian excursions into reparations finance and its indefensible demand for the trial of the former German Kaiser. There were many who were secretly relieved when Germany came into the open and informed the world of her intention to re-arm. At least such a declaration brought some clarity to the confused thought of Europe. And when Hitler went further and occupied the Rhineland it was deemed a natural and quite understandable sequence. The day came when a busybody Member of Parliament asked Lord Cranbourne in the House of Commons by whose authority Heligoland was being refortified. Mr. Eden's spokesman answered wearily, " By the authority of no one." The laugh was on the private member.

It is a far cry from the flush of victory of the last months of 1918 to the stern realities of the last months of 1936 and the spring of 1937. The Great War was of short duration by comparison with the great conflicts of the past. It extended just over a little more than four short, albeit devastating, years of time. But it was a very different kind of war from those which had gone before and had endured for greater lengths of time. Hitherto wars had been for the most part merely elaborate manœuvres on the part of professional soldiers. It was rather like a game of chess, the movements of armies causing temporary inconvenience to the civilian population, but more often bringing unexpected prosperity in their wake. Even the Napoleonic conception of war did not greatly disturb the daily life of the ordinary individual, and in the supreme effort of Leipzig there were fewer military involved than in the latter-day most commonplace action on the Western front. The Great War set a new standard in human conflict. There was scarcely an individual among two-thirds of the population of the world who was not directly or indirectly involved. In the case of the active belligerent powers it is fair to say that every national in the course of the four and a quarter years of struggle had to fulfil, or deny, his obligations in some form or another. The Great War was as much a war of peoples as of armies. Its ultimate effects on the generation who suffered it and on those who had the misfortune to be born during it have yet to be assessed by the student not only of history but also of medical and biological science.

The task of the historian may be the easier, for much was written down in the elaborate documents which defined, but did not contribute to, a peace settlement. When the " cease fire " sounded at long last, treaties were made on the lines of age-long tradition. The intervention of the American President and his enunciation of his now long-forgotten fourteen points were the opportunities of the casuists who were ultimately responsible for the draft of the Treaty of Versailles. A series of ideals were flung to the political and diplomatic wolves. The Peace Settlement, which is the cause of all our latter-day troubles, is the result.

It was generally forgotten that the World War was just as much a matter of concern for the peoples of the earth as for the armies which went into the trenches and the politicians who stayed at home. The professional diplomat and politician carved up Europe with something like gusto according to their own interpretations of the new-fangled doctrine of self-determination. It is very much to be doubted whether the dancing statesmen of the Congress of Vienna enjoyed themselves more than the banquetting politicians of the Treaty of Versailles. There is this to be said in favour of the Vienna settlement of post-Napoleonic Europe, the nations were still comparatively inarticulate, and imported King or Grand Duke was regarded as an expensive necessity but still a necessity. The peace-mongers of Versailles, having as their brief the armistice of Rhetondes, and lacking the authority of a Waterloo, proceeded to ignore the lessons of history, and to carve up the continent of Europe, erecting republics where Metternich created kingdoms, entirely oblivious of the fact that the world had experienced an industrial as well as an educational revolution and that its inhabitants were no longer an unthinking, inchoate chorus of voices. In this year 1937 the world suffers from the academic tragedy of the Peace Settlement. The lessons of history may have been known to the treaty-mongers. If they were, it is certain they were never appreciated and certainly never interpreted. A war of peoples was settled by a treaty which would not even have met the sequel of a war of professional armies. At Versailles great crimes were committed by comparison with which the delinquencies of the Congress of Vienna were venial sins.

There are few to-day who do not realise that the Peace Settlement was conceived in an atmosphere of hate and brought to birth in a spirit of unreality. The Treaty of Versailles in its spirit of " Delenda est Carthago " stands as a sorry memorial to the ineptitude of those who endeavoured to make peace without a spirit of goodwill and a sense of fairplay to an honourable foe. It is the sad tale of that treaty in its gradual and inevitable disintegration, linked with the fact that a different line of policy in pre-war years on the part of our own government might have made a better and less troubled world, which ought to be thought on more and more as we look for a solution of our present discontents.

From the moment when the late King Edward VII

by reason of his tremendous charm and tact and encouraged by his Cabinet persuaded one Loubet, President of the Third Republic, that the hostility of France towards England was quite ridiculous, and based on a long period of inexplicable misunderstanding, it has become the fashion in England in certain quarters to regard France as the friend and Germany as the enemy. Before the war that great "peace-making" idea was sedulously fostered and to implement its charm a great exhibition—now used for dog racing—was organised at Shepherd's Bush in the west part of London. The new-fangled idea of a world Olympiad was even called on to support this great new move which was to perpetuate peace—for a matter of six years. The theatre was called into service to emphasise the imminence of the German menace and every schoolboy, tragically approaching years of manhood, was fed with cheap penny magazines, in which the ex-Kaiser was either burning London or else landing on the foreshore of Kent. The time came when that great lawyer and statesman, Lord Haldane of Cloan, was held to public ridicule because he once described Germany as his spiritual home: he was deemed almost a traitor because he attended the German manœuvres in his capacity of British war minister. The fact that he was the creator of the pre-war Territorial army and the moving force behind the organisation of a potential British Expeditionary Force in the event of a European war was forgotten in the skilfully fostered mass hysteria which thought only of the German menace without giving a thought to what might happen from association with its hereditary enemy. There is no doubt that in August 1914 the great majority of the British people had been worked up into a fever of apprehension in regard to the intentions of Germany. The invasion of Belgium seemed to justify the prophecies of our false prophets and the manhood of the Empire willingly marched to the most abortive struggle in the history of mankind. There were not wanting signs in the trenches—and even on the home front where food tickets replaced the inconvenience of high explosives—that long before the end of the war men were wondering what this great war was all about. The private soldier in the front line learned respect for his equal and opposite number on the other side of No Man's Land. Artillery bombardment made equals of all men.

In the light of eighteen years of "Peace" who can deny that it was not the most abortive struggle in history? If we search the authentic records of our unhappy human story, we can surely never find greater reasons for unhappiness than exist in the world to-day.

The hour has surely come when we ought in the highest sense of patriotism to face up to the great problems which affect Europe at the present time. On the one side we have the enemy who was thought by the politicians to be so soundly beaten in 1918 as to be content to live in a state of humiliation for generations to come—not so resurrected in the space of eighteen years as to be the strongest potential foe—or friend—in Western Europe.

On the other hand we have a completely changed set of circumstances in the interior politics of our great war-time ally, France. The history of France since the war has been troubled like that of her formidable neighbour across the Rhine. For many years there obtained a chauvinistic, even jingo, spirit in the country. That sense of overweaning confidence and arrogance has passed and been replaced by one of anxiety and political uncertainty. Industrial conditions have so deteriorated as to make France one of the least stable of all the great European powers from a labour and employment point of view. The new orientation of her foreign policy initiated by M. Laval, in the light of the so-called German menace, has become in its turn a menace to all those who attach importance to the conservation of existing social order. Pierre Laval extended the hand of eager friendship to M. Stalin because he was looking for some extra guarantee of French military and territorial security. The coming to power of M. Leon Blum has put an entirely different complexion on the Franco-Russian understanding. The thrifty peasant individualist of the broad acres of France has been asked to share his political destiny with the prodigal product of the Russian Soviet who believes in world revolution and who is only distantly interested in the continued existence of the Third Republic.

Here is indeed a new order of things in Europe. It would be idle for anyone in a position of responsibility to ignore the fact that hundreds of Englishmen to-day view with the gravest misgiving the close relations between France and Russia. How can this understanding be reconciled with the spirit of Locarno? Should a breach of a great European document be overlooked because it is innocent, inoffensive France who is acting in the interests of her precious security? Is France to be forgiven everything and granted most things just because she was invaded by the enemy twice in sixty years? And must it always be forgotten that for 800 years her armies endeavoured to fight on anybody else's territory except their own?—and generally succeeded.

As a result of the last war, Great Britain lost nearly one million of her sons: at the end of the conflict the resources of Empire were wellnigh exhausted. The

National Debt, in spite of tremendous contemporary efforts, reached astronomical proportions and its burden must be borne for generations to come. Almost the only tangible gain from this long sacrifice was a mandate over some of the German colonial possessions, and this doubtful asset may yet prove to be a liability unless something is done to satisfy the aspirations of Germany's rapidly-growing population.

When we went to war, with the banal words of " Tipperary " on our tongues, we were convinced that the Germans were very devils incarnate. We believed, we even enjoyed in a sadistic, war-mongering way, stories of fearful atrocities in Belgium. Some journalistic firebrand of the kind who stayed at home, described the enemy as Huns, and many with German names hurriedly assumed Anglo-Saxon cognomens lest they should be confused with the hated, despicable enemy. The time came, however, when the soldier, in the trenches—and he after all was the most important factor in the fighting—began to have a very wholesome respect for his opposite number on the other side of the wire. When the British Tommy dropped Hun and substituted Jerry as a description of the German, an event of European significance took place, although in the heat of battle it was deemed of no consequence. At the same time there were many incidents between the British and French troops which led the British soldier to wonder if our gallant allies were as single-minded and honest in purpose as the reported speeches of statesmen at home would have the world believe.

Most great movements and changes of viewpoint in this age have small beginnings and there are thousands of Britishers to-day who conceived dislike of the French for some act of characteristic pettiness in the back areas. Towards the end of the war there had grown up a feeling that the French people had no great love for the British soldier and that feeling of suspicion persists. The French do not like us : they envy us our greatness. How much they really admire us can readily be derived from the most casual study of the French press of all shades of opinion at any moment when the British Government forgets France for an hour or two and decides to think of its own interests.

By the time the armistice came, both British and Germans were thoroughly sick of the meaningless slaughter. The advance to the Rhine was made in a spirit of relief at the termination of gunfire rather than in a spirit of jubilation at conquest. There was no demonstration of hostility, and the posting of black sentries by the French on the bridge-head of Mayence disgusted the British soldier, just as it eternally offended the German of all parties. The British people and the serving soldier, once the war was over, were prepared to give a hand to the fallen foe. It was like the act of a man who had fallen out with a former friend, soundly beaten him and desired to shake hands afterwards to restore a modicum of goodwill. It was a point of view which was immediately appreciated by the German people and has never been forgotten. At no time in post-war German history, no matter which party has been in power, has there been any animosity against Great Britain among the mass of the German people and from time to time there have been evidences of overwhelming friendship. The attitude of France towards Germany has never varied either during the war or since. Germany was the hereditary enemy and there could be no settlement, nor security unless she was kept permanently grovelling in the dust. It is a point of view which has never made any great appeal to the British people, and now that France is going back to Russian alliances and is endeavouring to re-create a balance of power on the lines which led to the Great War, it makes even less appeal.

There are many who have wondered if a different line of policy since the beginning of the century might not have prevented the European war. The Entente Cordiale with its incongruous membership of democratic Great Britain, bourgeois France and autocratic Russia was hardly calculated to placate the German Empire which might rightly consider itself menaced on both sides and on the sea. If Germany took measures to counteract such menaces, there was a certain feasible excuse. Germany has always been accused of having caused the war by her menacing, arrogant attitude. Yet I have never found the virtues of a milk-white dove in the policy of St. Petersburg before the bombardment. Speculation is nearly always fruitless, but some belated satisfaction may come from the thought that if Great Britain and Germany, with their enormous resources, had been on friendly terms in 1914 instead of ranged against each other, the Great War might never have taken place. There could certainly not have been formed a counter-combination of anything approaching such strength and such potential influence for good.

In a world of doubt like that which exists at present, the necessity for an understanding with the great German people is more pressing than ever. Germany stands for ordered Government and in the modern wave of revolution and disruption may well be the bulwark of ordered Government in Northern Europe. It may be said that the Nazi Government is aggressive and bellicose. Such a statement is often made and it would appear to have some justification after intensive study of *Mein Kampf*. But in actual fact Germany has not taken any deliberately hostile steps beyond asserting her authority in the traditional Rhineland. Hitler has declared that Germany is no longer interested in the ownership of Alsace and Lorraine and that for many years to come her people will be far too occupied putting their own domestic affairs in order to embark on wars of conquest. Moreover, the friendship of Great Britain—a natural friendship incidentally—would always exercise a controlling and restraining influence in any excess of patriotism on the part of the Germans. The new Germany has a very wholesome respect for Great Britain and the British. It is a sense of respect born in the trenches and fostered by a spirit of fair play in peace. There is plenty of evidence to show that the German people would welcome an understanding with Britain. At the moment they are given room for doubt on account of our undefined attitude towards France. At one moment the Prime Minister pushes our frontier to the Rhine : the next he solemnly pronounces against Continental commitments. Even Mr. Baldwin cannot have it both ways. The refusal of the French to disarm was responsible for the rearmament of the Reich, a fact which must not be overlooked and which the taxpayer finding money for more battleships should also not overlook.

Any scheme of close co-operation between Great Britain and Germany would inevitably be greeted with a tirade of abuse from across the Channel. It would be pointed out in terms of scorn that Great Britain was safeguarding her own interests at the expense of those of France. One wonders what steps France would take to safeguard the interests of Great Britain if they endangered her own security in the remotest degree. That opinion is one of realism : and the age of sentiment is past—or ought to be.

It is time that we came to an end of this dilettante era in our foreign policy. Are we to continue to pander to the whims and fancies of France whenever called on? Is the tradition of Versailles to pursue its evil way until the world is plunged into another war? At present our repeated flirting with any new suggestion made by France, always in her own interests, and generally against Germany, is causing the gravest disquiet in Central Europe. And while our statesmen are so anxious about French security, they are apt to forget British security. I am one of those simple people who consider British security to be of some importance, and I am convinced that its surest guarantee can be found across the Rhine.

CHAPTER XII

FOOTNOTE TO HISTORY

EXAMINATION of the salient features of European history from the period of the Heptarchy in our own country and the establishment of the Empire of Charlemagne on the Continent quickly shows that there was always a close contact between the Teutonic peoples, of which the Anglo-Saxons who founded the English state were an offshoot, and the more numerous family of German tribes across the water. The Norman Conquest did not materially affect the mainsprings of blood and population of the island: the island language remained and the use of Norman French was confined to the court where it still has picturesque survivals. Our island institutions were based on those of the great German family. In both countries they emerged from a feudal system which was later to be developed on different lines, centralised in the King in England, divided among the princes in Germany. Both the Anglo-Saxon and German nations come from the same stock. This cannot be gainsaid. As history went on its way a difference of circumstance caused the two peoples to develop differently. For one thing our island position gave us a greater sense of independence and self-reliance—traits which are to be found in the individual Britisher to-day. The constant internecine quarrels in the Empire and the incidence of the feudal system destroyed those qualities in the German people and imbued in their spirit a herd instinct; created a nation always willing to obey. It has often been said that the Germans are a disciplined people. That is not quite true. Of all nations in the world the one that most readily lends itself to and accepts discipline is the British. Our ingrained idea of law and order is sufficient proof of what I say. The German characteristic is one of implicit obedience and submission to authority. In these two respects our nations differ, but in spite of the widely diverging histories of Great Britain and Germany, the two nations still have a great number of things in common. Both peoples are progressive : both peoples have inquiring minds : both rate achievement of more importance than imagination. How true this is may be judged from the dull way cooks in both countries prepare good food.

Now it would be difficult to find any point in common between the British and the French peoples. There are thousands of instances of personal friendship between individuals but it may fairly be said that the much vaunted Anglo-French amity is a diplomatic myth. Let us be quite frank about this. The French do not like us and for our part we do not care for them. The discerning traveller will always go to France, for France is beautiful and the French have so completely solved the art of eating, living, and sleeping well. But the Britisher in France is always faintly suspicious that the local inhabitant is either laughing behind his back or just waiting an opportunity to add up his bill on the wrong side. The phlegmatic bearing of the British makes no appeal to the volatile French, who moreover very rightly regard our refusal to learn any foreign language, except perhaps Hindustani or Urdu, as evidence of our arrogance and even boorishness. And indeed the Britisher in France is something of a boor, or even a Pharisee who goes abroad to realise how much better he is and returns to thank his own particular island God that he is not as other men are. A Briton in Germany has none of that maddening superiority that he has in France. I have often thought on my travels that the subtle change of attitude is due to the fact that in Germany a Briton does not altogether feel himself among foreigners: he unconsciously senses some degree of kinship with those around him. But France will always be a very, very foreign land.

The French, moreover, are an envious people who still dream of their former greatness and wonder what will happen if their birth-rate goes on declining. In spite of outward democracy and the masquerade of a republic, the French are a military people who love show and spectacle. The most resplendent monument in every town is to some great military captain. They are right to be proud of their military history for they have produced some of the greatest leaders of all time from Condé, Turenne, Napoleon, Davoust to Ferdinand Foch and Hubert Lyautey. It is idle to think of Germany as having military instincts without acknowledging the fact that France also has ideas of military prowess. The French also realise that in the fight for world Empire, Great Britain got the plums and left France the Sahara desert. Things might have been so different if Montcalm and Lally had prevailed in Canada and India. The French envy us our sea power and our immense wealth. And with an accepted superiority of intelligence, insight, logic, and imagination, they cannot understand why a race of dullards in plus-fours can make their viewpoint a world viewpoint when they are so minded. It is even more preposterous than the mass strength of the unthinking military machine on the other side of the Rhine which, at any rate, does not lack direction.

It may fairly be said that the fundamental divergences between Great Britain and France from a racial point of view, as exemplified in historical times, have been demonstrated on numerous occasions since the end of the Great War. In the face of the common foe there was a semblance of unity during the actual years of fighting, but after the signature of the infamous treaty of peace in the Hall of Mirrors at Versailles, the British people took a very different view of the beaten enemy. The French invasion of the Ruhr in search of ephemeral reparations caused a wave of disgust among the British people because it was a perpetuation of the war idea and the British people had had a sufficiency of such mentality. The French people came to regard Raymond Poincaré as a heaven-sent saviour : the British people looked on him as a menace to the peace of Europe. No matter what the political complexion of the prevailing government in France, the foreign policy of the Third Republic remains the same—hatred and fear of Germany, and to safeguard the frontiers, any measures, likely to be efficacious, are good and worthy measures. After the humiliating terms of the armistice and their subsequent endorsement by the Peace Treaty, one might have supposed that the country which was most entitled to live in a state of fear was Germany and that the German people might be justified in their actions by fear of the French. The British people today are not greatly moved by the bogey of the German menace even though the head of the Reich is Adolf Hitler. On the contrary they are greatly disturbed at the attitude of France in persistently refusing to recognise any good intentions on the part of the Germans and in clamouring for measures for her own safety quite oblivious of the fate of the rest of the world.

In the light of the present-day situation it is interesting to go back into history and realise that the Entente Cordiale was an unnatural alliance and that when we fought the Germans on a big scale in 1914 we fought against our hereditary allies, as I have said, almost for the first time for 800 years. Our traditional feud with France is of much longer duration than the feud between France and Germany. It dates from the period of the Norman Conquest when the successful invasion of Duke William established a direct connection between our island and the Continent. To maintain his Duchy the usurping King had to fight not only Philip of France but also his own sons and feudatories. In fact, his death was directly due to his horse stumbling on burning cinders at the siege of Mantes. His successor Rufus had to spare time from his hunting in order to fight his brother in Normandy, and Henry the First spent three years away from England fighting France and Anjou for the possession of his continental dominion. Such wars continued intermittently for many years. Henry the Second fought in France from 1158 to 1163 and the whole story of the period is rendered sordid by the treachery of royal sons and brothers aided and abetted by the coeval Kings of France. By the end of the twelfth century the greater part of modern France was under the domination of the Angevin Kings, their absolute dominions consisting of Normandy, Maine and Anjou, and their dependencies including Brittany, Poitou, Aquitaine, Gascony, and Toulouse. These wars were of a purely dynastic and feudal character. They were fought in a spirit of personal aggrandisement and had little to do with the feelings of yeoman or serf in England. But the day came within a century or so when the wars assumed more national proportions and battles were fought between the armies of the two countries in a spirit of animosity that continued for generation after generation.

It was perhaps the long period of war with the Angevin and Plantagenet Kings which first began to bring the idea of the usefulness of union home to the people of France. The wars marked the beginning of the breakdown of the feudal system and the greater authority of the French King over the powerful nobility. A long period was to elapse before anything approaching unity was established, but the seeds had been sown. While the long struggle was in progress, the French part of the great Empire of Charlemagne had been almost completely divorced from the Empire which had become partially Germanised by the first three Ottos. The ancestors of Charlemagne were undoubtedly Franks, but the sympathies of this Titan of the Middle Ages were undoubtedly inclined to the German part of his vast dominions. He may be claimed for the Pantheon of the French, but he more rightly belongs to the Valhalla of the Teutons. There is no need to enter into the complicated story of the division of the Empire. It may suffice to say that by the period of the Crusades the Emperor was to all intents and purposes a German monarch whose will prevailed over his hundreds of princelings in Central Europe, with just that authority that corresponded to the individual who wore the imperial crown. The kingdom of Francia by reason of the aggressive wars of the Angevin Kings of England had been reduced to a shadow and the day was yet far away when the French King could talk on terms of equality with the elected ruler of the Empire. But the struggle between England and France continued and was frequently characterised by acts of base perfidy. And that perfidy was not always confined to English men-at-arms. In fact, there were many instances of the basest treachery on the part of the French Kings, and Bishop Stubbs was once moved to write of the cautious self-preservation practised by the French leaders in contrast with the knightly prowess of their German contemporaries within the Empire. He mentions the repeated failure to maintain the knightly word on the part of the French Kings as indicative of the more chivalrous spirit of the German or Teutonic peoples than the French. He even goes so far as to say that both the English and German Kings, as in the time of Tacitus, kept their hold on popular imagination for deeds of arms and leadership.

The development of England and France at this period followed very different lines, the French state becoming more autocratic, the English leaning towards an elementary Parliamentary system exemplified by the long struggles of the thirteenth century until the final establishment of the Model Parliament by Edward the First, rightly called the " English Justinian ", in 1295. The English Kings did homage to the King of France for their French possessions in accordance with feudal usage, but the first part of the fourteenth century saw the two countries at war again and this time the conflict lasted for a hundred years. The battles of Crécy and Poitiers and the capture of Calais make the reign of Edward the Third renowned in the history of English chivalry, and the English King assumed the title of King of France. In the next century Henry the Fifth triumphed at Agincourt in 1415 and five years later was acknowledged Regent of France by the French Court and married the King's daughter. The power of England was so great at this time as to rival that of the Emperor Sigismund, and had he lived Henry the Fifth might have been the leader of Christendom and reduced

France to an appendage of his island kingdom. The sequel was very different, for in the next reign there rose the inspired figure of Joan of Arc and the collapse of British rule in France. The proud possessions of Henry the Fifth were reduced to a few coast towns and a small district in Normandy around Bayeux. In the next century when the French recaptured Calais, our last foothold on the Continent disappeared.

We approach the period of the Reformation, that great religious upheaval which was to prove an age-long link between the English and German peoples. The significance of the Reformation must never be overlooked in a study of the relations of Great Britain and Germany and their reactions with France. The Emperor Maximilian had long waged war with France, and his grandson, the redoubtable Charles the Fifth, who had inherited the Spanish dominions of Ferdinand and Isabella, found himself ranged against the power of the now strong French monarchy under Francis the First. The struggle was more a war to the death between French and Spanish, rather than German influences, but while Europe was distracted by the contest Friar Luther nailed his theses to the church door of Wittenberg and the Reformation had begun. It is doubtful, if there had been peace in Europe, if the Lutherans in Germany and the Calvinists in Geneva could have flourished and prevailed. Likewise it is doubtful if Henry the Eighth would have openly defied Rome in the way he did if he had not seen the reformed doctrines rapidly gaining ground in Europe. (It must be remembered that only in 1521 the Pope had granted Henry the dignity of "Defender of the Faith" for having written a pamphlet against Luther.) But there would have been a bitter struggle, for the idea of reform was not new in England. Wycliffe had already been arraigned for heresy and Wycliffe was the true predecessor of Huss just as Huss was the mentor of Luther. The spirit of the Reformation symbolises in many ways a phase in the character for intellectual independence which was to be synonymous with Great Britain, Germany and other Northern countries for a long time to come.

The Reformation brought England and that part of the Empire, which is now for the most part modern Germany, into close contact. The more or less universal adoption of the reformed faith by the English after the severance of relations with Rome by Henry the Eighth and the divorce of Catherine of Aragon was a source of inspiration to the reformers, struggling for power in Northern Germany, who had just drawn up the Confession of Augsburg to which Charles the Fifth could not subscribe. By the time Luther died in 1546 the Reformation had made great progress both in England and on the Continent, and the Counter-Reformation failed to make much headway except in Austria which was won back to the Roman Catholic Faith. Scotland became Calvinist and John Knox preached at Geneva. The growing Puritan party in England were able to join in spiritual friendship with the Lutheran church in Germany.

But the end was not yet. The upheaval in religious beliefs had inevitably led to war. The French people were just as much affected by the new reformed doctrines as were the Germans and English and for nearly forty years the powerful Huguenots fought against their Roman Catholic adversaries. The Massacre of St. Bartholomew was but one incident in the long struggle. Nevertheless, when Henry of Navarre decided that Paris was " worth a mass " the religious wars virtually came to an end with a grant of religious freedom which lasted for nearly a hundred years until the infamous Louis the Fourteenth deprived the Huguenot protestants of their civil rights by revoking the Edict of Nantes. One result of the wars of religion, however, was to consolidate France into a strong military and commercial power and prepare the ground for that policy of aggression initiated by Richelieu and carried on for nearly two centuries.

A very different circumstance obtained in Germany where the wars of religion after the more or less abortive counter-reformation reduced the country to misery and ruin and left the Empire a miserable shadow of its former self. The Thirty Years' War, with all its vileness and tragedy, murder and rapine, is known to all students. It was left to a Swedish king to save the Protestant cause in Germany from the first great assault. It was given to Richelieu who has been aptly described as " Cardinal of the Huguenots " to make a military alliance with Sweden and use French Catholic forces to prevent the obliteration of the Reformed Faith from Northern Germany. It was an indication of the realistic policy of the France that was arising to such great strength in Europe. An alliance with the Hapsburgs and Spain to annihilate the Protestants of the north might have ultimately led to a menace of the French position, a threat to her security. Richelieu could not tolerate such a thought and so threw all his influence on the Protestant side although he was a cardinal prince of the Church. It is one of those curious ironies of history that the subsequent Peace of Westphalia was made possible by the foreknowledge of French intervention on a large scale, interference which was merely another milestone in the long history of the feud between Hapsburg and Bourbon which dated from the reign of Charles the Fifth and Francis the First. The settlement also brought to France the possession of Metz and a goodly part of Alsace and thus created a grave problem for future generations.

Many historians have endeavoured to interpret this intervention of Richelieu in the Thirty Years' War as evidence of the persistent "Protestant Policy" of France. Actually it was the policy of an astute opportunist but it served to convince Oliver Cromwell, now head of the Protectorate after the execution of King Charles the First, of the pacific and high-minded intentions of France. In his foreign policy Cromwell threw all his forces into the scale against Spain when it came to any foreign issue, and made overtures to France. Perhaps he was actuated by the fact that the exiled young Prince Charles was a frequent visitor to France and could be made a quite embarrassing weapon by the French Government if they were not kept in a sweet frame of mind. There was no evidence as yet to show the true nature of French intentions and Louis the Fourteenth had not yet given a taste of his fanatical Roman Catholic quality and his boundless territorial ambitions. Cromwell might have changed his mind if he had lived a little longer. But he died, and the Restoration came and Louis the Fourteenth interpreted his friendship for England by offering an army to Prince Charles (afterwards Charles the Second—a secret Papist just as his brother James, Duke of York, was an open believer) to restore Roman Catholicism in England.

A great deal of tremendous significance happened in the last half of the seventeenth century in the light of subsequent history (yes, indeed, of importance in the history of our own times). For one thing we begin to feel the influence of Brandenburg (or Prussia). We watch the creation of a complete personal autocracy in France and the business of royalty made into a "great, noble and delightful trade". We see England survive the Restoration as a Protestant state and prepare herself under the leadership of William of Orange to take a leading part in stemming the aggression of France.

Charles the First's interpretation of the Divine Right of Kings was a poor thing by comparison with the beliefs of Louis the Fourteenth. The *Grand Monarque* took his office of kingship very seriously. As Mr. H. A. L. Fisher writes in his illuminating *History of Europe*:

> Royalty was a divine office (to Louis XIV) entrusted by the providence of God to a divine agent, whose qualifications, as embodied in himself, merited, so he believed, the exalted trust.—Duty always came first, duty conceived in the grand manner, as labour for great and spectacular ends ministering to the splendour of France and the renown of its sovereign; for the two were identical.

Louis the Fourteenth did not beat about the bush when it came to his intentions. He was a royal advocate of aggression and a fanatical believer in the Roman Church. He carried out his ideas of religious intolerance by revoking the Edict of Nantes and so driving tens of thousands of France's most useful citizens from their homes to carry their habits of industry and thrift to other countries. When it came to war he was quite frank about his ambitions. He wished to emulate the great French soldiers of the past. "Perhaps to surpass some undertakings which they deemed impracticable. Luxemburg, Namur, Mons, Ghent, and Brussels were ever before me." He once said it was quite incidental to him that the forty years of war in which he involved his country were ruinous and ultimately devoid of result. He left behind him a vast monument in stone—the Palace of Versailles. Is history justified of all its ironies?

There is no great need to enter into details of the wars of William the Third and Anne against the forces of the *Grand Monarque*. The English and Dutch armies under the unimaginative leadership of the former Stadtholder fared indifferently well, but it is noteworthy that the campaign was fought on foreign soil so far as the French were concerned. When it came to the more expansive efforts of the war of the Spanish Succession, the arms of the French extended to the remoter parts of Bavaria, where the signal victory of Blenheim was lost and won and the other great victories of Marlborough were achieved in the Low Countries. No invasion of France of any consequence took place, but even so the French still sing a military lullaby, "*Malbrouck s'en va t'en guerre.*"

The history of the eighteenth century is the history of Franco-British hostility. As the century grew in years the new Prussian state went from strength to strength. At the same time our Hanoverian Kings in their maintenance of their German dominions brought the British people into close contact with the German people. Our latter-day ideas of gentility and sensibility may not endorse the forcible seizure of Silesia by Frederick the Great, but it is significant that in the subsequent wars Great Britain was allied with Prussia against France. It was in the campaign of the war of the Austrian Succession on the field of Dettingen in 1743 that a King of England last took the field as the head of his army and the battle not only took place in an invaded Germany but was also fought against the French. A year later a storm dispersed a French fleet which had assembled in the Channel for the express purpose of assisting the Young Pretender in the rebellion which we now know as the "Forty-Five" and which was designed to bring down the reigning house of England.

In 1756, at the outbreak of the Seven Years' War, George the Second made an alliance with Prussia, and while Frederick the Great was campaigning on all his frontiers Great Britain was able to lay the foundations of empire. It ought never to be forgotten that if it had not been for the heroism of the great Prussian King, the conquest of Canada by General Wolfe might never have taken place. In much the same way the victories of Clive in India and the capture of Madras from the French could never have happened.

Under Frederick the Great the Prussian state became a factor of the first importance in the polity of Europe. Whatever may be the judgment of history as to the character of this great soldier and pseudo-scholar, it ought never to be forgotten that the struggle he undertook in welding his people in a stern régime of blood and iron had also its significance in the creation of the British Empire. Although the Treaty of Paris of 1763 which terminated the Seven Years' War was in a measure lenient to France, the French did not forget and their resentment against Great Britain found a most curious expression in the American War of Independence. At that time France was governed in a manner befitting the worst traditions of the feudal system. A peasant might well be imprisoned for shooting pigeons that were eating up his grain—and livelihood—supposing that the pigeons belonged to the local seigneur. The least offensive critic of the oligarcical system could be thrust into obloquy by the issue of a *lettre de cachet.* Anything approaching a democratic parliament had not been summoned for scores of years and the bad, mad tradition of the palace of Versailles was maintained in all its pettiness of nobility and importunity of duns. Yet it was this same reactionary system which became indignant on account of the woes of New England. The day came when an enthusiastic but almost inarticulate nobleman, the Marquis de la Fayette, led a band of swashbuckling aristocrats to fight on behalf of the American rebels whose ideas were diametrically opposed to the least conception that ever emerged from the brain of a Bourbon. French intervention in the American War of Independence must always be an enigma to the historian. The day of the " Sans Culottes " had not yet come. After all the final peace treaty was signed at Versailles! Some Americans still think their patriotic souls migrate to Paris for burial and the Statue of Liberty continues to guide wandering ships to the safety of New York Bay. But one may wonder if there would have been such great enthusiasm for the subversive ideas of Washington and Franklin if there had not existed in the France of those days an animosity against Great Britain which transcended all ideas of what was then regarded as a state of established order. Anyone who imagines that contemporary France was acting in a spirit of goodwill and friendliness towards the rebel colonists when her own system of government was a negation of both, qualifies for the pillory of ridicule. France intervened in the American war because of her hostility to England. And in so doing she contributed to a considerable extent to the loss of the Eastern States to the British Empire.

Within a year or two of the loss of the American Colonies, England and Europe were faced with the problems arising out of the French Revolution. This great revolution, which had such a far-reaching result on the subsequent history of mankind, gave birth to a war and in that way was very unlike the latter-day Russian Revolution with which it has sometimes been compared. The Bolshevist uprising was made possible by the sufferings of war. The French Revolution was caused by sufferings in time of peace.

But even when the *ancien régime* was overthrown, the temper of the French people did not change in regard to England and the liberalism of the revolutionaries confined itself to the better safety of the newly-formed French Republic. Rosseau may have written that man was born free and that everywhere he was in chains. That was a general statement. It implied universality. But the French Revolution, when it came, was almost entirely a national movement and a national movement of the most pernicious kind when looked on with the eyes of contemporary states. To-day the aims and attainments of the French Revolution, as distinct from the Reign of Terror, would be deemed to be very modest experiments in social change, but the threat to established order at that period was enough to cause the revolutionary wars in which the ill-equipped French soldiers not only defended their frontiers with success against superior forces but also managed to carry the war into the enemy's country and impose the first of many humiliating treaties on the kings of Europe.

The age-long feud between England and France came to a climax during the revolutionary and Napoleonic wars. The conflict between the France of Louis the Fourteenth and England was of small moment by comparison. From the very first the French revolutionaries were abusive of England although England at that time rejoiced in the most democratic institutions of the world, those of the newly-established American Republic not even excepted. The British Government were uncompromising in their attitude towards the Republic and ten days after the execution of Louis the Sixteenth on the *place de la Concorde* the French Republic declared war on England. France is now very prone to suggest that she is not the aggressor. But in most instances in history France has been the maker of war and the menace to peace. The war which began on February 1, 1793, lasted, with two short intermissions, until the final victory of Waterloo in the summer of 1815. The people of England did not want the war when it began. In fact, for the first year or so the conflict was most unpopular and the Government found it necessary to suppress agitation by suspending the Habeas Corpus Act. But when the French armies became a real menace to England, then the people accepted the struggle without demur and fought to the bitter end. Certain it is that when Napoleon, first as revolutionary general and afterwards as First Consul, galvanised the ragged armies of France into a formidable military weapon there was no hesitation on the part of the British people in ruthlessly carrying on a war which threatened contemporary liberty.

All the wars of the Empire were aggressive wars of conquest and spoliation. The Emperor was a professional soldier with unlimited ambitions and he endeavoured to carry out his scheme for a great French continental empire without paying undue respect to scruple. He might well have succeeded if it had not been for the obstinate resistance of Great Britain, a resistance rendered possible by those precious twenty miles of water between Dover and Cape Grisnez. But that when the army of Boulogne was formed there was dismay and alarm in England is proved by the existence of the little round Martello towers on the south coast, little strong points which anticipated the pill-boxes of the Ypres salient by a hundred years.

The whole of our resources were thrown into the struggle with Bonaparte and the spectre of a successful invasion haunted the whole population. How great was the hatred and hostility between the two peoples may be gathered by an examination of contemporary caricatures published on both sides of the Channel. Never in the history of mankind has the brush of the political artist been dipped deeper in vulgarity and violence. No insult was too poisonous or suggestive to offer the French and the French replied with examples of native wit that were equally crapulous.

From the very first Napoleon realised that his dreams of continental domination could not be made substantial unless England was subdued. After the victory of Trafalgar, he had perforce to abandon hopes for command of the seas and an invasion of Kent on a large scale. He found a certain solace on that glorious morning when Soult led the line to victory on the field of Austerlitz. Afterwards he worked hard to find means with which to afflict England. His enemies by land were easy to subdue and thrones went toppling over, although some of them had had an existence of five hundred years. There was a time when England was the only enemy and the kings and rulers of Europe were edging each other out of the way in order to be first to greet the eye of the man who in England was always called the " Corsican Ogre ". Napoleon knew that the only way to get at the traditional nation of shopkeepers was through trade and in his Berlin Decrees and his complicated Continental System he imposed a formidable sanction against the commerce of Great Britain. There is no doubt that Great Britain suffered gravely from the effects of the Continental System before it broke down under pressure of its own weight. But she was able to keep the seas and maintain the struggle. Her fleets went about the world annexing little bits of territory which seemed desirable. And her army was landed in the Peninsula to inform Napoleon that England was also capable of waging war against him on land. In the end the Peninsular campaign proved to be one of the decisive factors in bringing about the defeat of Napoleon. The end of the long struggle is well known to all. It was English determination which kept the spirit of resistance to Napoleon alive through all those difficult years. If it had not been for the moral encouragement given by us to distressed Austria and humiliated Germany the battle of Leipzig could never have taken place. The Germans know the debt they owe to British statesmen at this period. They know how the existence of a powerful potential friend and enemy of France urged the patriots of Stein and Hardenburg to greater efforts towards the ultimate liberation of the German people. It was Great Britain which was largely responsible for finally putting an end to the French menace. The soil of France was invaded and Paris was twice captured. These military measures are sometimes held up by the apologist for France to show how much she has suffered in history. But what of the invasions of Europe by the revolution and the first empire? The devastation wrought by the French wars extended to the walls of the Kremlin as well as to those of Lisbon. For something like twenty years the French carried fire and sword all over Europe in their wars of aggression. That fact ought not to be overlooked.

The history of the nineteenth century is largely the history of the Liberal experiment. In the course of its progress a new Italy arose, unified for the first time, and Germany advanced towards an Imperial status of a far more coherent kind than had ever been found in the troubled story of the Holy Roman Empire. The new Europe was planned and that plan continued almost intact except in regard to the gradual expulsion of the Turks from Eastern Europe, until the outbreak of the Great War. The various wars against the Turks brought no territorial advantages to the new Germany and by adding to the extent of the Dual Monarchy of Austria and Hungary merely aggravated the problems of that unhappy combination. France underwent a series of experiments in Government of an almost kaleidoscopic kind, ranging from the antediluvian theories of the restored Bourbons to the umbrella bourgeoisie of Louis Philippe, from the stark realism of Napoleon as President and to the *opéra bouffe* of the Second Empire. Out of such things was the Third Republic born. Great Britain spent most of the century fighting Colonial wars and by the end of the century had brought more than a quarter of the world's surface under the protection of the Union Jack. By the time Europe awoke to the fact that Africa was theirs, except for the formality of carving it up, Great Britain had taken most of the parts that were worth possessing. The forces of Europe took a new alignment. The accepted ascendancy of Austria in German affairs received its death-blow on the battlefield of Koniggratz and thenceforward the biggest factor in German history was the kingdom of Prussia.

The foreign policy of England was directed towards the expulsion of the Turks from Europe and the checking of the power of Russia. For that reason a British army was sent to the Crimea side by side with the armies of France. For the first time in history British and French troops fought side by side in a first-class European conflict. But that co-operation did not disclose any great change in opinion between the two peoples. Almost before the smoke had faded away over the citadel of Sebastopol, there were grave misgivings and in a few years, in spite of the strange friendship of Queen Victoria for the Empress Eugenie, each move on the part of the French Government was viewed with grave doubt by the British Government. At the same time the new Germany and Great Britain grew closer together and this movement of friendship was emphasised by the marriage of the daughter of the Queen with the heir to the throne of Prussia.

The hereditary conflict between the French and Germans found warlike expression in 1870. The French have since ceaselessly complained of the ruthless invasion of their country by the German army and the subsequent peace. But in this connection one must remember that when the French troops marched to battle their cry was "À Berlin" and their staff officers were equipped with maps of German territory only. Furthermore, when Bismarck imposed his treaty on the French people it was not a treaty impossible of fulfilment like that which the Allies, largely at the behest of France, imposed on the Germans at Versailles in 1919. In fact, French peasants by delving into their stockings hidden in their attics were able to produce enough money to pay the indemnity of five milliards of francs in the matter of a year or two. It would have taken Germany several centuries to have found the reparations demanded by the treaty-mongers of Versailles. The French Emperor had at one time hoped of collaboration of England against Germany but he looked in vain. In those days there was no great desire to fight a kindred people for the benefit of a nation which had shown herself conspicuously hostile to our interests in the past.

Before the year 1900 had come to end a dramatic

century, France was the victim of intense Anglophobia. Coming late into the struggle for Africa she had sent her explorers and pioneers to the dark Continent and there was the celebrated incident of Fashoda. Colonel Marchand was obliged to surrender to perfidious Britain, territory which he had been the first to explore, and indignation ran high against us in France. Our prosecution of the Boer War did not assist matters and France thought of increasing her fleet to prepare against the British menace to her security. And it was in this lively atmosphere that the Entente Cordiale was born. It is nearly always forgotten that this alliance with France, for ever associated with the name of Edward the Peacemaker (although actually it was the work of Delcassé, Jules Cambon, and the Balfour Cabinet), was brought about because of the fear in Great Britain of continued French hostility. Perhaps it was a mutual fear. But it was definitely a fear. It was more or less an alliance with an enemy. In the excess of emotion it was hailed as a great step forward. But there were wise men in England, among them the late Lord Rosebery. He viewed with alarm this drastic departure from the traditional foreign policy of England. He noted that in the negotiations with France, Germany had not been consulted and Germany had the most powerful army in Europe and Germany had always been our friend, if not our ally in the past. He predicted that the Entente Cordiale with France would inevitably one fine day lead England into a war with Germany.

That prediction came true as a suffering world knows to its grave discontent. The war took place and ended in the exhaustion of the enemy and the imposition of a deplorable peace. Within a few years it was recognised that the campaign had been fought in vain and that the peace treaty had left behind it the causes of grave misunderstanding and the seeds of great wrath to come. And to-day we are still drifting, flirting with France, becoming maudlin over Geneva, trying to piece together the scraps of Locarno, knowing in our hearts that Germany is once more a great and decided nation and yet refusing to forget the lesson of the Entente Cordiale, that instrument of peace which led to the greatest war in the story of mankind.

CHAPTER XIII

STONING AT VERSAILLES

THIS book is a plea for a better understanding between Great Britain and Germany. I have endeavoured to give my impressions of the Third Reich. How difficult has been that upward path to recovery is known to all who have followed European events at first hand since the war. The fact that the Germany which was obliged to sign the Treaty of Versailles made any recovery at all is the cause of lasting astonishment to many, so vindictive were the terms of peace, so humiliating to the pride of a gallant enemy. To-day there can be no doubt as to the progress which has been made in Germany in the last three years. Germany is once more a great power. She is likely to be an even greater one. The complete change in the outlook and hopes of the German people is a proof of their tremendous heart and power of recuperation. It has been an even greater achievement than the recovery of Prussia under Stein and Hardenburg after the battle of Jena. At the same time the new Reich offers the hand of friendship to Great Britain, whose Government is apparently more concerned in carrying on military staff talks with France. It is forgotten that the policy of France since the war has been one of self-interest and that the only idea which is always present in the minds of the French Foreign Office officials is the inviolability of France. No matter who sinks, France must swim, and if a powerful country like Great Britain can be relied on to help in the safeguarding of French security so much the better. The fact that Great Britain has everything to lose and precious little to gain through such an arrangement is calmly ignored by the Quai d'Orsay. It is for the benefit of France. It is in the nature of a sacred trust. And the propaganda goes forth unceasingly that France is the friend, not Germany. Did you ever hear of one Codlin, and one Short?

Post-war history in the light of the relations of the victorious powers with Germany makes sad and sorry reading. The treaty was signed eighteen years ago this summer. The tragedy of Europe was that few people troubled to read it. It is true to say that once the war was over the great mass of the British people were anxious to return to work, try to live at peace with the world, and see how much could be repaired of the havoc wrought by four years of war.

In France, however, a spirit of hostility was carefully fostered. The French army was kept in being while ours was rapidly demobilised. Return to normal conditions was purposely hampered by the Government in case the civil population should forget the victory and the chance of revenge it offered. Propaganda was carried on *ad nauseam* concerning the devastated areas and unhappy martyred Pas de Calais. (Most of it already in process of being adopted by "rich" towns of England, many of which are now suffering from an even greater devastation than was ever produced by shellfire.) At the least provocation M. Raymond Poincaré stumped the country, emphasising the enormities of the enemy and keeping alive the feeling of hate. It was this same attitude which led to the famous outburst of one of Germany's delegates when he declared in the open conference, "We know what hate we encounter here." And the spirit of goodwill was hardly encouraged by the posting of Senegalese sentries by the French on the Rhine bridgeheads in their area of occupation and the command that Rhineland maidens should enter the military brothels to satisfy the desires of the black soldiery—an act which has never been forgotten or forgiven.

There is no need to examine in any great detail the various absurdities and anachronisms of the Treaty of Versailles. The settlement, if it had been drawn up expressly for the purpose of sowing the seeds of trouble to come, could not have been more skilfully contrived. It was a treaty drawn up largely by the French which had for its object the subjection of the German people for ever. Such a peace was bound one day to bring about its own destruction and rouse the subject people into revolt against it. One can only wonder why the German people delayed so long before throwing off their bonds. In the end it needed the inspiration of Adolf Hitler to capture the nation's imagination and make it realise its strength.

How grotesque was the peace treaty is well evidenced by the financial section. The reparations clauses make astonishing reading. Their compilation was the opportunity for financiers and experts to indulge in monetary astronomy. At one time in the lobbies of the conference there was mention of £50,000 millions as the minimum figure Germany would be asked to pay. The fact that it was doubtful whether there was so much money available in the whole world at the time was passed over, for the peace conference was wrapped in an atmosphere of unreality at all times. Even the Hughes-Cunliffe Committee estimated total reparations at £24,000 millions, and in 1919 hard-headed American experts put the figure at £13,000 millions. Incidentally, this was the figure fixed on at the Boulogne Conference twelve months after the treaty was signed. The story of the reparations settlements is devastating in its lack of purpose. Eight months after Boulogne, the experts lopped off another £2,000 millions from the sum total. This left some £11,300 millions outstanding. The Fehrenbach Cabinet in Berlin, who were perhaps better judges of German financial resources than any outside government, said they could perhaps pay £1,500 millions at a pinch. This suggestion caused a ring of derisive laughter in Paris, but I remember that a few weeks afterwards the experts solemnly announced they had decided that £6,000 millions would meet the case. Where, oh, where were the ciphers bandied about so freely in the conference lobbies? It is interesting to note that in England our chancellors had long since ceased to bank on reparations payments in making their budgetary estimates. The French did and we all know what happened to the franc.

It is instructive to recall the attitude which was taken by the British representatives on the Reparations Commission towards their French colleagues in those days. For six long years, from 1919 to 1925, Great Britain's delegation was led by Sir John Bradbury, now the first Lord Bradbury, and the official who achieved universal fame as the signatory of our wartime paper money. Sir John occupied extensive offices in the Hôtel Astoria, the hotel overlooking the Arc de Triomphe, from the roof of which the ex-Kaiser had planned to witness the triumphal entry of his army into Paris. His huge frame, expansive smile, tortoiseshell-rimmed spectacles, and carelessly worn clothes, became part of the political landscape of the French capital. He had none of the engrained fears of the Press common to most Treasury officials. In fact, newspapermen were often his confidants. At regular intervals he invited Paris correspondents to have a talk and these talks were always entertaining and often illuminating. Long before the French went into the Ruhr—and so committed the greatest blunder in modern history—he was often reduced to despair. Whenever he suggested a spirit of compromise he drew down on his head the reproaches, even vituperation, of his French colleagues. His mildest suggestion of some minor concession to a Germany he knew full well could not pay the fantastic sums asked for, was greeted with loud hints at traditional English treachery towards her friends. When Sir John received us, he would sit well back in his chair and remark that what he was about to say was actually based on appreciation of realities, but he was certain that it would not please his "French friends". And believe it or not there were responsible officials in the French Finance Ministry at that time who sincerely believed that Germany could pay all that was demanded of her in the reparations clauses of the Treaty of Versailles. They would point out that the treaty admitted Germany's incapacity to pay for everything. That had been a tremendous concession on the part of the victorious Allies. All Germany had been asked to pay for was compensation for damage done during what was officially described as the period of "belligerency". Those same officials were convinced that the German Government, as per treaty, could make a special issue in bearer bonds to an equivalent amount payable in gold marks on May 1, 1926, to account for the complete restoration of Belgium. Any attempt on the part of the British representatives to disturb that illusion was regarded as little removed from treachery.

For six difficult years Lord Bradbury tried his best to moderate French demands and he incurred a certain amount of odium. It must not be forgotten that it was the contumacy of the French in the matter of reparations that disturbed the world financial situation and prepared the way for the world crisis. Lord Bradbury's attitude was frequently contrasted with that of the British representative in the Rhineland, Lord Kilmarnock, an avowed Francophile, who, although obliged to say "No" to the more extreme demands of the French delegates on the Rhineland commission, would dearly have liked to have said "Yes". Lord Bradbury was in no sense partisan. He merely acted in accordance with the dictates of common sense and his own unrivalled knowledge of international finance.

Germany at this time was in a deplorable state. There was not enough money available to feed the population let alone set the wheels of production in motion. The mark—it was before the great inflation—exchanged at something like 5,000 to the pound. The straps of railway carriage windows were made of compressed paper. The few motor-cars which still kept the streets had tyres composed of anything but rubber. Food was scarce and soap was often unprocurable. The blackcoated worker had frequently to walk bare-foot to his office desk. Normally respectable girls, with their lovely flaxen hair, were willing to prostitute themselves at so much a month—a pound or two—in order to be assured of reasonable food and shelter. In many parts locomotives of railway trains depended on wood fuel and for years their speed was restricted to something in the neighbourhood of thirty miles an hour as a reminder that Germany lost the war and was not as other countries. At the same time

1937 VERSION OF GERMAN ROAD AND MOTOR COACH

[face p. 250

the treaty confiscated the German mercantile marine. Huge ships had been given to the Allied powers as compensation for war losses. They were put on the world ocean routes with the result that home ship-building practically ceased and the industry on both Clyde and Tyne is only just beginning to recover. Many of the coalfields of Silesia were lost to Germany for ever and the Saargebiets until 1935. The scrapping of the munition and aircraft factories threw tens of thousands on the unemployment market and the abandonment of conscription accentuated a labour question which had always been difficult to cope with. Moreover, Germany had no longer any colonies or territorial outlet in which to find homes for her surplus population or new markets, and at home she had been deprived of rich areas which had been handed over to various states, one of which had taken no part in the war at all.

Nearly every page of the treaty contains some evidence of the ferocity of feeling which was engendered by the atmosphere of the peace conference and carefully fostered by the French Government. It is all the more tragic when one thinks that this Carthaginian peace was directed against a people who were for the most part broken in spirit and had been reduced to penury. When the full significance of the treaty was revealed to them there was a natural revulsion and from that moment intelligent Germans who had been merely the victims of the war machine began to wonder why they had been singled out for such obvious injustice and aggression. From that spirit of wonder grew the present spirit of revolt. And the flames of resistance were constantly fanned by abortive attempts to impose the letter of the settlement. I travelled in Germany just after the war a good deal and I have always contended that, in the state of mind which existed among these crestfallen and humiliated people, if a reasonable treaty had been imposed by generous victors then Germany would be working at this moment in close co-operation with the rest of the world, that universal disarmament would have been accomplished long ago and Europe would have been spared the series of crises which have marked the post-war period. In the interval between the signing of the armistice and the peace treaty, death and desolation stalked the land. The blockade perpetuated the universal misery and the return of the army made the unemployment situation wellnigh intolerable.

A commentator wrote very truly of this period:

> Everything the German people had believed in lay in ruins. The German God had failed them. They had accepted hardships infinitely greater than those of the Allies and all to no purpose. Bewildered and starved they would have followed any leadership towards any ideal. All the industries lacked raw materials and there was no money to pay for their import. The four months after the armistice were more ruinous than any before. No work was done. Less food was available. Complete uncertainty prevailed as to the future. Starvation and despair in some quarters caused murder for the sake of a few marks.

I remember in those days that many of the population drank coffee made from acorns, and bread made from—well, it will never be quite known what. It would be difficult to find a parallel in human callousness on such a big scale. And when the German delegates eventually came to Paris for the signature of the treaty they were treated almost like criminals. They were taken hurriedly to Versailles and carefully concealed from the general public. A barbed-wire fence segregated them from the outside world. Armed sentries patrolled the vicinity lest at any time they should lose the impression of being kept under surveillance. Once when some Germans appeared for a moment in view they were greeted with a hail of stones by the good citizens of Versailles. Those hours previous to the actual signing are perhaps best forgotten by Europeans who wish to preserve some semblance of self-respect. In the palace of Louis the Fourteenth are inscribed the words, " À toutes les gloires de la France ". The treaty was drawn up in that spirit and the German delegates when they signed it were made to think so by a huge military display, meaningless salutes fired in the neighbouring park and pyrotechnics and bacchanalia at night.

Just as after the Congress of Vienna there was a series of minor conferences among the powers so there was a succession of conferences after the great Conference of Paris and the signing of the Treaty of Versailles. But there was this great difference. The conferences of the Holy Alliance met to implement the settlement of Europe. It may have been a wrong and unworthy settlement but at least it was a settlement. The endless conferences after Paris and Versailles met in a forlorn hope of trying to make a treaty work.

There was a bewildering number of conferences in the period immediately after Versailles. There was sent on tour what was afterwards facetiously described as the Lloyd George circus. They were spacious days and the British Prime Minister never went on travel unless he was accompanied by an imposing phalanx of secretaries, advisers, press representatives, and friends. For a year or two his little regiment was almost constantly on the move, and it was only at Genoa that it was finally disbanded and Mr. Lloyd

George prepared to pass into the political obscurity from which he has never fully emerged.

While the statesmen of Europe wandered about the Continent, the lot of the German population was still perilous and miserable. I remember in Berlin at that time people were still dying of starvation. Nearly every other child seemed to be suffering from rickets. The restaurants were patronised solely by war profiteers, and passers-by on the Linden used to press their noses to the windows to get a glimpse of the food and well-being inside, things they could never hope to get for themselves, for they had either fought in the war or not taken advantage of the novel war-time conditions to make money. The mendicancy was distressing and heartrending. Men who had once been in professorial chairs or held high positions in the Administration, gladly accepted a pair of old shoes or a cast-off coat from foreign journalists or members on the inter-Allied commission established in the city. But in Paris finance ministers of the stupidity of Klotz, who afterwards appropriately died in a madhouse, regaled the French people with stories of the unlimited wealth of the Germans and their ability to pay for everything they were asked. I made mental note then—I was living in Paris at the time—that the French were very dangerous people to be allied with.

Even in those early days the British Prime Minister was genuinely alarmed at the attitude of France. He did his level best to exercise a restraining influence on the so-called Gallic logic, and before he finally retired from power he became one of the best hated men in France simply because he did his best to look a little further than the following morning. To this day the French have never forgiven Mr. Lloyd George because he refused to join in the senseless campaign of hate against Germany. In many parts of France his name is anathema and I well remember the riot of abuse and ridicule which greeted any comedian who impersonated him on the vaudeville stage—for in France there is no Lord Chamberlain, and any statesman or politician is regarded as fair game for the red-nosed comic. I am convinced that when our great war-time Prime Minister records his memories of the days of the peace he will point out how ill advised was contemporary French policy and how it prepared the way for the wrath to come. After all, he himself had personal experience of how the French regarded the correct rôle of British participation in the Entente Cordiale. After all, he was hissed by the crowd in the Place de la Concorde because he refused to be party to impossible demands of the French Finance Minister, the amiable Paul Doumer, whose hatred of the German was second only to that of Poincaré, who lost four sons in the campaign and who himself fell a victim to the bullet of a crazy Russian refugee.

Germany had passed through the threat of civil war at the time of the Kapp Putsch. A failure to deliver the monthly quota of reparations had led to reprisals on the part of the French who advanced into Frankfurt am Main and Darmstadt. At the famous Conference of Spa when M. Millerand consented to meet the Germans in the conference chamber, the German delegates had offered to send labour and material into northern France to make good the devastated areas on the reparations account because they had no money—an offer which was indignantly refused on the ground that it was a characteristic piece of Teutonic impudence. The situation in Germany went from bad to worse and by the time of the Conference of Paris in 1921 it was plain to many that reparations were in the nature of an *ignis fatuus*. It was left to Mr. Lloyd George to intervene and test the true quality of French friendship for England when vital French interests are concerned.

Those were eventful and busy days. M. Briand was Prime Minister. His Finance Minister was white-haired Paul Doumer. M. Briand let his Finance Minister do the talking for he was never very proficient at figures, and in his heart he had a great humanity which was apt to be misunderstood by his fellow-countrymen as it was later at the golf links of Mandalieu and after the abortive attempt at reconciliation with Germany over the luncheon-table at Thoiry. M. Doumer entered the lists against Germany with all the authority of a great academic economist (the most dangerous species) influenced by an excessive patriotism. No one can doubt but that M. Doumer was the embodiment of the French politician of the more honourable type. His integrity was above reproach. He was an admirable *père de famille*, and had even written a book of moral precepts for the guidance of his sons. He was a man of invincible energy, a non-smoker and a teetotaller. He brought to the conference the hard, unrelenting outlook of a man who had been cruelly bereaved by the Germans and who was not likely ever to relax in his hatred of the enemy. When he rose to speak in 1921 he had the moral support of the equally pertinacious Poincaré, who had now been relieved of the Presidency, and was using his leisure to prepare the brief against Germany that was to end in the Ruhr disaster. M. Doumer was in astronomical mood. He demanded that Germany should liquidate her debts by paying twelve milliard gold marks, or £600,000,000, every year for forty-two years. This was altogether too much for David Lloyd George who had himself been a not unsuccessful Chancellor of the Exchequer. He pointed out that twelve milliard gold marks represented just before the war about two milliards of marks more than the total German exports and one milliard marks more than her annual import bill. How, then, in the name of reason, could Germany be expected to pay in her present situation on this preposterous scale? Mr. Lloyd George, as I remember, did not speak for long, but what he said was enough. If a bombshell had hit the conference-room, there could not have been more confusion and indignation. The British Minister also pointed out that to approach a scale of payment of this kind, it would be necessary to shift Germany's forests and coal-mines bodily from the other side of the Rhine, a metaphor which met with a very cold reception among the logical French round the table.

The next day the Paris political press excelled itself. I have never read such bitter invective, invective made all the more extraordinary in that it was directed against France's most powerful ally. When Mr. Lloyd George emerged from the Hôtel de Crillon, there was a hostile mob waiting for him under the arcades that had to be kept in control by extra armed police. The British delegates were the subject of catcalls wherever they went and for a day or two things were very unpleasant. The press attacks became so foul and vulgar in their abuse that Mr. Lloyd George's patience at last wore out and he complained to Briand. That sturdy old political warrior knew his France well and persuaded the British Prime Minister to take no notice. He pointed out that the French press was as perfidious and corrupt in reality as they temporarily imagined the

British Government and people to be. Mr. Lloyd George had his way on the major point. There was a compromise on the Doumer plan which whittled it away by about a third. In any case, it was soon to be forgotten altogether.

With two brief intervals since the war the attitude of France has been uncompromisingly hostile towards Germany. There were two moments when some sort of accord seemed likely—the period when Briand and Stresemann took to lunching together ; and the days immediately following the announcement of the Saar plebiscite figures when M. Laval publicly recorded his belief in German sincerity and so brought down on his head the usual storm of abuse from the French press, surely the most irresponsible press in the world when it comes to essentials. Apart from these two developments the legend of hate has persisted, and in all fairness, it must be said that it has not been reciprocated on the German side to anything like the same extent. For one thing Germany has no territorial or minority grievances with France. Herr Hitler has stated on more than one occasion that the question of Alsace Lorraine must be regarded as now definitely relegated to past history and that from the German point of view it no longer exists. Both before and after Hitler came into power, Germany has frequently offered a basis of peace by agreement and understanding. But her offers have always been rejected, for the French have assumed on each occasion that the Germans cannot be trusted. What particular evidence France has given since the war that she could be trusted to do anything but make trouble, is another matter. Germany became a signatory of Locarno. Germany joined the League of Nations. Germany entered into the disarmament discussions.

But she was never treated as an equal, and her exodus from Geneva was eventually inevitable even if Hitler had not triumphed in 1933. No republican government would have been able to continue to tolerate a situation as intolerable as that which prevailed at Geneva at that time for very long. There is a limit to all human patience—even that of the German people. The French frequently say they want peace and goodwill with Germany, but it is a very difficult thing to be friendly with a neighbour whom you think and call a blackguard. There is not a great difference between the mentality of official France in 1937 and 1921. France has never forgiven her allies for not helping her to keep Germany in perpetual subjection. The French, who are said to be a logical people, assumed that history could be ignored and that it was possible to keep a great people like Germany for ever under the iron heel of a conqueror.

When one thinks of the French as a peaceful, warm-hearted people, their hysterical behaviour just after the war ought to be remembered. I recall one incident very vividly. There had been the international court sittings at Leipzig which witnessed the farce of "trying" the German war "criminals". The late Lord Hanworth, then Sir Ernest Pollock, travelled to Saxony as His Majesty's Solicitor-General and the trial was held in accordance with the letter of the Peace Treaty. In the end, to the intense fury of France, the German war criminals were exonerated. French officialdom was exasperated, to say the least, and at a moment when feeling ran high, I went to Nomény to witness the presentation of the Croix de Guerre to the mayor of the frontier village by M. Bonnevay, then Minister of Justice. The inhabitants of Nomény had acquitted themselves gallantly in the face of the enemy and a medal was to be their treasured reward. In the course of his oration, M. Bonnevay became eloquent concerning the Leipzig tribunal. Raising his voice, he cried, " France will hold a special court for the re-trial of these war ciminals who have been exonerated by the Leipzig tribunal. The French military court is the proper court for the trial of crimes committed by soldiers." M. Bonnevay, as Minister of Justice, surely ought to have known something about legal procedure, but why did he stipulate only a French military court ? Had France no allies during the war ? Actually, of course, M. Bonnevay's ludicrous outburst was quite typical of that streak of French arrogance which persists to this day and which endeavours to convince the inquirer that the war was really won by France with a little help from some other states.

Before Mr. Lloyd George finally retired from the political scene he tried to teach M. Briand to play golf. In so doing he almost completely wrecked the French Prime Minister's career, once and for all. Unhappily the result of the incident was to drive the one moderate French statesman with any influence away from power for several years, and leave the field open for the reign of Poincaré, and the invasion of the Ruhr, a crime and a folly which I am certain would never have been countenanced by Aristide Briand, the pig-keeper of Cocherel. In those days golf was still almost exclusively associated with the wicked British, and it was but natural that the Welsh wizard should attempt to distract M. Briand from his immediate task of browbeating Germans by wasting time on a golf links. How absurd it was was evidenced in the conference when Mr. Lloyd George severely rated the ill-fated Dr. Rathenau, who had been particularly long-winded in his complaints about the cost of coal deliveries and the upkeep of the army of occupation, by reminding the German minister that it was the German nation and not the Allies who were being asked to pay reparations. The Conference of Cannes marked the end of the Entente Cordiale. Since then the European situation has passed through many vicissitudes. The broad basis of Locarno was tried and failed, and who is to blame, France or Germany, has not been decided, although it is difficult to associate the Franco-Soviet pact with the strict interpretation of the Locarno agreements. To-day our Foreign Office is pursuing a persistent policy of friendship with France, while in many quarters it is thought that matters have almost come to an arrangement that could be described as an unofficial military alliance. And our attitude towards Germany is taking on something of the intransigeance and arrogance of the Quai d'Orsay.

The Conference of Cannes is important in our study of Anglo-German relations, although it took place as long ago as the early days of 1922, because it might have resulted in a British guarantee of the French frontier which would have completely changed the situation and altered the whole trend of European politics.

At the time when Mr. Lloyd George came to the Riviera, it could rightly be said that he had the whole of Europe at his feet. I was on the station platform at Cannes when he arrived from Paris and he literally jumped down the three steps of his sleeping-car. He had an agility astonishing in one of his years for he was then nearly sixty. He exuded vitality and his high spirits were infectious. There was a group of friends on the platform to meet him and in the confusion no one noticed Mr. Winston Churchill, who was busily engaged in looking after an easel and colour-box. He had come to paint the Riviera scene on canvas and not to participate in the Conference. At least in the end he got something tangible out of his visit. "The sun! The sun!" cried Mr. Lloyd George to me. "We so seldom see the sun at home in winter like this, do we?" And it was in that gay spirit of sunshine that he carried on throughout the troublous days of the forthcoming Conference.

The Villa Valetta where Mr. Lloyd George stayed was, ironically enough, built by a German before the war. In the interval before the opening of the Conference Mr. Lloyd George spent the time motoring along the Corniche roads or playing golf at Mandalieu or Cannes. The authorities at Cannes realised the immense publicity value of having a European Conference in their midst. They used the propaganda value of the circumstances to the utmost, and it may fairly be said that from that moment the little town has never looked back. The Lloyd George circus at least assured prosperity for one small community if it failed to bring about tranquillity between nations. The actual conference took place in the famous Cercle Nautique, one of the oldest clubs on the Riviera coast. It was an undistinguished building but its fair-sized rooms gave it an advantage over the ordinary hotel. There was a tremendous gathering of international figures at Cannes during the second week of January. Stately Marquess Curzon installed himself in a discreet hotel that stood back from the Croisette, half-hidden in palm trees. M. Briand took a suite overlooking the sea at the Hôtel National, then the last word in Riviera elegance. He was able to watch Sir Laming Worthington Evans play lawn tennis on the hard courts below. M. Loucheur brought his tennis rackets to Cannes but very wisely did not unpack them. Mr. Lloyd George and Sir Robert Horne were inseparable, whether it was on the golf course or picnicking in the Gorges du Loup. And hidden away in his own hotel was Dr. Walter Rathenau, Germany's Foreign Minister, whom destiny had marked out for the assassin's bullet about twelve months later. One might add that a very saturnine figure wandered about the lobbies of the Cercle Nautique and ventured occasionally into the *salle de boule* at the Casino. He was an Italian journalist named Benito Mussolini.

The Conference was made the occasion for the destruction of a plan to replace the Entente Cordiale with a new pact of guarantee. The proposed new pact went further in some ways than the previous alliance. It offered to guarantee the Rhine frontier from invasion. One of the side-issues of the negotiations in Paris previous to the signing of the treaty had been a tentative Anglo-American guarantee of the inviolability of the Rhine in the interests of France. The proposal was abandoned because President Wilson began to realise that such a measure would find no favour in Congress. During the many talks at Cannes, Mr. Lloyd George hinted at some form of unilateral treaty whereby Great Britain would bind herself to give a guarantee of security to France in this respect, and M. Briand looked on the proposals with favour.

But there were those in Paris who were not prepared to put trust in the policy of the British Prime Minister. Mr. Lloyd George had become suspect. He had been wise enough to suggest some concessions to the enemy and that was sufficient. While M. Briand was in Cannes endeavouring to arrive at a *modus vivendi* for Europe, there were members of his own Cabinet who thought he was being brought under the magnetism of the Lloyd George personality. M. Briand was adopting an altogether too compromising attitude towards the general situation, and his enemies in France were convinced that the spell of the Welshman must be brought to an end. While M. Briand was endeavouring over the luncheon-tables of obscure restaurants in the back streets of Cannes to reach some permanent settlement not only in regard to reparations but also for the future security of France and a guarantee of permanent peace in Europe, his enemies in France got busy. (Those who are now rejecting the offer of German friendship for a renewal of old alliances with France, ought to bear this last incident very much in mind.) There were hints that M. Briand was inclined to toy with the idea of some arrangement with Germany. He was being urged thereto in his close contacts with the perfidious Lloyd George. He had been carried away by the arguments of Rathenau. He had put credence in the argument of the falling mark that would soon begin to fall as down a chute and had never for one moment realised that Germany was entering on a policy of inflation in order to escape payment of reparations. The fact that the British Government was prepared to commit itself to a tangible guarantee for the security of France was passed over. It was much more significant that M. Briand was weakening in his attitude towards Germany. That there was never any ground for such suspicions is another story. Briand was acting as a citizen of Europe and not solely as a citizen of France and that was quite sufficient. M. Poincaré, from the outside, and M. Louis Barthou, from the inside, led cliques both of the Cabinet and Senate and Chamber which intrigued against the absent Prime

Minister. Politics are always a dirty game but in France they are sometimes positively unclean. In a day or two an intense feeling of opposition had been whipped up among the rank and file of the Nationalist members which spelt the doom of the head of the Cabinet in much the same way as similar manœuvres have brought down many a good wise man in France before and will certainly do so again. The German Foreign Minister, Herr Rathenau, had asked for a moratorium on account of the decline in the value of the mark, and it began openly to be stated in Paris that M. Briand was in favour of concessions to the Reich. That was quite sufficient to clinch the arguments of the treacherous Barthou. M. Briand, when he spoke on the long-distance telephone to Paris, began to realise that his position was in danger and that the muddle-headed Alexandre Millerand, the new President of the Republic, and a man who himself dreamed of the supreme power that was to bring about his downfall two years later, was siding with his enemies.

It was at this moment that there took place a fantastic golf " match " on the Cannes course at Mandalieu. It was a tremendous trifle. During his eight or nine days on the Riviera holiday-making previous to the Conference, Mr. Lloyd George had indulged to the full his passion for golf. Scarcely a day had passed without his appearance either on the course at Mandalieu, a course where one has to hit straight and hard, or at Cagnes, by Nice, where the fairway is almost as wide as a desert, and where the Prime Minister, I believe, one afternoon did a hole in one. Mr. Lloyd George thoroughly enjoyed the sunshine and the amenities of Cannes and the spirit of the open air entered into all his thoughts. So it happened that one day after a particularly trying session of argument with the German delegates, he suggested luncheon at the golf house of Mandalieu. M. Briand accompanied him, and afterwards, in an expansive moment, the French Prime Minister said he would like to try his hand at this ridiculous game of golf which his British friends liked so much. It was in a spirit of the utmost goodwill and joviality that Mr. Lloyd George volunteered to give M. Briand his first lesson in golf, and in company with Lord Wester Wemyss, of armistice fame, and Lord Riddell, his Fidus Achates during many conferences, the two statesmen made their way to the first tee. Naturally there were many correspondents present in the vicinity, for wherever the two ministers went they were always trailed by newspaper men. M. Briand addressed the ball with an attitude of contempt, and to his intense astonishment his mighty swing just succeeded in rolling the little white ball a matter of a few yards. The game proceeded for about two or three holes and then the French Prime Minister gave it all up in disgust, grunting something about the absurd ideas of British people who could find pleasure in tramping over the countryside knocking about an insignificant white indiarubber ball. It was all so trivial, this incident, but at the same time so very human. But that afternoon on the links prepared the moment for M. Briand's departure into the political wilderness for a very long time.

The special correspondents of the Paris newspapers, already well aware by their editors of the " change of feeling " in the corridors of the Quai d'Orsay and the lobbies of the Chamber, made political capital of the golf game at Mandalieu. Feelings in France were then running so high against defaulting Germany that this lapse of the Prime Minister from the pressing problems of the hour was interpreted as something like treachery. The cables to Paris that night hummed with derisive comment, and it was freely stated that the Prime Minister had forgotten his duties to France in his infatuation for the crafty Lloyd George. The Paris press made the most of the story. Photographs of M. Briand, walking out to the tee with his British colleagues, were published by nearly every newspaper in the country. The enemies of compromise in the Chamber took umbrage at this grave dereliction of conduct and M. Briand, scenting trouble from afar, caught the night train back to Paris. The sequel is well known. Briand, without mentioning the trifling affair at Mandalieu, overwhelmed the Chamber with an eloquent defence of his policy. His false friends quivered under the lash of his tongue. But the great orator from Brittany knew that his triumph would only be ephemeral and he decided to resign forthwith. He went into the wilderness and left the field of international affairs open to reaction and Raymond Poincaré.

It is significant that the British offer of a guaranteed inviolability of the Rhine was not renewed when Poincaré once more became Prime Minister of France. But Poincaré did not care very much. He assumed office and immediately made it known that so far as he was concerned nothing had happened of consequence in Europe since the signing of the treaty—that dread *Journée de Versailles*.

CHAPTER XIV

COAL AND BAYONETS

TWO significant things happened in Europe about the same time as M. Briand handed in his portfolio to M. Millerand. They were hardly noticed at the time.

A young man in Munich had formed a party with the avowed object of defiance of the peace treaty and the re-establishment of Germany as a great power, free and equal in relation to all other peoples. His name was Adolf Hitler. He was the son of an Austrian customs officer and had won the Iron Cross as a corporal runner in the Sixteenth Bavarian Infantry. He had started his political campaign in an obscure beer-hall in Munich. He had invented the symbol of the swastika as the emblem of all true Germans. And only recently he had felt himself strong enough to emerge from the obscurity of beer-gardens into taking the grounds of the Crown Circus to hold the first mass meeting of what was to become known as the National Socialist German Labour Party.

At the same time, the obscure Mussolini returned to Milan to prepare for the great events to come.

It bears small relation to the present theme but it may also be recorded in passing that a third great event was taking place in far-off Turkey. One Mustapha Kemal, now called Ataturk, had begun to defy the Allies in the way Germany has subsequently done. But he had better fortune, for quite soon the great ones of the earth assembled at Lausanne to make a new peace treaty with the new Ankara Government, and less than twelve years later their successors were to meet together at neighbouring Montreux to make still more concessions to that same revised arrangement.

There was one more full-dress conference of the old kind before Mr. Lloyd George finally disappeared from power. It took place at Genoa and was designed to be a grand effort to settle the problems of Europe once and for all. There was to be a general understanding between France and Germany, and Great Britain and Germany. A new world was to emerge from the grave deliberations. Moreover, an approach was to be made to Soviet Russia. (Moscow sent the late M. Chicherin as her chief delegate.) In those days the very existence of the Soviets was something of a mystery. No one knew precisely what the word meant or what the Russian Government stood for or aimed at. It was regarded as very daring on the part of Mr. Lloyd George to suggest meeting anyone connected with Red Russia, and when a distinguished Czarist diplomat appeared on behalf of the Red Government, there were many who were, to say the least, a little disconcerted. The conference yielded none of its expected fruits, mainly because Mr. Lloyd George reckoned without Poincaré. In the end Germany was driven into the arms of the Soviets out of a sense of mutual protection, for in those days both states were looked on by their allegedly more civilised neighbours as something like pariahs.

The outcome of Genoa was really tragic. There had been a sharp stiffening of attitude in Paris and instead of the compromising spirit of M. Briand, the cold relentless spirit of Raymond Poincaré was felt. The last named was now Prime Minister once more and he sent to Genoa his henchman and political disciple, the same Louis Barthou who had plotted against Briand. He was instructed to oppose any suggestion on the part of Great Britain which in any way favoured Germany. It is true no direct move was made from Paris to wreck the conference, but it was always apparent that the new government had made up its mind to pursue its vindictive policy towards Germany. There was to be no concession. It was a hopeless position and the conference after five weeks of life naturally showed signs of wilting. When the Russians announced the treaty with Rathenau signed at Rapallo, the end came. M. Poincaré sent a farewell message of the cheerful nature that if the Germans did not resume payments of reparations forthwith then the French army would march into the Ruhr, whether Great Britain, Belgium, or Italy liked the move or not. It was also suggested that France did not approve of an alliance between Germany and Russia. Europe had to wait for another ten years before Laval and Blum thought otherwise of the Soviet Union. Mr. Lloyd George returned to London to wait the end of his coalition.

Into the Ruhr marched the poilus in due course. The moment the first battalion had crossed the boundary, modern Germany began to arise. That was on January 11, 1923. Ten years later almost to the day the Nazis were advancing in triumph towards a United Germany, strong in faith, resolute in will. I have often heard the argument put forward that Germany is Europe's aggressor and that France must be permanently on her guard against another invasion. But what of the invasion of the Ruhr? Surely that was the oppression of the weak by a mighty, invincible host. If ever there was an act of aggression, surely this was one. It also happened to be an international crime.

It created animosities which may never completely fade away. When Lloyd George said the invasion of the Ruhr was like digging for coal with bayonets, he completely defined the situation. If any further proof is needed of France's aggressive policy towards Germany in those days one can find it in the plans of Marshal Foch for a riparian frontier on the Rhine and the encouragement of the treacherous Separatist movement in the Rhineland by French agents at this same period. Because things happened fourteen years ago that do not quite fit into our latter-day statesmen's picture of France, they should not be forgotten or glossed over. It must be remembered that one of the main preoccupations of the German Republican Government in those days was to escape from the merciless aggression of France and the impossible demands of French chauvinists. M. Poincaré must have known that he could not force the Germans to come to heel by occupying the Ruhr. It is fair, however, to say that, once in the Ruhr, he had no intention of marching out again. And all the world now knows that the inflation of the mark was not a diabolical move on the part of Germany but a dire necessity.

The invasion was decided on with the cold relentless calculation that was so typical of Poincaré—"That horrid little man," as Lord Curzon once tearfully described him. Indeed, if in subsequent times the action of Hitler in creating the Third Reich can be described as putting the clock back, the action of Poincaré in the Ruhr may fairly be defined as nearly stopping it.

Great Britain, now under the Premiership of Mr. Bonar Law, to her everlasting credit was no party to the invasion. Exactly a week before the troop movements began, Mr. Law addressed the British correspondents in Paris at the Hôtel de Crillon. The French Government had made all their preparations for the invasion on the grounds of exacting reparations. The British Government had first of all demurred and then had openly objected. Mr. Bonar Law wished to state the case of his Conservative administration and he did so very briefly in a short speech that has become history :

> The French proposals compromise the recovery of German credit and we cannot therefore accept them. But this need not impair our friendship with France. His Majesty's Government have examined the French proposals with the closest attention and are of opinion that not only will they not achieve the end in view, but that they are fraught with grave danger for the economic future of Europe. With deep regret, therefore, the British Government cannot be further responsible for them.

At the same time it must be placed on record that the day before the invasion the German mark stood at 48,000 to the pound. In four weeks—by the end of February, 1923—it stood at 480,000 and by June at 4,800,000. After that the mark became simply a financial jest. In September the quotation was 480,000,000 and before the end one could obtain a whole suitcase full of beautifully printed paper money for a silver shilling. In fact, shops were opened in the heart of London to market million-mark notes at so many a penny. For sixpence one could obtain almost as many marks as existed in the whole Reich before the war. And for half a crown you could buy enough paper to cover the walls of a room.

I witnessed at first hand many scenes of misery among the German population during the days of inflation, scenes of misery that were emphasised the more by the fact that anyone with foreign currency could live like the proverbial milord for a few shillings a day while the majority of Germans just went hungry. Germany was suddenly transformed into a land of milk and honey for everybody but the unfortunate German who depended for his existence on the value of the mark. In the occupied areas the ordinary private soldier with his shilling or two a day deserted the official wet canteens and their rows of barrels of English beer—often in imperfect condition—for the restaurants of the city of Cologne. There he could buy bottles of rare hock and German champagne for the price of half a bitter. The soldier went from his billet to parade by taxi, for it was cheaper than going by tram and so much less tiresome. There were some abject cases of exploitation of the mark by an influx of British civilians who came over in swarms to this earthly paradise, but the authorities took very firm measures and to this day the Germans of the Rhineland declare with pride and satisfaction that in the time of trouble the British army was full of forbearance and sympathy. In fact, it was that attitude which has made the name of the British soldier respected all over the Rhineland and which caused to grow up something in the nature of affection. Everything was cheap. It was impossible to spend very much. You could give a dinner-party for two or three people at the best hotels in Berlin for five shillings. And sixpence, or maybe ninepence, was quite enough to pay for a room with a view.

The tragedy of the German inflation was the suffering it inflicted on the innocent population. The great mass of the people had been engaged in the war like the people of every other nation because their rulers told them to. They had suffered like all the others except that in their case the horrors of death and bereavement had been accompanied by physical starvation. Then after some years of uncertainty they were to lose even that little which the war and reparations had left them—the relics of their private fortunes and savings. It must be remembered that when the mark was inflated and the Government printing presses were revolving with insane speed, the mark was still legal tender for the amount written on its face. Thus even in the early days a man who had, shall we say, a little nest-egg of two thousand pounds put away for his old age suddenly discovered his total fortune to be worth about twopence. The Germans are a thrifty people and it is the ambition of every citizen to have a little money put by. This money disappeared completely and one can imagine that to the vast majority of people it seemed as if the bottom of the world had fallen out.

I well remember the time when you paid for a seat in a cinema with a bar of soap, for soap was better than any number of marks. If you took a tram journey of any distance in Berlin it was most probable that by the time you had completed your journey, the conductor would be asking you for a few more million marks—the exchange having fallen again in the interim. One had to go to the bank with a big bag to obtain the equivalent in paper marks of a few pounds. In all the big cities people sold all their treasured possessions and pawned their household goods at the grocers' or butchers' in exchange for food rather than traffic in the worthless paper currency. In all big centres of population suicides became commonplace and the pavements were crowded with beggars. And they were not professional cadgers, but men and women who had known, if not wealth, at least comfort, and who were forced to stand in the gutter in the hope that someone would give them a chunk of bread or a slice of sausage. And it is well to draw a veil over the scandal of prostitution

ON THE ROAD TO HEIDELBERG

[face p. 274

which was universal in Germany at that time, a scandal which was all the more appalling because it was the result of desperation and starvation and had no recreational, or vicious, significance.

It was the Ruhr invasion which began to rouse the Germans from their long period of despond. It was the Ruhr invasion which occasioned the first big manifestation of the new Nazi Party in Munich. Adolf Hitler planned a march on Berlin and he was encouraged by the war-time chief-of-staff, General Ludendorff, who had not yet brought to perfection his new Pagan creed of the German Nordic God. Bavaria was rapidly falling under the sway of separatism and the opinion of the Bavarian Catholic peasant was far removed from the internationalist spirit that was fast gaining ground in Prussia. There was a danger of a possible split between the Germanic peoples, of a possible union between the Rhineland, Bavaria and Catholic Austria as opposed to the Bavarian north. It was an intolerable prospect to a man like Corporal Hitler, who had looked on the Pan-Germanic ideal as something more precious than Holy Writ ever since he had been obliged to live on the meagre wages of odd jobs found on the streets of Vienna. The French separatist agitation in the Rhineland was also making rapid headway. It was to assert the solidarity of Germany against the occupation of the Ruhr and the plots of the French that Hitler mustered his brown-shirt followers and embarked on what has become known as the Beer Hall Putsch. The *coup d'état* which was to have opened the way to Berlin and result in the establishment of a new administration under the swastika failed dismally, as we all know. Behind the barricades loyal soldiers opened fire at the word of command, to Hitler's intense astonishment. Seventeen brownshirts fell and Hitler himself in stumbling broke a collar-bone and was thus put out of action. Three months later, in February, 1924, he was condemned by court-martial to five years' detention in the fortress of Landsberg. His gaolers and followers supplied him with books, pens, ink and paper and during the eight months he served as a political prisoner, this indefatigable man with a mission wrote *Mein Kampf*—perhaps the most controversial book of modern times. If his coup had not failed, it is certain that the book would never have been written. And the coup would never have been attempted if the French had kept out of the Ruhr.

After the massacre of "Bloody Easter" at Essen, German passive resistance in the Ruhr began to weaken and afterwards the French may be said to have attained the mastery of the area. But all their invasion did was to aggravate and not solve the reparations question. A man who was to leave his mark on European politics, Dr. Stresemann, Foreign Minister in the Cabinet of Chancellor Marx, was obliged to admit defeat. Germany was completely bankrupt and the mark was no longer accepted by anyone even within the German frontiers. We were close to Dr. Schacht's rentenmarks and the Dawes and Young plans. But they do not bear greatly on the theme. After the Ruhr, Europe from a political, as distinct from a financial point of view, took on a new aspect. Reparations may have caused the Ruhr disaster or they merely served as an excuse for the invasion. But that same Ruhr invasion temporarily ruined the Reich and in the depths of despair, as so often happens in history, a nation found a sense of unity.

February 11, 1923, was one of the most important dates of the present century.

CHAPTER XV

"DESCENSUS FACILIS"

THE Ruhr situation became intolerable, but it might have lasted much longer had Poincaré remained Prime Minister of France. Actually he was succeeded by the radical Mayor of Lyons, Edouard Herriot, who was more amenable to reason although not possessed of any wide viewpoint on European affairs. To this day, in spite of his alleged advanced views, Herriot continues to be an ardent French nationalist in all things. It was fortunate, however, that Herriot succeeded to power, for there had been a change of government in England. The idealistic, compromising Ramsay MacDonald had become Great Britain's first Socialist Prime Minister and had taken to himself the additional duties of Foreign Secretary. Had Poincaré remained in office, Mr. MacDonald would have been defeated at all points for his temperament could not have stood up against the cold steel mind of the Lorrainer. Mr. MacDonald was no Lord Curzon, who was more than a match even for Poincaré on occasion. With M. Herriot it was different and after a few preliminary setbacks, plans were made for the Ruhr evacuation at a full-dress London conference. (It was primarily a reparations conference, but there is no need to emphasise this aspect in discussing the question of further Anglo-German relations.)

It is almost forgotten that the plans for the evacuation were finally outlined in the Cabinet room of No. 10,

Downing Street. No British ministers were present. M. Herriot took the Prime Minister's chair and the German and Belgian delegates sat round the historic Cabinet table. I believe the incident of having such an international gathering in this room in the absence of British ministers is unprecedented in the long history of the famous house. M. Herriot was being openly criticised in Paris for his willingness to discuss evacuation even at this time, and the French press found in the pawky humour and rough Gaelic charm of Mr. MacDonald characteristics similar to those of Mr. Lloyd George, of unpleasant memory.

It was during these talks in London that German statesmen made their first contact with the British public and gave evidence of the desire for friendship with Great Britain that is so manifest to-day. (The movement for a close understanding did not begin with Hitler, be it remembered.) That was a strange period, for the German Chancellor and his Foreign Minister, Dr. Stresemann, were frightened lest there be a hostile demonstration. They really thought that Londoners six years after the armistice were still full of war hatreds.

I was on the platform at Parkeston harbour, Harwich, when the German delegation arrived. It was a bitterly raw morning and the German ministers shivered as they made their way to the train. The party consisted of Dr. Marx, the Chancellor of the Reich, Dr. Stresemann, Dr. Luther, Finance Minister, and Dr. von Schubert, Commissioner General at the German Foreign Office. They were met by Dr. Sthamer, then German ambassador in London. As the party walked along the quayside, the delegates looked rather sheepish and not a little suspicious. It was a memorable occasion in history and they were aware of it. Dr. Stresemann told me afterwards that he was positively scared and was agreeably surprised during his week or two in London that few people paid attention to the delegates after the novelty had worn off. Dr. Stresemann did not know the Londoner. As a matter of fact, when the delegates reached Liverpool Street, the station was packed with city workers hurrying to their offices and shops. Only a few dawdlers took the trouble to watch the arrival of the close-cropped German Foreign Minister who was shortly to become a world figure as one of the joint architects of Locarno.

On the day of the fateful meeting at No. 10 I had a long talk with Dr. Marx. He had created a very favourable impression in London, far more so than Dr. Stresemann, whose strange, elusive personality proved baffling to many. Dr. Marx, however, with his benign smile and curiously shaped spectacles, instantly inspired confidence, and all the time he was in the capital he was personally very popular. He impressed one with a sense of honesty and earnestness, and he had that rare faculty in a German of putting the stranger at his ease in a moment. He declared himself to be an advocate of peace and understanding. "I want the British people to understand the German people," he said. "That is my aim in life.

"It was with great joy when we arrived here a fortnight ago that we found we were being admitted to the conference on equal terms. In Germany we are conscious of having been given second place for so long. We have been so helpless. Perhaps that is why the occupation of the Ruhr caused us so much unhappiness. We came to London to be helpful and promote peace and I hope we have succeeded in our object."

M. Herriot stayed in London for almost a month without intermission during the long negotiations and was radiantly happy at the prospect of returning to his favourite restaurants in Paris and Lyons with something dramatic and successful to talk about in his expansive way. He was bubbling over with enthusiasm when I saw him before his departure. He was convinced that the Conference would lead to a new Entente with France and said so emphatically. He added, " France and England must be united to settle all the problems of Europe which are still outstanding. I still hope that this conference will be the beginning of a new era in European politics. Although there is certain to be opposition to the Protocol (reparations settlement) and the Ruhr evacuation agreement in the French Parliament, I am sure they will not be defeated. The effect of the London agreement will be far-reaching and we have made a great stride in the direction of peace and understanding all round."

There was a great deal in what M. Herriot said. If Europe had continued on the course of conciliation after the London Conference, we might have been spared many of our present troubles. But there was opposition to the Ruhr evacuation in the French Parliament and it became obvious that, although the withdrawal took place according to plan, the French Parliament would not admit Germany on equal terms in an all-round understanding. Later, another attempt was made to bring about a Franco-German agreement by M. Briand and Dr. Stresemann. It was also to fail to bear fruit for very long. After that the two countries were once more to drift into varying degrees of antagonism until the present impasse was reached; and Great Britain is confronted with the question as to which side she should support in order to ensure peace in our time.

The Treaty of Locarno has become so much

associated with our own Foreign Office, where a room is named after the agreement, that we are apt to think that the whole system of mutual assistance pacts was a British idea. Sir Austen Chamberlain when he came back from the Swiss resort was greeted as an international hero and the reception he got befitted great achievement. But it ought to be remembered that if it had not been for German persistence there would never have been a Locarno agreement at all. It is a fact that in the very early days of his Foreign Secretaryship—he was made Secretary of State after Mr. MacDonald's defeat—he did not look too kindly on the idea of coming to an agreement with Germany and it was only the pressure of influential colleagues in the Cabinet—Lord Balfour, Lord Curzon, Lord Birkenhead, and Mr. Winston Churchill—which persuaded him to modify his attitude. Sir Austen has always been ardently Francophile. He is a man of prejudice and suffers from other defects of his own qualities.

In spite of her tremendous sufferings and the injustice done her by the Ruhr invasion, Germany still worked for an understanding with the Allies. I had a long interview with Dr. Wirth, who had been one of the post-war German Chancellors, just about this time. He said quite definitely that Germany wished to work in harmony with France if only France was agreeable. And concluded: "We want to work on lines of political development with the nations that fought us. Certainly my own party in the Reichstag will do all in its power to further friendly relations between France and my country." In this connection it is interesting to recall that it was Chancellor Luther who was the first to put forward the so-called "initiative" suggesting a pact of mutual guarantees among the Western powers. It is a fact that should not be forgotten by those who contend that German foreign policy since the treaty has been recalcitrant and aggressive. The first German " initiative " addressed to the Foreign Office was given as cool a reception as the plans presented by Hitler for some basis of settlement of outstanding difficulties since he became Reichsleader and Chancellor. It was just not trusted because it came from Germany. The Luther initiative agreed to accept the territorial status of the Rhine as laid down in the treaty and accepted the demilitarised zone. It asked for a pact of mutual security combined with an arbitration treaty. That was in the month of January. It was on December 1 that the Locarno Pact was signed in Whitehall and it was almost exactly on the lines of the suggestions made by Dr. Luther which were more or less snubbed. Dr. Luther was not deterred by the unhelpful attitude of the British Foreign Office. He prepared a second initiative and sent it to the Quai d'Orsay where, strange to say, it met with quite an eager reception. The ground was prepared and all was going well, for Sir Austen Chamberlain had been obliged to make a closer study of the first initiative. And then cobbler President Ebert died and at the subsequent election Field-Marshal von Hindenburg was elected President of the Reich. There was universal consternation and it was openly declared that Germany had gone back overnight to the mentality of 1914. In actual fact the suspicions were groundless for the German people sincerely desired peace provided they had a square deal. Hindenburg, already very old and hard of hearing, looked with no favour on Luther's scheme, which he thought would mean an indefinite period of subjugation for Germany, but opinion was too strong for him and he had to give way. It may be said that Hindenburg gave more trouble to his own government than he ever gave to those of the other powers. As we all now know the lakeside idyll of Locarno took place and Germany took her place among the family of nations once more. Sir Austen Chamberlain was made a Knight of the Garter. Locarno marked a climax in latter-day history. The world thought that at last a permanent basis of peace had been reached and enthusiasm knew no limits. Here was a document mutually agreed on which maintained the territorial frontiers of France, Germany and Belgium as laid down in the Treaty of Versailles. The three powers agreed not to attack each other or resort to war except in circumstances of legitimate defence. In the case of Great Britain there was a solemn obligation to come to the aid of any of the powers that had been the victim of aggression in defiance of sworn obligations expressed in the pact. It seemed a foolproof scheme.

There was one snag, however. Germany must join the League of Nations, and there was grave misgiving in Germany concerning this step, and in Geneva there were many powers who had not been consulted at Locarno, who were determined to oppose any such election. Geneva, which was to have been the peace-ground of the world, began to make the difficulties which have led Europe to its present state of political chaos. It was into the hands of the League that the Locarno Treaty was given for safe keeping and it was members of that same League which were the first to break the Locarno spirit. The first time Dr. Stresemann went to Geneva, he was kept kicking his heels about the peace city while Brazil objected to admission of the Reich. In the end he had to go back to Berlin empty-handed, soured in temper and quite disillusioned. It was not until September, 1926, that Germany entered the League on the basis of a permanent seat on the Council. By that time there had been a revival of the bad old spirit of intrigue, temporarily stayed by the Locarno agreement. France was feeling for Allies in Poland and among the members of the Little Entente as additional guarantees of her security—a move hardly in accordance with the pact. Nevertheless, Germany came in and was prepared to work in harmony with Geneva on the understanding that she was treated as a free power and on terms of equality with the other great powers.

It was on September 8, 1926, in the dreary surroundings of the Salle de la Réformation in the older part of Geneva, that Gustav Stresemann took his place as Germany's first representative at the League of Nations Assembly. (Her last incidentally was Dr. Josef Goebbels.) There were scenes of great emotion of the kind Geneva so dearly likes and Dr. Stresemann was given a tremendous reception. He made an appropriate speech. Afterwards came M. Briand, then at the height of his career and the inspiring genius of Geneva and the League in which he had a fanatical trust. To his everlasting honour the great Briand had worked for collaboration in the face of bitter opposition of the French nationalists just as Dr. Stresemann, in spite of many rebuffs at Geneva itself, had carried out his pro-League policy in the face of German nationalists (not yet National Socialists) in the Reichstag. The eloquence of Briand rose in praise of the League. He declared in that resounding voice which no one who ever heard it is likely to forget:

"Those who indulge in irony and detraction at the expense of the League of Nations, who daily cast doubt upon its soundness and time after time proclaim that it is doomed to perish, what will they think if they are present at this meeting?"

The question echoes down the years. What do they think? In that moment of enthusiasm and inspiration at any rate the world was entitled to think that the past was forgotten and that Germany had been received freely and equally among the powers of the world. I maintain that it was due to the fears and animosities of the French that the noble ideal of their fellow-countrymen was not fulfilled in its highest degree. For the sorry story of the last decade began to be told so very quickly afterwards.

There is no need to be expansive about the famous luncheon at Thoiry, when Briand and Stresemann outwitted the press for a few hours and sat down in a small *auberge* across the frontier to enjoy a *chateaubriand.* (It is said that an enthusiastic German attaché anxious to return honour to Briand later included in the menu a beef steak which was described as a *Schloss Stresemann.*) Both statesmen were good trenchermen and perhaps in the warmth of their very real, albeit newfound, friendship, they made many extravagant promises, one to the other. No one knows exactly what happened at Thoiry, but there were rumours which were never contradicted that Briand agreed to the immediate evacuation of the Rhineland and the termination of the tenure of the mines in the Saar. Nothing of the sort happened. Emotions died away, and when a little time had passed, Briand realised that his countrymen were still not disposed to look on Germany as anything but an hereditary enemy. At the time when so much goodwill prevailed, the franc was falling dangerously—like the mark a short time previously—and France was looking for outside help. France is always humble in such circumstances. But Poincaré was to return again, stabilise the franc and embark on the same policy as before. And Briand was gradually to disappear from the political scene, to die finally in eclipse.

I have dwelt at some length on the events which accompanied the signing of the treaty, the immediate post-war conferences, the invasion of the Ruhr, the pact of Locarno and the entry of Germany into the League because I have long felt that although these things happened only ten years or a little more ago, in this age of very short memories and extreme opportunism they are apt to be too readily forgotten. But they are of very great significance to all who have a genuine desire to understand the present situation in Europe and to appreciate why our human story remains such a very unhappy one.

We draw nearer to the world crisis and all the evil it brought about. At the same time we observe the grave disappointment felt in Germany at the unsatisfactory results of her membership of the League. After M. Poincaré had dramatically stabilised the franc and for the first time in many years persuaded the French people to pay their taxes regularly, the goodwill of Thoiry—if it ever existed in real fact—completely disappeared. The demand for reparations was made with the old insistence and Germany, then ruled by a socialist government in the accepted sense, felt compelled to adopt an independent policy. From this time date the beginnings of rearmament of the Reich and the skilful measures of the late General von Seeckt in making the Reichswehr the most formidable professional army in Europe from the point of view of extreme efficiency if not of numbers. No one can deny there was secret rearmament in Germany long before Hitler came to power. In fact rearmament was well advanced when the Führer took office. But surely in the light of events, Germany was justified.

For her there was no equality of rights although she had a permanent seat on the League Council. She looked around and saw every other nation armed and ready, but by the terms of the treaty she must perforce remain defenceless. It was a situation that no country with history and tradition behind it could accept without protest or without some measures to redress the balance. Even if rearmament did not begin on a big scale until some years later, it must be remembered by critics of the Hitler régime that it was begun by a Germany ruled by a Reichstag elected by secret and free ballot.

The whole world steadily advanced towards financial catastrophe and in Europe the reparations problem lingered behind the scenes like an evil spirit. In Germany the nationalist element, later to be concentrated and vitalised in the Nazi Party, grew in strength as the monetary position grew more and more hopeless. In France there was the insistent demand for payment, payment, payment, which at length reached such a pitch that in future the French suggested that of any moneys or goods delivered by Germany, France should have the major share. England ought to agree to such an arrangement because England was so very wealthy.

It was to combat this point of view that the hard-headed Yorkshireman, Mr. Philip Snowden, travelled to The Hague to take part in the last important reparations conference which was to happen before the final wiping of the slate at Lausanne. The man who was to become known as the "iron chancellor" was not swayed by any sentiments that Europe should be run for the benefit of France at the expense of Great Britain. He had noted with some disgust that Great Britain had sacrificed fifty-seven per cent of her French debt, eighty-five per cent of her Italian debt, and had paid £116,000,000 to the United States in a matter of five years. When the French put forward their request for exceptional treatment, he dismissed their claims as " grotesque and ridiculous ", two adjectives which have become historic in European history. It was the swan song of reparations ; it was the prelude to the world crisis ; it paved the way to the final amortisation of the whole reparations question that was to take place at Lausanne in the not so distant future.

In the spring of 1931 the great crisis came on the world like a damp shroud, destructive of fortune and hope, a kind of creeping paralysis. Its effect was universal. It drove England off the gold standard and brought into existence the National Government. In France it led to widespread public nervousness and opened the way for incredible political and financial scandals. In Germany it brought ruin and an unemployment situation that drifted gradually towards internal disorder and political disintegration. But even in these moments of dread and disaster, while in England we were thinking of how best to save the economic situation, in France politics took first place as always. It was well known that by this time the Hitler Party had 107 seats in the Reichstag. We were not very exercised in mind about the fact, but in France it was deemed of more importance than any world crisis for Hitler stood for the revival of Germany as a great power in reality and not by mention in treaty. France saw her opportunities of manipulating the financial problems of Europe to her own advantage and to the loss of republican Germany—and took them.

While we at home were facing bankruptcy, our faithful ally was preparing her plans for a new attack on Germany. The Reich had committed the dastardly fault of making a customs union with her kinsfolk in Austria. The dreaded Anschluss came into being and was regarded in France as a menace to world peace—as if the world had nothing else to think about at that time but such an interpretation of French security. In England we were indifferent. We realised that Austria was too weak to live alone, but France looked on the union as a possible accretion to Germany's national strength and therefore it was not to be thought of. In her attitude France was warmly supported by her allies in the Little Entente, all three of which had profited by the false doctrine of self-determination at the time of the treaty to include in their own boundaries millions of people and tens of thousands of square miles of territory that ought properly to belong to Germany, Hungary or Austria. In Paris, lonely, aged Aristide Briand watched the decline and fall of that policy of appeasement he had spent so long in creating. In a very short time he had to bear the full brunt of the venom and hate of his fellow-countrymen. The weekly papers were filled with scurrility about the pig-keeper of Cocherel. A third-rate comedian could be certain of bringing down the house in a boulevard music-hall by some oblique reference to the grand old man of French politics. Grotesque caricatures of the champion of Locarno looked down from every newspaper kiosk. Rarely, even in France, has there been so much public ingratitude towards an elder statesman, and in this case it was the very last of the elders. The mercurial Herriot, then in opposition in the Chamber, led the attack and won the applause of the mob. The Government was forced to fight the Anschluss and the fact that Great Britain was indifferent was quite sufficient to revive the hoary slogan, " Perfide Albion ". The British Foreign Minister, then Mr. Arthur

Henderson, suggested that the whole question of the customs union be referred to The Hague Tribunal under the well-known Optional Clause. By the time the justices had made up their minds, the financial situation of the world was indeed parlous. But the judgment stated that there was nothing illegal in the formation of an Anschluss between Germany and Austria. There was something like explosion in the Quai d'Orsay. But time was on the side of the French. The plight of Austria became so desperate that the Credit Anstalt was unable to meet its commitments and Austria appealed for a loan. With generous gesture, France said she could not support such a loan unless the project of the Anschluss was abandoned. It would be hard to find a more glaring example of political blackmail. It was all the more flagrant when it is realised that the Bank of England was willing to contribute to the proposed loan without making any political conditions.

There were other similar gestures. When Hungary appealed for aid, no aid was forthcoming. Hungary was too hostile to the Little Entente. When Germany could no longer meet her payments under the modified Young Plan, France refused to accept President Hoover's suggestion of a moratorium on international debts for a year. And of course no one can deny that our gold standard crisis was largely aided by the substantial withdrawals of gold reserves from England by the Bank of France. However, one has the consolation of knowing that within a year a stroke of the pen was to wipe out all reparations payments apart from some small token.

Let no one in England think that the French were sorry in their hearts when England came off the gold standard. The exact reverse is the case. There was a satisfaction that sneaked all over France that at last the proud English pound sterling had been humiliated. I was in Biarritz at the time England went off gold. I have not forgotten the general attitude of the populace towards the Englishman who had only pound notes, so very desirable on the Saturday morning, so very contemptible on the following Monday. In Paris a millionaire friend of mine was requested to leave his luggage as security in an hotel he had patronised for years because he was anxious to return to England to look after his interests and had not enough French francs to pay his reckoning.

No one can assert that France behaved either with dignity or generosity to friends and enemies during the height of the world crisis. But even her skill in intrigue could not stay a whirlwind. The universal hold-up of credits and destruction of trade had brought Germany almost to the international bankruptcy court once more. So much had happened, however, since the previous impoverishment. The German people, although they might be torn between conflicting political faiths, were no longer the subservient nation of 1923. They had begun to realise their strength, and although there was to be a fierce deplorable political conflict among themselves, there was to be no show of undue weakness to the outside world. When all the turmoil of the immediate crisis had sorted itself out, there was a Germany standing in the background of Europe which had to be reckoned with, a Germany that could fight out her own internal battles and emerge the more strongly.

The most obvious form of international retrenchment in such circumstances was disarmament and at long last the time was deemed ripe to call together the Geneva disarmament conference, foreshadowed by the treaty and which had been in expert preparation for seven years. The Conference began and Germany sent her representatives to Geneva in the early days of 1932. Hitler was not yet in power. He had no majority in the Reichstag. It was questionable whether he would obtain such a majority and there were many experienced observers who were willing to lay odds against his ever obtaining real power. In a previous volume—*Geneva Scene*—I have outlined at some length the story of the unhappy Geneva conference. Even at that time of universal distress, France and her Allies were not disposed to take a broad view. Germany still remained the foe, and every time there was a suspicion of progress, there were expostulations at Germany's secret rearmament by representatives of nations who were already fully armed and had no intention of cutting down their forces. Germany left the conference because she was not admitted on terms of equality of rights. When she came back there was a promise of equality that was never kept. A few months passed and by that time the nationalist forces had overcome their opponents in the Reich and were able to present a united front to Europe. Germany left the conference for ever, quitted the League of Nations, assumed the equality in reality she had been promised in theory, and showed the world she was a great power. Hitler was Chancellor of the Reich.

CHAPTER XVI

BY WAY OF HOPE

IT is a stock argument among those who persist in their advocacy of agreement with France and a revival of the old-time balance of power that Germany is the aggressor, that her native instinct is bound up in militarism and that her policy is a menace to European peace. For them France stands out as the champion of liberty and democracy, the essential bulwark of peace.

But what are the facts ? On what occasion since the war has Germany assumed an attitude of aggression ? She has assumed an attitude of defiance on more than one occasion, but that was a natural consequence of an unjust and unworkable peace settlement. But defiance can hardly be said to be synonymous with aggression. And if one looks into the question of defiance and the tearing up of the peace treaty, it would appear that great justification lies with the Germans. It is a fundamental law of contract that a bargain can only be maintained provided it is agreed on by two people freely and willingly. A contract that is forced on one of the parties by pressure of circumstances cannot be said to be a sound contract. Such a contract was the Treaty of Versailles, a treaty that was grotesquely harsh and impossible of ultimate fulfilment. Moreover, it ceased to have the same value when Germany was admitted back into the family of nations on terms of equality. The treaty fell down of itself. When the Lausanne conference finally ended the reparations problem, an important part of the treaty became void. Other sections were bound to be abrogated in the course of time.

Germany has been accused of deliberately breaking her pledged word, a word that in any case was given in a moment of humiliation and helplessness. But that word was given on a general understanding actually recorded in the peace terms that there should be a universal scaling down of armaments as a means of settling the outstanding difficulties in the way of permanent peace. The victorious allies, while ultimately agreeing with the principle of German equality, ignored that part of the treaty with the exception of Great Britain, who embarked on a policy of reduction of arms that has left us in our present defenceless position. There was never any question in Paris of serious French disarmament, and even at the height of the disarmament conference, French ideas of disarmament were that France should be left more powerful than her neighbour across the Rhine. It was on that issue that the conference broke down and brought about all our woes. Surely here was an abrogation of the Treaty of Versailles in a vital respect, an abrogation of which Germany for once in a way was not guilty.

It was only a matter of time before Germany re-established herself. The fact that her re-establishment came about under the auspices of Adolf Hitler ought not to blind us to the essential issue that Germany would have torn up the treaty eventually no matter who was in power. In fact, if the extremist elements had prevailed, I have not the least doubt that the disruption would have been much more drastic and that we should have real reason by now to fear German aggression both from a military as well as a political point of view. The treaty could not last for ever. No treaty is hall-marked with permanence, especially a treaty like that of Versailles. Study it carefully and you are forced to wonder why it lasted so long.

One must look at the situation from the point of view of Germany. There she lay on the other side of the Rhine with heavily armed powers on all three landward sides. In her state of unpreparedness, her frontiers were open to invasion by anyone who cared to mobilise an army. Yet in theory she was supposed to be the equal among nations. What guarantee had she against an aggressor? Sometimes it must have sounded very strange in Berlin when Paris was loudly demanding security and more security. Berlin at any rate had none. It was an intolerable situation and it came to an end in due course. The principle of conscription was re-introduced, the demilitarised Rhineland was re-occupied with a skeleton force. They were gestures of self-respect, gestures which assumed the equality of rights which had been talked about so much. But they were not gestures that were accompanied by immediate evidences of aggression. On the contrary each move was accompanied by an offer of some peaceful settlement. Germany asked time after time for some agreement among the powers by which her national, sovereign rights would be respected. But her enemies have ignored those overtures just as they have every other peace move that has come out of the Wilhelmstrasse for years past.

And those who think of Germany in terms of aggression might do well to remember the many causes of discontent that continue to weigh on the German people. There is the so-called Dantzig Corridor that divides Germany into two parts and separates East Prussia, the cradle of the modern Empire, from the rest of the country. The great city of Dantzig, although a

German city, is no part of the Reich. There is the festering sore of the Upper Silesian coalfield, a division of territory that cannot possibly be justified. There is the enormous German minority in Czecho-Slovakia. And there is the Colonial question. When one considers just these four issues—and there are others—one begins to wonder at the patience of the German people, for the German people are strong and they might reasonably be expected to express themselves a little more forcibly in regard to such manifold injustices.

But this great people, so often accused of aggression, has submitted with fortitude and forbearance for a period of nineteen years to conditions which we in England would have found quite intolerable. And now they have resumed their arms and taken on themselves the dignity of a great people once more, are we still to go on treating them as the erstwhile enemy who was beaten once and if necessary will be beaten again? Are we to break with history once more and continue to disregard any gesture of peace and understanding simply because it happens to emanate from Berlin and is therefore unacceptable to Paris? This is the vital question of the hour. It must not be confused with domestic politics. The Government of Germany and the form it takes is a matter for the Germans to decide. The question of Nazism does not arise. It so happens that under the Nazi régime, as I have been at pains to point out, Germany has become a great power in the world once more; the Nazis have given something back to Germany which previous political régimes failed to give; the great social reforms of the Third Reich are moulding the German people into the most unified race in Europe. And that great unified people are looking for peace and see in friendship with Britain a basis for peace not only for themselves but for everyone else. Our close co-operation with France at the expense of Germany can only serve to exasperate a situation which may soon grow desperate. And is it worth it ? Must we for ever go on backing the wrong horse ?

INDEX

For Product Safety Concerns and Information please contact our EU
representative GPSR@taylorandfrancis.com
Taylor & Francis Verlag GmbH, Kaufingerstraße 24, 80331 München, Germany

www.ingramcontent.com/pod-product-compliance
Ingram Content Group UK Ltd.
Pitfield, Milton Keynes, MK11 3LW, UK
UKHW020019200926
475702UK00014B/1972
* 9 7 8 0 4 1 5 8 4 8 8 8 6 *